Thomas Aquinas and Karl Barth

REVISIONS

A Series of Books on Ethics
General Editors:
Stanley Hauerwas and Alasdair MacIntyre

Thomas Aquinas and Karl Barth

Sacred Doctrine
and the
Natural Knowledge of God

EUGENE F. ROGERS, JR.

UNIVERSITY OF NOTRE DAME PRESS
Notre Dame   London

Manufactured in the United States of America

Library of Congress Cataloging-in-Publication Data

Rogers, Eugene F.
    Thomas Aquinas and Karl Barth : sacred doctrine and the
natural knowledge of God / Eugene F. Rogers, Jr.
        p. cm. — (Revisions)
    Revision of thesis (doctoral)—Yale University.
    Includes bibliographical references.
    ISBN 0-268-01889-8 (alk. paper)
    1. Thomas, Aquinas, Saint, 1225?-1274. In Epistolam ad Romanos
expositio. 2. Barth, Karl, 1886-1968. Römerbrief. 3. Bible. N. T. Romans—
Criticism, interpretation, etc.—History. I. Title. II. Series.
BS2665.T543R64 1995   94-42830
227'.106—dc20   CIP

∞ The paper used in this publication meets the minimum requirements
of the American National Standard for Information Sciences—Permanence
of Paper for Printed Library Materials, ANSI Z39.48–1984.

Book design by Will H. Powers.
Typesetting by Stanton Publication Services, Inc., St. Paul.

To Victor Preller

Contents

Preface
Acknowledgments and Disclaimers

The present book hopes to accomplish two things: to carry out a fresh reading of Thomas Aquinas on the nature of theology, and to uncover his affinities with Karl Barth. In the second respect it belongs to the genre of systematic-theological dialogue. I take the mammoth study of Otto Hermann Pesch as a model.[1]

Jeffrey Stout writes that "we have at least two clusters of topics that might motivate interest in something called 'the meaning of a text'... namely the alternative idioms of authorial intention and contextual significance, either of which can stand in for talk of meanings and be explicated further if the purpose at hand requires."[2] In the present case, I specify the authorial intention by close readings of Thomas's own theological texts. Meanwhile, I specify the contextual significance in terms of modern systematic or constructive theological concerns, Catholic and Protestant, and the concerns of modern American religious studies, all of which attempt in various ways to enlist Thomas for their own purposes, as I do.

I hope to be just historical enough to understand what Thomas says in terms of his own usages and not in ours, to realize that Thomas Aquinas did not have the Enlightenment to go by.[3] I also hope to be historical enough to recognize the presence of stages in Thomas's development, specifically between the beginnings of the *Contra gentiles* and those of the *Summa Theologiae*, so that readers do not mistake the project of the one for that of the other. Thomas Aquinas did not exempt himself from the observation of the very first question of the *Summa* that human inquiry takes place "over a long time."

I distinguish different stages in Thomas's career and in Western intellectual history, however, more for systematic-theological or constructive than for historical purposes. Historical remarks remain in the background. The purpose is not to give a neutral report of what Thomas says that would be useful to all comers. I do not seek Thomas's intent as an end in itself.

Rather I seek Thomas's intent for particular purposes and with a particular sort of charity.

For I also hope to be systematic enough to suppose that Thomas has something to say to current theologians, with whom he would want to be in conversation, and that he—in common with the goals of the newly founded Order of Preachers (Dominicans)—had allowed himself to be formed by a reading of the scriptures, particularly Romans. Thomas did have Romans to go by, even if he lacked the Enlightenment. Or better: he could not stand outside Romans' *Wirkungsgeschichte*, but became himself part of it.

Stout continues: "The more interesting the text, the more readings we shall be *able* to give without simply repeating ourselves and our predecessors, and the more readings we shall *want* to give....Let us then celebrate the diversity of interpretations as a sign that our texts are interesting in more ways than one. The only alternative would be to have texts that weren't."[4] But that does not mean that anything goes, or that there is no way to interpret badly or to get things wrong. The variation of interpreters' interests and purposes "would be cause for worry only if interests and purposes were themselves beyond the pale of rational appraisal and critical revision."[5] Thomas too regards the end or purpose as the principal circumstance in the evaluation of a human act.

This book has two purposes. Agenda I is to interpret Thomas Aquinas on the nature of theology during the last stage of his authorship, by attending to the equation "sacred doctrine is [an Aristotelian] science" of the *Summa theologiae*, and testing the interpretation in the light of Thomas's commentary on Romans. Agenda II is to uncover affinities between Thomas and Karl Barth. The two purposes interpenetrate each other and complicate the structure of the argument. Neither could be sacrificed without loss. For one, in Stout's terms, attempts to specify Thomas's intentions in light of the modern context, while the other attempts to address the modern context in light of Thomas's intentions. It would in any case be impossible to achieve an entirely unalloyed case of one or the other.

Although I hope that both arguments are fairly well complete, only one of them could occupy the foreground. An attempt to give Thomas and Barth equal billing would grow too long, and the interpretation of Barth is (I think) less controversial than the interpretation of Thomas. Agenda I therefore predominates and tends to dictate the structure. This is first of all an essay in Thomas-interpretation, and second of all an essay in controversial irenic. With respect to Agenda II (the comparison with Barth), therefore, I suggest more than I assert. I have confined my interpretation of Barth almost entirely to the brief remarks of the *Shorter Commentary on Romans* because it follows the lead of the *Church Dogmatics,* and does so in the order of a text that Thomas also comments on. Readers primarily interested in the comparison have complained that the interpretation of Thomas's Romans commentary has grown too detailed; other readers, more interested in the interpretation of Thomas, have regarded the detail as precisely what makes the book most valuable. Those of the first sort who are willing to take my word for the interpretation of Thomas and are eager to get on to the comparison with Barth may skip chapters five and six. The presence of two lines of argument does complicate the attempt to structure things entirely according to Agenda I. Advantages compensate for that. Agenda I (the interpretation of Thomas) contributes plausibility to Agenda II, and Agenda II (the construction of convergence) contributes significance to Agenda I.

By no means do I exhaustively survey alternative approaches and secondary literature. For the bulk of the secondary sources—Catholic, Protestant, and religious studies—assume a reading that I am trying to *displace.* They ask questions that I am trying to *unask.* It is hard to unask questions while entertaining them. I have therefore kept explicit engagement with rival readings to a minimum, although the deployment of the Romans commentary seeks implicitly to make them more difficult and to shift the burden of proof. I have preferred to rest the argument more on the power of its own inherent rationale than on its ability to demolish alternatives. The epilogue does attempt to credit and explain what is good in rival interpretations. Stout puts it another way. "What originally might be counted as evidence of drastic disagreement on a single topic now seems to show only that there are too many distinguishable topics present to sustain much substantive disagreement at all.... Too much divergence ceases to be divergence altogether: it merely changes the subject."[6] By passing over large bodies of literature in silence, I have sought to keep from changing the subject.[7] In the nineteenth century the process had already begun by which interpretations of Thomas ceased to be interpretations of the same thing and came to diversify the very topic of conversation.[8] An Epilogue will tender speculations of its own on why the common Thomas-figure of Barth and Vatican I was never diversified *enough.*

This book began in George Lindbeck's Aquinas seminar at Yale University. When it had become a programmatic essay, I shared it with a short-lived group organized by Joe Mangina and called the Theological Irregulars, where Serene Jones and Kendall Soulen offered early advice. I was fortunate enough at that stage to receive additional advice and criticism, some of it searching, from Alasdair MacIntyre and Otto Hermann Pesch. As a paper at the American Academy of Religion it benefited from the support of Bill Werpehowski and the response of Greg Jones.

The essay became a dissertation at Yale University. I would like to thank my adviser, George Lindbeck, and my readers, Kathryn Tanner, Nicholas Wolterstorff, and David Kelsey. Lindbeck first introduced me to Corbin and offered important suggestions as to the structure of the whole. Joseph A. DiNoia, editor of *The Thomist*, provided encouragement (and a manual *Summa*) when Part I was still chaos. Joe Mangina, Cathy Kaveny, and Peter Casarella offered moral support. Robert F. Goheen, as administrator of the Mellon Fellowships in the Humanities, also afforded me encouragement, and a year's financial support.

As the dissertation became a book I have Stanley Hauerwas to thank, who ripped the manuscript out of my hands in characteristic eagerness to publish it, as well as Alasdair MacIntyre and David Burrell on behalf of the University of Notre Dame Press. I wish also to thank Jim Langford and Carole Roos, my editors.

At St. Anselm College Dennis Sweetland gave me my first full-time job and provided funds for reproduction of the manuscript. Michel Corbin was kind enough to bear with my spoken French for an hour at the Institut Catholique. Xavier Montasterio supplied a list of typing mistakes in the Latin. Bruce Marshall and Robert Jenson helped me to eliminate errors and improve the argument.

At the University of Virginia I have benefited from a summer research grant and from a presentation to Robert Wilken's theological discussion group, with responses from David Novak, Daniel Westberg, and Robert Scharlemann. Westberg has been a good conversation partner and fellow Thomas scholar. Scharlemann rescued my application for the summer grant by alerting me that someone had mislaid it. I am grateful to my student Donna Bowman for preparing the index.

Derek Krueger has been a companion to me also in the preparation of manuscripts, his desk abutting mine.

Finally I wish to thank Victor Preller, who retires this year. When I was an undergraduate at Princeton he taught a seminar on Thomas in 1984, the notes for which, ten years later, I still refer to. In addition to his book he has generated an oral tradition, to which this essay owes a great deal.

For what follows I say with Thomas *"et per longum tempus, et cum admixtione multorum errorum."*

Author's Note

On the advice of my editor I have kept Latin and German to a minimum, citing them only where English would be misleading or ambiguous.

References to the *Summa* will most often appear in the text, like this: I.1.1–10; that is, Part I, question 1, articles 1 through 10. Numbers without a title will always refer to the *Summa theologiae*. The *Summa contra gentiles*, on the other hand, I will always call the *"Contra gentiles,"* reserving *"Summa"* for the *Summa theologiae*. Usually I will also cite parts of articles if I am referring to an objection ("obj."), a reply to an objection (*"ad"*), the *sed contra* (*"s.c."*), or the body of the response as singled out from the rest ("c" = *corpus*). Note the reservation of "response" for the body of an article and "reply" for an answer to an objection. For long parts of articles, beginning, middle, and end appear as *"in init.," "in med.,"* and *"in fin."* "Prol." cites one of the prologues to each of the four Parts, I, II–I, II–II, and III. "Proem." cites a proemium or introduction to one of the questions, usually a programmatic or transitional remark. The proemia give definitive lists of the matters to be discussed (the articles) in a question, and, as original with Thomas, carry more authority than the titles, which are not.

For the sake of consistency and of the best possible fit between the sources and my exposition of them, all translations are my own except where otherwise noted. I also sometimes *alter* the translation of the same passage from quotation to quotation, in order better to anticipate different nuances of the exposition. In rendering Thomas's quotations from the Vulgate, I have tried to strike a balance between consistency with the translations I have made to further the exposition, and consistency with the familiar ring of verses in the reader's ear. Therefore I have conformed my translations of biblical verses to those of the RSV where Thomas's text allows it, but not otherwise. In the first case we will come to, 2 Corinthians 10:5, for example, the RSV has "thought" where the Vulgate has *"intellectum,"* and Thomas's context clearly requires the rendering "understanding."

For Thomas's scriptural commentaries I give the biblical book, chapter, and usually verse, preceded by *"In,"* and usually followed by the paragraph number of the recent Marietti editions, unless the verse is clear from context, in which case I confine the reference to the paragraph number. Thus: *In* Rom. 1:20, §118. Although the use of biblical verses is anachronistic—Thomas did not have them—it is more useful for readers to know where he is in the biblical text than where he is in a *lectio* (as in the chapter: *lectio* citation). I do usually refer to nonbiblical commentaries by book (bk.) and *lectio* (*lect.*).

I have in all cases consulted a text in the Leonine tradition. Where not otherwise noted I have consulted the most recent complete edition, that of Robertus Busa, *S. Thomae Aquinatis opera omnia ut sunt in indice thomistico additis 61 scriptis ex aliis medii aevi auctoribus,* 7 vols. (Stuttgart-Bad Cannstatt: Friedrich Frommann Verlag-Günther Holzboog KG, 1980). The edition is a bibliographic oddity because it is sometimes listed as an appendix to the index, *Index Thomisticus: S. Thomae Aquinatis operum omnium indices et concordantiae in quibus verborum omnium et singulorum formae et lemmata cum suis frequentiis et contextibus variis modis referuntur quaeque auspice Paulo VI Summo Pontifice consociata plurimum opera atque electronico IBM automato usus digessit Robertus Busa SI* (Stuttgart-Bad Cannstatt: Frommann-Holzboog, 1974–1980).

For convenience I have often used the manual edition of the Lenonine text of the *Summa* in the Biblioteca de autores christianos (Madrid, 1961). (The most recent Leonine text, used by Busa, appeared in 1948.)

For the commentary on Romans as well as other on other letters traditionally ascribed to Paul I have used *Super epistolas S. Pauli lectura: Prologus. In S. Thomae Aquinatis doctoris angelici super epistolas S. Pauli lectura.* Ed. P. Raphaelis Cai, O.P. 2 vols. Turin: Marietti, 1953. I retain the Marietti typography except that I omit the dashes after paragraph numbers and render boldface with small capitals.

All translations from Thomas are my own. Occasionally I have consulted the following:

Commentary on the Gospel of St. John. Aquinas Scripture Series, vol. 4, pt. 1. Ed. James A. Weisheipl. Albany, New York: Magi, 1980.

Summa Theologiae. "Blackfriars ed." Facing English and Latin. 60 vols. New York: McGraw-Hill, 1963–76.

Summa Theologica. "Die deutsche Thomas-Ausgabe." German above Latin. Trans. the Dominicans and Benedictines of Germany and Austria. Graz, Vienna, Cologne: Styria, 1933–.

The Summa Theologica of Thomas Aquinas. "American ed." Trans. Fathers of the English Dominican Province. 3 vols. New York: Benzinger, 1947–48.

A translation of Thomas's Commentary on Romans is in preparation by Steven C. Boguslawski.

References to the works of Karl Barth appear in the notes.

Thomas Aquinas and Karl Barth

1

Three Audiences and Two Agendas

I

I have addressed this essay to three audiences.

A. As a contribution to *Catholic* theology, the essay spends most of its length interpreting Thomas Aquinas. It seeks to promote a genuinely "evangelical" Thomas, in the German sense of the word, as one who in the *Summa* speaks always and everywhere as a theologian rather than a philosopher, or, as the *Summa* puts it, who seeks there to contribute to the theology that pertains to sacred doctrine rather than the theology that pertains to metaphysics. It presents sacred doctrine as a matter of "taking every understanding captive into obedience to Christ," as I.1.8 has it, or as an exposition of what the Romans commentary calls the "gospel grace of Christ"—and therefore evangelical in the Lutheran sense.[1] I call that "the evangelical Thomas." In carrying forward the portrayal of an evangelical Thomas, the essay seeks specifically to render him both more scripturalist and more christocentric (or better, in a sense it develops, *christoform*) than any Catholic interpretation I know of, and closer to Barth.[2]

B. As a contribution to *Protestant* theology the essay interprets Thomas in the direction of Karl Barth.[3] Barth objected to natural theology, but he did not regard Anselm as doing it, and he deployed Anselm in his struggle to get beyond the Enlightenment.[4] But Thomas, despite the Five Ways, also objected to what he called *theologia naturalis*.[5] To Protestants, this essay attempts to show that Barth might have applied his positive reading of Anselm also to Thomas; he might have found in Thomas, too, resources for getting beyond the Enlightenment. In the attempt, I end up interpreting Thomas in non-standard but, I think, textually compelling ways. Both Barth and Vatican I were reactions against the Enlightenment, but they were different ones, and Barth reacted even more strongly to the reaction of Vatican I than to the Enlightenment itself. Gilson reads Thomas in the tradition, however attenuated and controverted, of Vatican I's attempt to

3

deploy the Middle Ages against the Enlightenment. This essay attempts to read Thomas also in the tradition of Karl Barth's attempt to deploy the Middle Ages (in the person of Anselm) against the Enlightenment. An Epilogue will speculate (but only speculate) about the relation of the two attempts.

c. Or a reader may regard this essay as contributing to the reception of Thomas, in religious studies departments of colleges and universities not related to churches, by an American scene animated by Victor Preller, Jeffrey Stout, Alasdair MacIntyre, and George Lindbeck.[6] Their insistence on a pluralism that appreciates communities' irreducible particularity prepares a *public* place not just for a deracinated Thomas, but for a Thomas with theological integrity. Their critique of Enlightenment epistemology helps us explain where the Neo-Thomists went wrong. Their suspicions tell us of what sort of foundational readings to be skeptical. And their American neo-pragmatism tells us how to retrieve Thomas for current uses. While MacIntyre is becoming more Catholic book by book, and Stout listens for theology's "voice,"[7] they both have room to appreciate more fully how Thomas's theological commitments ramify also through his philosophical and ethical work. Although this essay will address none of those authors directly, it is a third purpose of it to render the depth and breadth of Thomas's theological commitments more difficult to ignore.

I take the last possibility a little further, that of reading the essay as a contribution to the relation of theology and religious studies, since I will leave it undiscussed in the body of the essay.

It is possible to regard the age of religious studies as the culmination of a development that reached an important milestone in John Locke.[8] He addressed people with no will to believe except on the basis of proof. But people with no will to believe except on the basis of proof are a characteristically modern phenomenon. Thomas Aquinas might have compared such people to debaters who fall into sin when they debate out of doubt (II–II.10.7c and *ad* 3)[9]—or to demons, who have no will to believe, even on the basis of proof (II–II.5.2 *ad* 3). So far removed was his time from modern notions of objectivity. Although Thomas also believed that one might debate with unbelievers to learn from them, and that one ought to interpret the scriptures in accord with the best deliverances so far of relatively independent natural science, he understood, as do postmodern thinkers from Thomas Kuhn to theologians of liberation, that the devices and desires of the heart have a great deal to do, for good and for ill, with the assent or dissent of the intellect.

Thomas distinguished two sorts of God-talk (*"theologia"*), the God-talk that belongs to metaphysics (for the late modern period, read "religious studies"), and the God-talk that belongs to sacred doctrine (for the present purpose, read "theology"). The two versions of God-talk overlap in material content, and their distinction consists precisely in that they consider their material under a different formality, as hearing and sight. In some ways they complement each other. Theology need not be intellectually irresponsible, and religious studies need not denigrate the claims of faith. But the division sounds as if it must still leave each formality hermetically sealed off from the other, one fideistic and one scientistic.

One could say that part of Thomas's innovation was to pursue the inseparability of form and matter so that the formal rationale came to influence the definition of the material. For purposes of theology, Thomas defines all things as *revelabilia*, which does not mean merely things that might be revealed. Rather theology regards all things as belonging to the one world depicted within the Bible,[10] as biology regards all things as they bear upon life. Any and everything is potentially subsumable under that description, even if never mentioned in the sacred pages; that, for Thomas, is a consequence of the doctrine of creation. He sees his charge as a teacher of sacred doctrine in the presence of Aristotle as a charge *to consider nothing God-forsaken.* That is the point, by the way, of the Five Ways: to leave no human or physical motion unrelated to God. Thomas's project suggests a way of parsing the relationship of theology and religious studies. It is the office of religious studies *to leave no human phenomenon unexamined, even human religiosity.* It is succeeding very well in the fulfillment of that charge. Theology however has abandoned to secular culture the investigation of large parts of the world, so that, contrary to its charge, it treats much of the world as effectively God-forsaken. Thus it often fails in its office *to consider nothing God-forsaken, even human religiosity.* The account here offered of theology in Thomas and Barth hopes to encourage theology in that task.

II

The book has two agendas, first to interpret Thomas, and also to compare him to Barth. I take them in reverse order.

Agenda II takes as its challenge and motivation to uncover some of the affinities (indeed, to create a convergence) between Karl Barth and Thomas Aquinas just where both modern Barthians and modern Thomists would have thought convergence least likely: on the natural knowledge of God. It seeks to do so on the basis of their reading of Romans 1:20 and its context in Barth's *Shorter Commentary* and Thomas's *Super epistolam S. Pauli ad Romanos*, where each of them ends up saying surprising things about the natural knowledge of God under the pressure of following Paul. Thus read, Part I supplies plausibility for the reading of Thomas on Romans to follow by showing what scripturalist and christoform resources exist in—or more strongly, govern—the methodological reflections of the *Summa*. Part II simply executes the reading of Thomas on Romans. Part III makes the comparison of the two commentaries (Barth's and Thomas's), arguing a convergence, and the Epilogue speculates about why students of Thomas and Barth have almost universally failed to see it. In Agenda II, all three Parts of the essay contribute to the construction of a convergence between Thomas and Barth on the natural knowledge of God. Part of what I hope to do is provide a reading of Thomas's theological procedure that resembles in a smaller way Barth's account of Anselm's.[11]

Such a reading is significant because Barth is at once the most intrepid recent defender of the sort of scripturalism that I believe Thomas to share, and a most confident detractor of Thomas on the grounds that Thomas deserts that scripturalism for the natural theology Barth abhors. To the extent that I can defend the suggestion, made occasionally by Corbin, of a *convergence* rather than an opposition between Thomas and Barth, I will have helped to change the terms of the debate. Since my primary purpose (Agenda I) is to explicate Thomas, the argument for such a convergence will remain largely implicit until the penultimate chapter. In an epilogue I will sketch a way of reading neo-Thomist and Barthian reactions to Kant that will seek on intellectual historical grounds to relativize some of the obvious objections to a convergence. The main consideration in favor of it will remain the reading of Thomas as it proceeds in Parts I and II. Nevertheless the following considerations should provide grounds for the suspension of disbelief until the reading is complete.

The clash is promising. The Five Ways have constituted for a millennium the now celebrated, now notorious, now controverted, now all-too-plain climax of natural theology. Barth sums up one evaluation of them as follows:

> Natural theology was able, ... after the rediscovery of Aristotle, to get the upper hand over medieval theology, which at last and finally became apparent in the formulas of the First Vatican Council (in the canonization of Thomas Aquinas as its supreme achievement [*Spitzenleistung*]).[12]

Since the comment comes in the midst of a portrait of natural theology as dogmatics' most virulent disease, wherein the castigation of the *analogia entis* as *"the* invention of the Antichrist" has been repeated only a few pages earlier,[13] Barth's characterization of Thomas's achievement as a *"Spitzen-leistung"* becomes a superlative of disapprobation. The summit reached becomes that of a tower of Babel.

Yet where something very like the natural theology of the Five Ways appears in the *Super epistolam Sancti Pauli ad Romanos lectura*, it cannot be functioning as a *Spitzenleistung* of any sort of natural theology of which Barth could disapprove. In a letter at the end of his life, Barth writes: "On the contrary, I would gladly concede that *nature* does objectively offer a proof of God, though the human being overlooks or misunderstands it. Yet I would not venture to say the same of natural *science,* whether ancient or modern."[14] If that is the division, then Thomas's arguments belong on the side of "nature" rather than on the side of "natural science," because for Thomas, concrete nature is already shot through with grace, and Barth's notions of science, both ancient and modern, are held captive to modern notions of a natural science that defines itself as immanent to this world. But when *Thomas* defines natural science in his commentary on the Prologue to John, it comes under sacred doctrine, serves the doctrine of creation, and remains open to the explication of the world as having a source and an intelligibility that transcends it. "Natural science," he writes, "considers things as proceeding from God."[15] Obviously *that* is not the sort of "natural science" Barth had in mind. And in Barth's own *Shorter Commentary on Romans* (which Barth intends to match the account in the *Dogmatics* and enjoys the advantages of brevity and verse-by-verse organization), an explicit openness to natural theology appears, which, however narrow and hedged round with conditions, only leaves a space for the sort of natural theology that Thomas offers. It is indeed for just that hedged and narrow open space, with just such conditions as those on which Barth places the emphasis, that Thomas offers a natural theology.

When Barth arrives in his commentary at Romans 1:20, he finds himself compelled to admit, with caveats and reversals, that

> the world which has always been around [the Gentiles], has always been God's work and as such God's witness to himself. Objectively the Gentiles have always had the opportunity of knowing God, his invisible being, his eternal power and godhead. *And again, objectively speaking, they have always known him.* In all that they have known otherwise, God as the Creator of all things has always been objectively speaking the

proper and real object of their knowledge, exactly in the same sense as undoubtedly the Jews in their law were objectively dealing with God's revelation.[16]

In some ways that statement sounds as if it goes far beyond what Thomas would say. Barth does not distinguish God's essence where Thomas would, for example. In other ways, Barth's attempt to qualify his claims by dialectic rather than distinction will cause him to seem to take it back.

The discipline of having to follow Paul (within, to be sure, a certain very broad tradition of interpretation which they themselves help to define) will make each of them, Barth and Thomas, model his presentation of certain issues in natural theology less upon his own situation and preferences than he does in his more systematic works, and more, instead, upon the moves of Paul. That presentation will in turn render more visible theological similarities of argument, agenda, and approach that situations and circumstances might otherwise becloud. Barth and Thomas will each seek to execute what we may call the "material moves of Paul."[17] Thus by "material convergence" I mean in this case just such a pattern of argument as Paul executes first and Barth and Thomas follow, as it were, at a distance.[18]

I seek to discern a common underlying pattern *just when* differences of vocabulary, emphasis, and time threaten to cover it. Under the influence of Paul their common teacher, Thomas will talk about the ineffectiveness of natural knowledge of God under certain sinful conditions and how it serves to prove the necessity and sufficiency of grace, conditions that go unmentioned in the tightly circumscribed article on the Five Ways; under the same influence Barth will talk about the possibility of an objective natural knowledge of God, a possibility that goes unmentioned in the differently directed polemic of *Church Dogmatics* I/2 and II/1, except to seem denied. Each must intentionally or unintentionally press his own questions upon Romans, but Romans will in turn with greater or lesser influence press its questions upon each one. It is by attending to the latter pressure—that of Romans, or of a tradition of reading it, upon its commentators[19]—that I hope to discern a convergence in the matter of natural theology. Natural theology as a Christian discipline finds its home, both Barth and Thomas would agree, in Romans, and I hope to see the concept behaving more similarly in Barth and Thomas when they place it there, where it is at home, than in other contexts, where they marshal it for distinct purposes under different circumstances. Indeed Thomas seems to deploy the actual phrase *"theologia naturalis"* much more rarely and in a potentially much narrower sense than Barth, although it sounds every bit as negative.[20]

III

Agenda I, on the other hand, is to present a reading of Thomas Aquinas in the period of the *Summa* as more scripturalist and christoform than he is usually understood. On that reading of the essay, Part I elaborates this hypothesis: In the *Summa*, at least, Question 1 structures or sets up sacred doctrine as an Aristotelian science so that *the more Aristotelian it is, the more scriptural it is*, and *the more Aristotelian it is, the more christoform it is*. Part II deals with a more or less implicit objection that the Five Ways of Question 2 of the *Summa* tacitly set up a second, rival way in which sacred doctrine counts as Aristotelian science. Question 2 cites Romans 1:20 as warrant for the demonstrability of the proposition "God exists," and adduces five cosmological arguments for asserting the truth of that proposition.[21] Thus I devote Part II of this essay to Thomas's commentary on Romans 1, where cosmological arguments also appear, or to the scriptural "home" of the Five Ways. Part II thus serves as a test of the hypothesis elaborated in Part I. I find the logic of Thomas's commentary on Romans compatible with the interpretation offered of theology in the *Summa*. Part III, instead of rehearsing the hypothesis, raises the stakes for its significance and answers certain objections by an explicit comparison with Karl Barth's *Shorter Commentary on Romans* (not the hermeneutical manifesto of 1921, but the theological commentary of 1956).[22] An Epilogue speculates about why friends and foes of Thomas had to interpret him in ways that left him much less compatible with Barth than he is in my reading. Under Agenda I, therefore, all three Parts contribute to the reading of Thomas.

If it is true that the *Summa* is as scripturalist as I think it is, then we can regard it as a compendium and abbreviation of the scriptural commentaries for those whom the Prologue calls "little ones in Christ," so that in case of dispute about how to take a passage of the *Summa* we could turn to scriptural commentaries where the same material is discussed, especially when the warrant for the *Summa*'s discussion in the *sed contra* locates an article's scriptural home. We ought, that is, to regard the scriptural commentaries as keys to the *Summa*, and the *Summa* as inviting us into the commentaries. More radically: we ought to regard the scriptures as keys to the

Summa, and the *Summa* as an invitation to scripture. It is here that Part II takes up the thread. Specifically, I am aiming for the scriptural warrant for the Five Ways.

Or again: If there is one place in the *Summa* where the skeptic sees Thomas's scripturalism in retreat, it is in the Five Ways. Generations of students have passed over Question 1 to give pride of place to Question 2. It is Question 2 read as if in isolation that functions to define the scientific character of Thomas's theology, and it is a very different scientific character from the one I will argue is to be found in Question 1. Gilson for example regards it as "extremely important" that those things that are "purely rational" in Christian beliefs "can be extracted from their theological context and judged, from the point of view of natural reason, as purely philosophical conclusions." Furthermore, that "enables us to understand how strictly metaphysical knowledge can be included in a theological structure without losing its purely philosophical nature."[23] Such a reading provides an immediate challenge to readings like mine (including those of Corbin and Preller). For one might find the criterion of consistency reversible. One might argue, that is, that a certain other reading of Question 2 tells us what Thomas's "real" intention is, and that Question 1 ought to be read so as to cohere with that, instead of the other way around. It is one purpose of the test that occupies Part II to make readings like mine more nearly irreversible by putting Question 2 into its scriptural context.

The symmetry is striking: Thomas's warrant for the Five Ways (precisely: for the demonstrability of God's existence at I.2.2) is Romans 1:20, and in Thomas's Romans commentary—*Super epistolam Sancti Pauli ad Romanos lectura*—immediately before 1:20 there appear similar cosmological arguments (*In* Rom. 1:19, §115). If we put the commentary on Romans 1:20 into context, we will have put Thomas's natural theology into context, even in its most prominent form. If scripturalist considerations control the claims for the natural knowledge of God in the commentary where it is at home, and I am right about how to relate commentary and *Summa,* then they also control the claims for the natural knowledge of God in Question 2, and the burden of proof becomes much heavier upon the nonscripturalist reading.

The opening of the *Summa* tells us that Thomas intends us to use it in part as an aid to reading scripture. Among many things that impede beginners in sacred doctrine, the Prologue tells us, one is that the things they need to know get presented in the order that the exposition of the biblical books requires. It is therefore among other things to present that matter in a disciplined order that Thomas writes the *Summa* (prol.). Although Thomas can sometimes treat sacred scripture and sacred doctrine as synonyms (*"sacra Scriptura seu doctrina,"* I.1.2 *ad* 2 *in fin.*) as when he assimilates them as founded upon God's revelation and as together opposed to the theology that belongs to metaphysics, it is of sacred Scripture that he speaks when he names sacred doctrine's authority (I.1.8 *ad* 2 *ca. fin.*) and sacred Scripture that he characterizes as having no superior (I.1.8*c. in med.*) He never suggests that reading the *Summa* ought to *replace* reading the scriptures. Rather it ought to serve them. That is also of course what his prior training as a *magister in sacris paginis* and his vocation as a member of the Order of Preachers would lead us to expect.

It is a second stated purpose of the *Summa* to organize and simplify the disputations arising from commentary on scripture just when they threaten to overwhelm students—just when, that is, they threaten to lose their roots in the interpretation of scripture. The *Summa* thus executes a moment in a cyclical progress of understanding from scripture to disputed question and back, a movement in which however *sacra scriptura* rules. It is no accident therefore that a large if largely neglected and even untranslated portion of Thomas's output as an author also consists of the sort of scriptural commentary, the *lectura*, from which first *quaestiones disputatae* and then the *Summae* themselves can be observed to arise.

The exception will prove the rule: one has only to dip into the questions as Duns Scotus, say, will have transmogrified them, to see that soon the apparatus will take over and a love of logic and distinction, with which there is nothing wrong in itself, will begin to multiply the questions for their own sake and not because they arise from the *lectio divina.*[24] The trend must already have begun when, in the prologue to the *Summa*, Thomas announced his intention—executed more successfully for himself, less successfully for even his immediate successors—to counter it: "We consider that beginners in this discipline...are impeded by many things, in part, indeed, by the multiplication of unuseful questions, articles, and arguments" (prol.). As Thomas would be the first to admit, of course, to characterize questions as "unuseful" implies only that he finds them useless for some particular end, which it is an office of the opening phrase of the response of the *Summa*'s first article to specify—namely, useful for human salvation (I.1.1)—and not that they might prove useful for some other purpose, like the development of formal logic. Nevertheless it is just in respect of purposes like these that Thomas's prologue and practice require us to distinguish him from many of his followers and fellows, and it is just his evangelical allegiance to his purpose that causes him to stand out among them.

In homage to that origin and authority Thomas still characterizes the "mode of this science" as "narrative" (and that necessarily).[25] Indeed when we come to read his prologue to his *Lectura super epistolas S. Pauli* we will find that even there, where we moderns would expect methodological considerations, we get instead repeated attempts to see Paul and his successors in the Church as latter-day participants in such biblical narratives as that of the Flood, just because that is this discipline's proper method (in the modest sense of that word). Yet almost no one ever reads the *Summa* in the way that Thomas's training and vocation, stated intention and executed authorship suggest: as an aid in reading *scripture*. On the contrary, interpreters often treat scriptural warrants in the *sed contra*s as so many tags on which tradition constrained Thomas ever so quaintly to hang a putatively independent argument—while they treat rarer and explicitly less authoritative Aristotelian warrants as highly significant. Yet sacred doctrine's very structure as a science points us nowhere else, I argue, than to such scriptural warrants, as the science's first principles.

Thomas composed the last *Summa* between 1266 and 1273. He wrote it in order, reaching the end of the *Prima* by 1268 (Viterbo), before his second regency in Paris. He seems not to have revised quotations and citations of Aristotle as Moerbecke translated him afresh. Whether Thomas also seems not to have revised his *own* text substantively is an issue I have not seen raised.

He commented on Paul's letters at least twice. The text we have of his commentary on Romans comes from the second series and counts as an *expositio* rather than a *reportatio*. That is, Thomas himself took responsibility for its final form, rather than a mere student listener. Or so far historians agree. Raphael Cai, editor of the Marietti edition, dates the two series of Pauline commentaries as once in Italy between 1259 and November 1268, and again at Naples between October 1272 and December 1273. According to him, our text of the *lectura in Romanos* dates from the latter series, and we have it in Thomas's own hand.[26] According to James Weisheipl, who gives the best annotations in English on Thomas's bibliography, our version of the Romans commentary dates rather from the second Paris regency (1270–72), also after the completion of the *Prima* (1266–68).[27]

Whatever the dating, we can be sure that both the *Summa* and the Romans commentary before us come *after* the *Contra gentiles* (1259–64). Therefore they both date to the *same* part of Thomas's authorship as Corbin divides it up; they date to the last "figure" of sacred doctrine as *scientia* that, according to Corbin, Thomas anticipates at various places after the beginning of the *Contra gentiles* and works out systematically in question one of the last *Summa*.[28] I do not need to advance any hypotheses about the influence of the *Summa* on the Romans commentary or vice versa, only to distinguish them both from the views of the early part of the *Contra gentiles*. All serious datings allow that.[29] That the matter of the Romans commentary elucidates the matter of the *Summa*, and vice versa, is to be proved in the doing.

I

"Sacred Doctrine Is Scientia":
A Hypothesis Elaborated and
a Partial Test Prepared

2

"Sacred Doctrine Is Scientia":
A Reading of Question 1

Hypothesis elaborated

Question 1 of the *Summa theologiae* (I.1.1–10) sets out the last of Thomas Aquinas's several systematic attempts to describe what sort of discipline theology is and how it proceeds. This chapter undertakes to read that question afresh. It attends to how Question 1 relates the intellectual practice of the Christian community to the revelation in Jesus Christ as biblically narrated, or, in the *Summa's* terms, how Question 1 relates sacred doctrine to sacred scripture. I propose that Question 1 commits the *Summa*—in possible distinction from earlier works of Thomas—to a much higher view of the Bible than usually supposed, one deeply if tacitly christoform. Furthermore, Question 1 makes Thomas's Aristotelianism nothing other than a term of that relation. That characterization applies especially to his use of the Aristotelian concept of *"scientia"* to define sacred doctrine. Indeed, it is just the concept *"scientia"* that Thomas deploys, in no less than four nuanced ways, to say how the teaching of the community depends systematically upon the revelation in Jesus Christ.

I develop that claim as a double hypothesis: In the equation "sacred doctrine is *scientia*" (I.1.2), Thomas has structured or set up sacred doctrine so that (1) *the more Aristotelian it is, the more scriptural it is.* That relation requires as a presupposition that (2) *the more Aristotelian it is, the more christoform it is.*

Let me anticipate two objections immediately. On the basis of what texts ought we even to entertain the hypotheses? Granted Thomas's Aristotelianism, why relate that commitment to his use of scripture? The answer is a promissory note: because the hypothesis renders the two articles on scripture that close Question 1 not just ancillary but integral to that question. And granted that Thomas first addresses christology at length in the Third Part of the *Summa*, why should we look for christoformity in the other two Parts, where his silences on the matter may run for hundreds of pages?[1] Why would Thomas leave a crucial christological presupposition to be recalled for long stretches without repetition? Because he thinks more like a mathematician and less like an after-dinner speaker: the christological presupposition can very well go without saying when Thomas programmatically announces it, like a negative sign before a parenthesis, and therefore constantly implies it.[2] By programmatic remarks I have in mind two that enclose all that lies between them under the sign of Christ. The opening parenthesis is the remark that "Christ, as a human being, is the way that has been stretched out for us into God" (via nobis tendendi in Deum, I.2 proem.). That is so, objectively, whether readers recognize it or not. Thomas does not cease to lead the reader on that way, just because he does not often look down at his feet. The closing parenthesis refers to that same via, "the way of truth for us, [which Jesus Christ] has demonstrated to us in himself" (viam veritatis nobis in seipso demonstravit, III prol.). The great parenthesis opens immediately after Thomas considers the scientific character of theology in Question 1, and closes only at the beginning of christology proper. It encloses everything else in the Summa. It encloses everything after Question 1 that is not itself explicit christology. Everything in the Summa is either christology, or marked with a christological sign. Everything that is not christology follows a road that Christ has stretched out, and everything that is not christology leads to the christology that stands at the road's end. For Jesus Christ is also "the consummation of the whole theological enterprise" (III prol.). Nor does he cease to be the fulfillment toward which it tends while it is on the way. Reminders and specifications occur along that way, as Thomas's tight articular structure allows and demands them, as when he remarks that it is "the mystery of Christ's incarnation and passion" that provides "the via for the human being coming to beatitude" (II–II.2.7 in init.). The Summa's christological reference is either explicit, or explicitly marked; it is either fulfilled, or on the way to fulfillment.

But the architectonic argument merely forestalls preliminary objections. The technical, Aristotelian means by which Thomas makes good on those claims—the way in which he renders Christ theology's via and consummatio, its form and end, not only by architectonic structures, but also in its procedure, deep in its very character as a science, is the burden of the main argument.

A short version of the main argument goes like this: A science is the more Aristotelian, the more it proceeds from first principles. Unitary first principles take propositional and real forms. For sacred doctrine, those first principles are respectively scripture and Christ.

A discipline counts the more as an Aristotelian science the more it attends and returns to its first principles; sacred doctrine, in the *Summa*, takes its axiomatic first principles from sacred scripture (I.1.8). The assertion about scripture leads into the assertion about Jesus Christ not only for Christian but also for Aristotelian reasons. For Thomas's Aristotelianism is realistic enough that propositional or noetic first principles participate in real or ontological ones.[3] Thus in I.1.2 Thomas says more accurately that sacred doctrine takes its first principles from "the divine revelation." And he does not locate the divine revelation immediately *in* sacred scripture, but he refers to a divine revelation "upon which sacred scripture is *founded*" (I.1.2 *ad* 2 *in fin.*). The divine revelation upon which sacred scripture is founded, it will become clear, is Jesus Christ. Thomas presupposes what Vatican II would take as its theme, that it was neither tradition nor scripture that God primarily chose to reveal, but God's very *self.*[4] The incarnation will become in Thomas's hands a new reality that founds a new science. And as an Aristotelian science may honor its first principles by mounting demonstrations from them, so sacred doctrine, in the *Summa*, finds its "most fitting" demonstration in Christ incarnate (I.2 proem. and III prol. with the *"convenientissimum"* of III.1.1 *s.c.*). Aristotelian demonstrations participate in the christological demonstration by analogy. Or so goes the argument.

I say that Thomas *sets up* sacred doctrine as *scientia* to emphasize his deliberate, authorial shaping of theology's intellectual form. If Michel Corbin is right, Thomas's thinking did not spring fully formed like Minerva from the head of Jupiter, but developed, so that from the *Sentence Commentaries* through the *De Trinitate* and the *Contra gentiles* to the final *Summa* he tried out different notions of how the intellectual practice of the church might function as a discipline.[5] Corbin himself uses the metaphor of different "figures" of theology or of its undergoing various Hegelian moments.[6] One could say that Thomas "construes" sacred doctrine as *scientia*, since when Thomas casts it as *scientia* he parses its grammar and explains its sense. Yet he does more. He nudges and changes entire problematics. In Question 1 he erects and readies for use a new intellectual apparatus, enabling an innovation in his developing craft and crucial to the *Summa's* theological project. Sacred-doctrine-as-*scientia* is the new set-up as a unity.

If we see in sacred-doctrine-as-*scientia* primarily an attempt, from outside theology, to relate faith and reason, or theology and philosophy, then we will misunderstand it. To relate theology and philosophy may have been the project with which Thomas began the *Contra gentiles* (although if Corbin is right, not the project with which he ended it),[7] and misreadings regularly arise from assimilating the *Summa of Theology* to the one *Against the Gentiles.*[8] In the *Summa theologiae,* however, Thomas does not use *scientia* primarily to relate biblical and extra-biblical knowledge, although he is never afraid to enrich the former with the latter. Rather, in Question 1 Thomas is working *within* sacred doctrine to specify a relation internal to it, a relation within sacred doctrine between the revelation that founds it and the explication that constitutes it. The *Summa* uses *scientia* as a tool to relate theology and Jesus Christ.[9]

The *Summa* represents an essay to *co-opt* Aristotelian *scientia* for the interests and purposes of sacred doctrine. In so doing the *Summa* undertakes to fulfill the charge to sacred doctrine that Thomas hears in 2 Corinthians 10:5, a verse that he frequently repeats and that he quotes as a characterization of sacred doctrine as a whole. It charges him "to lead back every understanding captive into obedience to Christ,"[10] "which certainly happens when a human being places all that he knows in the service of Christ and of the faith."[11] Aristotle offers just one of those captive understandings.

Nor, if Thomas understands Paul's charge aright, can the captive prove the Trojan horse in sacred doctrine that Thomas's Protestant and Orthodox detractors fear. The construction "the more Aristotelian, the *more* scriptural, the *more* christoform" seeks to allay that fear. It counters both the suspicion that the more sacred doctrine is Aristotelian, the *less* it can be scriptural or christoform, and the confidence that sacred doctrine can rest upon an Aristotelian first philosophy untransformed. It indicates rather how Thomas *so* co-opts Aristotle into the service of Christ as to constrain him *only* to lead readers more into scripture and Christ. The second clause, not the first, could stand alone: Sacred doctrine is scriptural. The Aristotelian *index* to that scripturalism is optional. Thomas characterizes the index "as if inferior" (I.1.5 *ad* 2). How can the inferior avoid becoming rival? Is that not precisely what happens almost immediately, when Question 2 offers the famous Five Ways, which have appeared to many to admit into sacred doctrine proofs from metaphysical as opposed to scriptural first principles for the existence of God, by trading on a distinction between philosophical "preambles" and theological "articles"? Such a test of the current Part of this essay is the task of the next. Here I can only reply that more familiar, rival readings, based on Question 2, seem to involve Thomas in self-contradiction. For to exempt Question 2 from Thomas's scripturalism has

the undesired effect of exempting it from his Aristotelianism as well, if
sacred doctrine counts as Aristotelian *scientia* precisely by attending to
scripture as to its first principles. Thomas determines in the *Summa* of theology *not* to treat *scientia* as a method in its own right, but as an instrument
for expressing the relation of sacred doctrine to Jesus Christ. Circular as it
stands, the reply is a promissory note that it is the purpose of this Part to
redeem.

The more Aristotelian...

When Thomas comes in I.1.2 to ask whether sacred doctrine qualifies as
scientia, he presupposes an exacting, Aristotelian notion of *scientia*. The
entire article, both the question and the answer, both the objections and
their solutions, presuppose that the scientific character of a discipline
depends upon its proceeding from first principles. The phrase *"procedere
ex principiis,"* in various forms and abbreviations, appears some half a
dozen times. Although the burden of the article is that sacred doctrine
takes its first principles from a higher science, that possessed by God and
the blessed, here we take up the prior question: what *are* first principles,
that Thomas finds them a fit instrument for articulating the procedure of
sacred doctrine? What does it *mean* for *scientia* to proceed from first
principles?

Proceeding from first principles does not mean merely deducing conclusions by syllogistic reasoning, even though Aristotle was the first to formal-
ize the process. It does include such reasoning. But so to narrow it misses
something crucial about Aristotle's realism. We moderns tend to take it for
granted that first principles are simply propositions: that-clauses, reducible
to words on paper, and that Aristotelianism is exhausted in arranging them
by means of categories and syllogisms. For Aristotle, however, and for a
strict Aristotelian like Thomas, who was engaged in most of his Aristotle
commentaries while he was writing the *Summa*,[12] first principles do not
exist primarily on paper, and the propositional aspect does not exhaust
their relations among themselves. First principles pervade everything that
is. For that reason it is no paradox for Aristotle to locate first principles
indifferently in two places that we moderns tend to regard as poles apart: in
the mind and in things in the world.

On account of that modern polarity, a mere catalogue of the Aristotelian uses of the phrase "first principles" would look like a series of

category mistakes, apples and oranges, propositions and things. "[F]irst principles...include beliefs and propositions. But Aristotle also regards things—non-linguistic, non-psychological, non-propositional entities—as first principles."[13] No category mistake, the concept of a first principle "unites what contemporary idiom divides."[14] First principles are unitary beginnings (*archai*) that make both things and ideas work. They identify a single necessity, of which we are accustomed to distinguish two aspects. Aristotle regards as first principles both propositions about the four elements, and the four elements themselves, without sharp distinction.[15] Propositions about real atoms, and the real atoms mentioned in the propositions, reflect the same first principle, manifest in two ways. Birds fly through the air and ornithology makes sense in our minds by a single necessity in two aspects.[16] The phrase "first principles" may refer to the single necessity; that is its original, integral sense. Or it may distinguish the two for purposes of analysis. So in his commentary on the *Physics* book II, Thomas specifies that "After the Philosopher, in the first book, investigates the *first principles of natural things*, here he investigates the *first principles of natural science*."[17] That is not two sets of principles, one for things and one for thinking, but one set of principles in two contexts. Although Thomas's theological commitments will require further refinements, for the time being we may call the two aspects real (thingly) and propositional. *Scientia* proceeds from unitary first principles in *both* aspects, propositional *and* real.

In order to maintain the real aspect against propositionalist distortion, we need to pursue it onto another level, onto the level of form. "First principles," "form," and a third term, "final ends," are three interrelated ways of talking about the same Aristotelian insight. Both things and thoughts, for Aristotle, are on the way *from* something *to* something, and the whole journey hangs together. Things enjoy an organic development, so that the beginning pushes toward the end, and the end pulls from the beginning. The beginning is a first principle (*archê*), the end is a final principle (*telos*), and the way in between is an inner principle, or form (*morphê*).[18]

First principles inhere in actually existing things as their forms, and thingly forms begin in actually existing things as their first principles. Real first principles aim, and forms guide—first principles drive, and forms structure the development of things in the world toward their end. It falls to first principles as forms of things, therefore, to secure a fitting or in-itself-intelligible passage of a thing from source to end. As its form, a first principle provides a thing with a track or path or plan along which it can run in its passage. On the level of actually existing things, first principles, as forms, are keys to the natures of things; for to have a nature is just to possess an internal principle of change.[19] The inner principles or forms are sources of intelligibility or enjoy intelligibility in themselves, whether anybody notices it or not. The corresponding first principles, therefore, found sciences, whether anybody practices them or not. The first principles of birds, say, manifest themselves in birds' formal structures—wings, feathers, beaks, nests—whether or not the same first principles manage to manifest themselves also in the formal rationales of a developed ornithology. Forms give developing sciences threads to trace; ends give them forms achieved; natures, in short, give sciences something to be *of*.

Because the principles of existing things already exist in the world, and because the principles of *scientia* are the selfsame ones in different guise, intelligibility too, or followable structure, exists in itself, can show itself in the world without first showing itself in us, belongs to the structure of reality and the nature of things. It is that feature of Aristotelian science that makes room for division and debate. "Nothing prohibits that which is more certain with respect to its nature (*certius secundum naturam*) from being less certain with respect to us (*quoad nos minus certum*) on account of the weakness of our intellect, which 'blinks at the most evident things like a bat in the sunshine'."[20]

In Aristotle we may, without paradox, even reverse the usual attributes of real and propositional first principles. It is usual to say: On account of form, structural relations exist within and among things; on account of the same form, explanatory relations exist within and among propositions. But we can also say: On account of form, structural relations exist among propositions, and explanatory relations exist among things. In short, one thing can explain another. One thing can even explain another without explaining it to us.

In that case we have a science waiting to be discovered. In contrast to our modern ways of thinking about science, an Aristotelian science is identically the *real* or thingly as well as the mental set-up or structure. It is as if Aristotle had derived *epistêmê*, "knowledge" or "science," from *epistêma*, "something set upright," something as physical as a monument or the ornament on a prow, a concrete structure.[21] Ornithology is not just *about* birds and *in* minds; ornithology is also, concretely, *in* birds. We may, in Corbin's usage, call ornithology a "real science"[22] because it enjoys a real aspect—a "non-psychological, non-linguistic, non-propositional,"[23] thingly aspect. "Real" does not so much bestow an ontological compliment as it corrects against propositionalist reduction. For it is the one form that elaborates itself at once in minds and things.

Should anyone object that sciences are not only discovered but also invented, Aristotle would demur, and point out that like discovery, invention too is the working out of a singular form. Form does not grant us unmediated access to reality, but form humanly grasped must be linguistic, and linguistic formulations depend for their proper context upon the total state of the mind in which they inhere, which is determined by moral, historical, and cultural matters, among other things (I.85.5 *ad* 3). That goes for faith, too (II–II.1.2 *in init.*). Form is not foundationalist in the modern sense, and does not exclude interpretation. Indeed, it is one of form's purposes to furnish an explanation for the fact that interpretation is ineliminable.

It is the same thing to say that an inner principle elaborates itself in minds and things, as to say that minds and things undergo development in response to integral first principles. Just then, in Corbin's words, "an object shows itself, . . . a real source of light presents itself, . . . true principles are apprehended."[24] Just then a discipline exists, in Corbin's word, with *scientificité*, with real scientific character. A real science enjoys its scientific character "not just on account of the play of categories, judgments, and syllogisms in it";[25] it enjoys scientific character just "*because* an object shows itself, because a real source of light presents itself." Then, in short, a science proceeds from first principles. It proceeds from first principles that belong alike to propositions and things, that cohere with inner and final principles in the self-elaboration of form. The mere play of categories, judgments, and syllogisms, on the other hand, cannot supply a science with an object or a real form, cannot furnish it with real first principles.

A few short steps can carry one rather far from this view. It is possible first of all not only to distinguish the propositional from the real aspects of a science, but to abstract them. One might go on, after abstracting the one from the other, to a second-order reflection on propositions as such, how they operate, on the play of categories, judgments, and syllogisms in general. One would then be attending to discourse itself, to the process by which human minds proceed from more to less known in language and over time. In so doing one would prescind from the real forms that give these propositions content and make this science distinct. There would be nothing wrong with that movement; only one would by now have left the realm of real (thingly) science and entered the realm of logic. One would thereby have left the realm as well of any particular propositional science, for logic is marked in Aristotle as "common to all sciences," peculiar to none.[26] For logic *abstracts* from the very features—those peculiar to a distinct form—to which a science *attends*.

That brings us to a new distinction that runs athwart the one between a science's propositional and real aspects, which analyzed the twofold expression of a single form. The first distinction, to put it crudely, was between the world and the mind, both of which may be logical, and both of which have content. The second distinction, crudely, is between content and structure, both of which may arise from the world, and both of which may arise from the mind.

The new distinction arises now that we have one procedure that attends to form, whether propositional or real, and one that abstracts from it. To stress the difference Corbin calls the first procedure, the one that attends to form, scientific or principial, and the second, which abstracts from it, discursive, reflexive, or logical.[27] Here again the two aspects, scientific and discursive, are finally inalienable from each other. The discursive aspect, or logic, is inseparable from any real science, and belongs to it by a natural necessity, as a shadow follows and retraces a body that it cannot, however, replace. "Discursive" has a technical meaning in Thomas. It describes the process of a finite mind in "running" (*discurro*) from one conclusion to another, one at a time, in order, rather than all at once. A correct running from one conclusion to another is what logic seeks to provide. Logic studies this running itself, finite thinking; it is discourse about discourse. Unlike a real form, logic's reflexive work is not itself a new source of light. It secures the necessary or negative, not the sufficient conditions of truth.[28] An Aristotelian science does not proceed from first principles on account of the inalienable play of logic in it, but logic is inalienable from it just when *scientia* proceeds—organically, if you will—from first principles. It is first principles—*archai*—that give rise to a science, not isolated logic. It is first principles, not logic, that give a science its properly scientific (i.e., its particular form-governed) as opposed to its reflexive or discourse-specific character. When Thomas writes that a science "proceeds from first principles," he is not remarking on its discursivity or its logic. He is remarking on its deep connectedness with a concrete object that gives it rise. "Briefly, in strict Aristotelianism sacred doctrine is not founded as a science by the fact of drawing its conclusions from first principles, but by the first principles' very *existence*."[29] When you have logic, then you have logic. When you have a set of first principles, then you have a virtual or elaborated science. In the *Summa*, a science is the more Aristotelian the more it is principled, not the more it is reflexive. A merely reflexive or discourse-immanent discipline could in theory confine itself to manipulating its signs; a discipline proceeding from Aristotelian first principles requires some reality to give it light. In the *Summa* a discipline is the more *scientia* the more it attends to first principles holding thingly and propositional aspects together.

Corbin renders the thesis about Thomas's historical development in a way that heightens its importance for us as readers. Thomas occupied other intellectual positions, which he abandoned. If we fail to understand his progress we may be left behind in them. Corbin argues that Thomas came to *replace* an emphasis on a science's reflexive aspect with an emphasis on its principled aspect, and that the change came with the *Summa*.[30]

In earlier works, Thomas had described the dependence of sacred doctrine upon God in terms of subalternation or quasi-subalternation. A subalternate science took its first principles from another, as music from arithmetic. In the *Summa* the example remains, but the previous explanation has disappeared, along with its accompanying terms of art. The reason, according to Corbin, is that earlier Thomas *had* thought of a discipline's scientific character as proceeding from its reflexive aspect, from its deployment of categories, syllogisms, and judgments. In the *De Trinitate* he had offered the definition that "the character (*ratio*) of *scientia* consists in that from certain known things other, unknown things are recognized (*cognoscantur*)" (*De Trin.* q. 2, art. 2). And that definition had seemed to *explain* the subalternation of disciplines in terms of the process of deduction, a logical aspect, or in terms of *following another's knowledge* rather than *borrowing another's principles*. The theory called subalternation located the continuity of scientific character, the bearer of *scientificité*, on a subjective rather than on an objective plane. Yet while the musician who takes her first principles from arithmetic can also study arithmetic, if she pleases, and follow the deductive links that bind them to higher first principles, the student of sacred doctrine has no independent access to the first principles it takes from the *scientia* enjoyed by God. So Thomas introduced the qualification of "quasi-subalternation" in concession to the disanalogy.[31] But to take a science's first principles from another that one cannot, in principle, ever seize for oneself, precisely *breaks* the discursive aspect. That the first principles of sacred doctrine are true is a judgment human discourse cannot make, so that quasi-subalternation, so conceived, is no subalternation at all, but rupture. With that the scientific character to be established is not established but ruined.

It is a new appreciation of Aristotle, according to Corbin, that gets

Thomas out of the bind. Real first principles can relate to each other, without their relation depending on our knowledge of it. So Thomas omits the definition of *scientia* and the related terms, not because they are false, but because they highlight an aspect of *scientia* (its discursivity) that proves unhelpful to his project. Scientific character now proceeds from first principles not on account of the (discursive) *linkages* they boast with a higher science, but on account of the (principial) *light they shed,* even if it lies beyond us.

The change shows us, in other words, that Thomas now interprets *all* sciences as proceeding from so many revelations, small "r," or from the self-manifestations of real forms, real first principles. We may even gloss the scientific or principial character of a science as its revelatory character. We do *not,* as Thomas used to think, have a distinct science when we have logic; logic is common to all. We have a distinct science when we have a distinct *revelation,* be it ever so worldly; or, to put it in uncontroversial terms, when we have a distinct form. It is distinction of form that diversifies sciences: "Things that relate in distinct ways to their matter pertain to distinct sciences."[32]

That is not only better theology but better Aristotle. According to that account, sacred doctrine is not a deficient science for proceeding from Revelation: it is rather for that very reason a proper science; indeed, science *par excellence.* To proceed from first principles does not mean, except incidentally, to proceed logically. *To proceed from first principles means, in the* Summa's *version of Aristotle, to proceed from formal "revelations."* According to that account, furthermore, to read the *Summa* as basing the scientific character of sacred doctrine merely upon its discursive, logical form, is not only to misread the text, but to foist upon it the very mistake that it is trying to correct.

In reading the *Summa,* therefore, we may not replace talk of a scientific character that proceeds from first principles with talk of a discursive character that abstracts from them. (For sacred doctrine, that will mean we may not elide sacred scripture in favor of pure deduction.) And when we talk about first principles we may not reduce them to their propositional aspect. (For sacred doctrine, that will mean that we may not separate sacred scripture from Jesus Christ.) In applying the original, integral, revelatory notion of first principles to sacred doctrine, Thomas Aquinas exploits real and propositional aspects in their identity and difference. At least since John of St. Thomas (d. 1654), however, commentators have been reducing the scientific or revelatory character of sacred doctrine to a merely discursive one. Instead of *sermo de Deo* we get *sermo de conclusionibus.*[33]

As a corrective, we must listen for the possibility that Thomas may be speaking of first principles or even sciences also in their real, principial, revelatory aspect. In article 7, for example, Thomas insists that "an entire science is contained virtually in its first principles [*tota scientia virtute contineatur in principiis*]." A controversy attends the interpretation of that pregnant sentence. Corbin uses it as a prooftext for the generative power of real first principles.[34] A footnote at that point in the Blackfriars edition, on the other hand, limits the text with a discursivist gloss. Two sorts of arguments move us beyond such interpretations-by-assertion. One argument is from the context of the remark in the article, and the other is from a related usage of the pivotal word, "virtual."

In the text we observe that it is the presupposition already of objection 2, for example, that sacred doctrine considers real states of affairs because scripture does so; the body of the article shares that presupposition as it responds. It is the burden of the response's initial exposition, furthermore, that a scientific discipline relates to its subject as a human power (like vision) relates to its object, where vision regards qualities (like coloration) "proper to the object seen." Because everything considered (*"omnia pertractata"*) in sacred doctrine is related to God as (real, not discursive) beginning and end, "therefore it follows that God is really [*vere*] the subject of this science." Only in that context does Thomas go on to speak in a new register, marked in some editions by a long dash, and in the text by the particle *"etiam,"* of the science's propositional aspect in the articles of faith. In short, the *omnia pertractata* are real; the *articuli fidei* are propositional; and the phrase *tota scientia* sums up *both* aspects as contained virtually in the first principles that are revelatory of it.

A confirming argument arises from the range of the word "virtual." To alienate the *virtus* or power of first principles from the form that exists in things is to alienate us human beings from our bodies and confuse us with angels. In I.58.3 Thomas considers the way in which *scientia* is virtually contained in first principles *for angels.* Angels differ from human beings in lacking matter. They also enjoy more powerful intellects than we do; they may work by intuition or seeing things at once, as God does. (Following Augustine, Thomas calls it "morning knowledge.") Since they lack matter, angels have no contact with bodily reality through sense impressions and must receive them infused by God.[35] Should God favor them with infused sense impressions, angels can also deploy discursive reasoning, as human beings do, moving from more to less known over time (called "evening knowledge"). In a sense, however, angels do not themselves encounter first principles in what we have been calling their real aspect, that is, in concretely formed matter. In another sense, the realest real is the intention in the mind of God. For angels, therefore, *scientia* can be virtually contained in first principles *only* as abstracted from their real or material aspect. But for human beings, to abstract first principles from their real aspect not only forgets the way in which human *minds* work, but leaves human *bodies* out of *scientia*. Leaving human bodies out of the process would cause a defect in the *scientia* sought by faith, since it would thereby cut the bodies of the faithful off from the process of redemption. To be a human science is to be principled in a way that does not violate human nature but respects God's purpose in making the world and human minds for each other: God did not make the world for the angels. Human science must therefore keep things and propositions together on account of the human creaturely nature and God's creatorly will. Hence for theological reasons, too, first principles contain a science wholly and virtually, or in power.

So far *procedere ex principiis*. All science arises from small-"r" revelations; sacred doctrine too arises from a revelation; therefore sacred doctrine counts as science, even science *par excellence*. Now I turn to an objection on another front. Does Thomas's implicit syllogism covertly level out the difference between formal "revelations" and Revelation? Does the move really raise Aristotle to competence in theology, or does it reduce theology to the level of any other science? The answer to the question involves Thomas's invention of *"revelabilia"* as a category for sacred doctrine's formal objects.

In Aristotelian Latin distinct forms often make words ending in *"-ibilia."* It would be a mistranslation to say that *visibilia*, say, are simply things that can be seen.[36] For their *form* of visibility remains even if there were no one to see them. Thus it is precisely in the nature of things that individual Aristotelian sciences get delimited by the "x-ibilia" that they consider. *Not* all things possess the intrinsic property of being visible, or edible, or audible. The only science that considers all things whatsoever, in abstraction from their various formalities, or intrinsic x-ibilia, is metaphysics, the most universal science. Or better, metaphysics considers things according to their universal characteristic of intelligibility, as *intelligibilia*. For Aristotle it is analytic that things are intelligible, that *res* count as *intelligibilia*. And since Aristotelian inquiry ends with "that which is," to consider things as things is nothing other than to consider them as *intelligibilia*. Or, for human beings, "that which is" is an abbreviation for "that which is *intelligible.*" So are we made. Interpretation is built into the one world. It is possible to imagine other completions. If "that which is" stood for "that which is edible," or if eating were built into the world for us, then we would be different creatures—say, goats. For Aristotle there is no other category into which all things whatsoever could go, except that of *intelligibilia*, and no science that could consider them all, except metaphysics.

In the act of understanding the *intelligibilia* and the intellect, sharing a form, are one.[37] For things and knowers actually befit each other. Since for Thomas and for Aristotle to have a nature is to be driven by a form toward an end, and since for Thomas and for Aristotle human beings reach their end by *themselves* ordering their actions and intentions toward their end (I.1.1, II–II as a whole)—as opposed to rocks, which find their end by a proper motion involuntary to them, and animals, which find their end by an instinctual activity not deliberate in them—the form driving human beings actually propels us toward understanding, where "understanding" means our mental grasp of first principles as intelligible forms. For *we*, unlike rocks and animals, must have understanding in order to order our intentions and actions toward our end. The understanding that we reach for and the intelligibility of things have the same first principles and the same form. Jonathan Lear puts it like this: "[Aristotle's] inquiry into nature revealed the world as meant to be known; the inquiry into [the human] soul revealed [the human being] as...meant to be a knower. [Human being] and world are, as it were, made for each other."[38]

A science is the more Aristotelian, therefore, the more it accounts for or discovers that integrity, that mutual fittingness, that quality of belonging to each other, of human beings and the world. It is in unitary first principles that the integrity resides. A science *accounts for* its integrity by tightening the logical and descriptive links that, in human minds and language, join mind to thing, the psychological aspect of first principles to the real. A science *possesses* its integrity in returning to the really existing things that, in the extramental world, embody first principles as forms, and, as a formal "light," illuminate the mind. It is part of the development of forms in the world to manifest themselves and, in the presence of knowers, to render themselves better known. A science is not the more Aristotelian the more it deploys syllogisms, unless the syllogisms connect to first principles that reveal the real. That is the way in which it marks a science to *"procedere ex principiis.*" It proceeds from them both logically and really, as a form elaborates itself in an intelligible structure.

Integrity lost

Lear speaks of the world as "meant" to be known, the human being as "meant" to be a knower, and of the two as made "for" each other. In Aristotle that relation implies intentionality only as a trope. Intentionality raises two new problems for Thomas that we have yet to address. One is what it means for a human being to have something in mind; this is a complex issue that I have, so far, ignored. Another is what it means for God to have a will. We take up the second first. Although Aristotle speaks of the divine, and understanding partakes of it, there is no will behind the "meant" to be or the making "for." The whole point of form is to explicate teleology without intention,[39] as of the unmoved mover to explicate causation without extension.[40] Both *telos* and prime mover attract, that is, without willing.

For Thomas, on the other hand, "everyone speaking of God intends to name 'God' that which has universal providence over things" (I.13.8 *ca. fin.*). In a series of small steps that go a long way, Thomas uses Aristotle against himself to move from teleology without intention to teleology centered on Christ. The result is a transformation that Aristotle would lack the tradition to understand. In the first step, Thomas plays on the Latin words to render providence a part of prudence, the virtue which for Aristotle orders means and ends, the most intentional, we might say, of virtues (I.22.1). It is then but another short step to see God's highly intentional prudence in the biblical character of Wisdom. Thomas goes on to refer providence to the one whom Wisdom calls "you, Father" (I.22.1, *sed contra* and corpus)—which identifies Wisdom as the Logos. So christology has assumed teleology, rendering Aristotle's account a deficient, reified case of itself. For Aristotle human beings were made by impersonal form for the world; for Thomas human creatures were made for God by God, a person capable of direct address in words like "Father."

Article 6 of Question 1 anticipates that move. In answer to the question, whether sacred doctrine is *sapientia* or wisdom, Thomas departs from Aristotle to describe the wisdom of *scientia* not as a reflection of the orderliness of nature, but as a reflection of the ordering of the Creator. Metaphysics was wisdom because Aristotle finds the world well ordered to human understanding. Sacred doctrine is wisdom, on the other hand, because "the highest cause of the entire universe, which is God, is called maximally wise" (I.1.6)—and precisely *not* because we find the world well ordered to our understanding. To find it well ordered is a desire frustrated without revelation; Thomas's providence, unlike Aristotle's teleology, is illegible short of revelation. The reading of providence requires the reading of God's intention in relating things. But God's intention in relating things is found in the literal sense of scripture, or perhaps more often, in spiritual senses founded more or less christologically upon it (I.1.10).

We may regard the whole problem of the return of Aristotle into the consciousness of the three great religions that accord some authority to Genesis as the problem of how to bend or break or co-opt Aristotle to the articulation of God's radical transcendence. David Burrell has compared and contrasted the responses to this problem of Maimonides, Ibn-Sina, and Thomas in his book *Knowing the Unknowable God*. Chenu has catalogued the responses of Western Christian theologians in the thirteenth century. Victor Preller has used Thomas to explore and articulate the way in which "'referring to God' is a *most* peculiar thing to intend," just when God outlies the reach of the human intellect.[41] Stylistic peculiarities in the articles on creation in Question 46 show how Thomas is struggling. Objections multiply to eight or ten. Thomas calls his opponents by name. Syntax stretches beyond the bounds of normal Latin and resorts to the medieval definite article, "*ly.*" But to pursue the matter of those articles in detail would take us far afield. Suffice it to say that the Aristotelian unity that Irwin and Lear describe can also be described as coming apart, for Thomas, for two reasons that are consequences of the doctrine of intentional creation *ex nihilo*.

For Thomas, unlike Aristotle, the structural first principles of the world—its set-up—lie radically outside the world, in the mind of an unreachable God. And for Thomas the intellectual first principles of the understanding—that which the human creature demands and desires—lie radically beyond our capacity. Thomas constantly implies and frequently expresses those views, both on the level of knowing, since "a human being is ordered to God as to some end that outstrips the comprehension of reason" (I.1.1) and on the level of being, since "the object...of the human appetite...is not found in anything created, but alone in God" (I–II.2.8). For Aristotle, in other words, *that which is* marks the home of first principles and the end of inquiry; for Thomas, on the other hand, it is God in which all things have their home and that marks inquiry's end, and what

God is remains "entirely unknown to the human creature in this life [*omnino ignoto homini in hac vita*]."[42]

Yet Thomas will rarely highlight the disagreement with Aristotle. He prefers to co-opt him by using one part of Aristotle against another. So Thomas marshals the *De anima*, for example, to his own purposes: "Now the object of the intellect is 'that which is,' that is, the essence of a thing, as it is said in *De anima* III [430b27]." So far, so good. Now, without so much as a raised eyebrow, the twist: "If therefore the human intellect, recognizing the essence of some created effect, recognizes of God only *whether* God is, then the perfection of the intellect does not yet arrive at the first cause, but a natural desire for inquiring into the cause remains to it.... And thus it will have its perfection by union with God as object, in whom alone the beatitude of the human being consists" (I–II.3.8). Aristotle would already have stopped at "what is," which Thomas has relativized into "created effects of God." But Thomas can push further: since "in this life we do not recognize about God *why* [*quia*] God is, and so are united to God as to One unknown" (I.12.13 *ad* 1), the union must take place by faith, which "proceeds not from the vision of the believer, but by the vision of the One Who is believed" (I.12.13 *ad* 2). Thomas has in a few sentences taken several steps beyond Aristotle. First he used the *Metaphysics* to move from teleology to christology; now he uses the *De anima* to move from "that which is" to the effects of God, from the effects of God to the unknown essence of God, from the unknowability of God to faith, and from faith to "the One who is believed." Each time he uses Aristotle as a ladder to be lifted up to his level from behind and replaced before him to climb to the next. So Thomas finesses out of Aristotle an articulation of the Creator's radical transcendence. For Aristotle, what is most knowable in itself becomes, eventually, most known to us, and is for that reason divine; for Thomas, what is most knowable in itself remains, in this life, least knowable to us, just because it is the Creator.

Yet in a new and more radical way Thomas does maintain or restore the Aristotelian unity between the knower and the most knowable, between the desire and the desired. He articulates the loss and manages the reconstruction of the integrity of an Aristotelian science, embedding it, as he does so, into a sacred doctrine that subscribes to creation *ex nihilo*. The reconstruction requires another distinction. It turns out that Thomas uses *scientia* in four ways.

For Aristotle it is among the virtues of first principles to hold the four aspects together, even if he must sometimes distinguish them; for Thomas it is among the requirements of earthly sacred doctrine that he keep the four distinct, even if *scientia Dei* and Aristotle keep them together. Thomas does honor the demand for unity: only the doctrine of creation *ex nihilo* requires him to move the locus of unity outside the world. To put the four aspects back together again therefore also requires him to move the locus of inquiry outside the world, where our minds cannot reach.

For Aristotle: the demand of the human being for intelligibility, the natural desire to know, is answered by *first principles as the end of a program of inquiry;* the effective structure of the soul that results from such intelligibility consists in *first principles as acquired forms or habits of the soul;* the academic discipline or logic-informed study that embodies that intelligibility derives from *first principles as the propositional axioms of deduction in an inquiry provisionally or finally in good order;* and the intelligible structure of reality to which that intelligibility corresponds arises from *first principles as the forms of natural things.* We have, in sum, first principles in four aspects: as the end of inquiry, as habits of the soul, as the axioms of a discipline, and as the forms of things.[43]

Four aspects of first principles lead to four aspects of the intelligible structure that we are used to calling *"scientia"* in only some of those aspects. As the end of inquiry, *scientia* answers the human desire to know. As a habit of the soul, *scientia* conforms the mind to reality. As an academic discipline, *scientia* formalizes deductions from axioms. And, since the form that is knowledge and the form that drives things are one and the same form, we can even say that, as a structure of reality, *scientia* informs the development of things. If the last aspect sounds odd, it is because, as Lear puts it, "'philosophical activity' is a name we give to substantial form only belatedly: form was operating as a basic force long before humans...were in a position to indulge their desire to understand."[44]

In another respect, however, we *are* used to thinking of knowledge as causative, namely when it works creatively in the mind of God. "The *scientia* that God has is the cause of things [*scientia Dei est causa rerum*]," Thomas says in I.14.8. That is already to introduce a Thomistic distinction where Aristotle knew none. Aristotle does not distinguish in principle between the knowledge that God has and the knowledge that human beings have in this life. The divine mind, like the human, is a place where forms reside, even if, in the latter case, in total unity. In Aristotle it is a residence that possesses an intentionality neither more, less, nor other than form. For "intentionality" could only be another of form's aspects, but not anything more primitive. In a similar way some modern literary critics ascribe an intentionality function to an "implied author" inferred from the form of the text. In a similar way, too, Freud can be interpreted so that psychoanalysis aids individuation as the coming to self-consciousness of a human form.[45] The divine, for Aristotle, has forms as a rational but not a voluntary structure, as Mind but not as Will. Thus for divine and human minds to have that form is *the same thing;* there *is* nothing more than to grasp form. On the contrary, to distinguish the understanding of God and the understanding of human beings would be, for Aristotle, to divide, to dis-integrate the form, to divorce it from its worldly home. Aristotle is paying no empty compliment to human beings, but acknowledging the form's integrity in its manifold working out, when he says that the understanding of first principles is divine.[46] Creativity in the world belongs to form, the same in us as in the divine mind, when we grasp it.

We have already begun to pull a thread out of the Aristotelian unity. The four aspects have already begun to unravel, so that the real or causative aspect of *scientia* has become hard to explain in strictly Aristotelian terms. In Thomas God has not only mind but will, not only form but intention. The causative aspect of *scientia* is clearer in Thomas than in Aristotle, if under *scientia* we recall what Thomas says about *scientia Dei.* "For the *scientia* that God has relates to all created things as the *scientia* of an artisan relates to things made. And the *scientia* of the artisan is the cause of the things made." So far Aristotle could also go, if all we had were an analogy. But Thomas uses Aristotle against himself. "For since an intelligible form relates to opposed things (since the *scientia* of opposed things is the same), it does not produce a determined effect, unless it is determined to one thing by the appetite, as it is said in the ninth[47] book of the *Metaphysics....* Hence it is necessary that God's *scientia* be the cause of things *according as it has will conjoined to it.* Hence the *scientia* that God has, as the cause of things, is wont to be named 'the *scientia* of approbation'" ("*scientia approbationis*"; I.14.9). That is the approbation that God expresses in Genesis 1 when it repeats the refrain (vv. 4, 10, 12, 18, 21, 26, 31), "And God saw what God had made, and it was good," where for Thomas "seeing" indicates possessing *scientia.*

Thus Thomas, unlike Aristotle, distinguishes sharply between the knowledge that God has and the knowledge that human beings have in this life, as between Creator and creature. The science possessed by God and the blessed (I.1.2) is reserved for the next. And the discipline available to us in this life, sacred doctrine, is a science *borrowed* (I.1.2) and taken on authority (I.1.8). Sacred doctrine is a science with believers only. That situation constitutes a contradiction in terms to Aristotle. Yet in this life we are united to the subject of sacred doctrine only in the habit of faith, not in that of *scientia* (I.12.13 *ad* 1). And the same person cannot have faith and *scientia* of the same thing in the same way at the same time: the answer to the question, whether those things that are of faith can be known (*scita*), is "no" (II–II.1.5).[48] Victor Preller reports that "*scire* is never used in connection with cognitions of God through natural reason": the word is "*cognoscere*."[49] Call it Preller's rule. For Thomas makes it a strict rule of properly formed speech in sacred doctrine that in this life human beings have *scientia* only "*circa res humanas*" (II–II.9.2). "*Circa res divinas*" human beings can have only faith. The exception proves the rule. For when Isaiah (11:2–3, II–II.9.1) counts *scientia* among the gifts of the Spirit, Thomas *denies* that *scientia* concerns divine things (II–II.9.2), because it is *scientia* only of *whether or not* some propositions are to be humanly *believed*.[50] For the things to be believed have the aspect of something temporal in the soul of the believer; that is, they count as *res humanas* (II–II.9.2 *ad* 1 *in init.*). Among the perfections of *scientia*, sacred doctrine lacks the one Thomas calls its *plena possessio* by human beings (I–II.68.2c). That is, although the *discipline* of sacred doctrine is a science (I.1.2), the *habit* (II–II.1.5) is not. Thomas presents us with a paradox. In sacred doctrine we have a science without scientists.[51]

The demand of the human being to know cannot be answered simply by *scientia* because the source of the intelligibility of the world and the end of the program of human inquiry lie outside the world, in God beyond creation, and beyond the reach of human powers, whose "what is" remains entirely unknown to us in this life. Thus in sacred doctrine the appropriate inquiry must begin not by collecting and evaluating the previous results of students of an extratextual natural world who have gone before, but by collecting and evaluating the previous results of students of revelation, interpreters of a world-defining text, who have gone before.

I do not mean to set up a thoroughly modern and unThomistic contrast between a scientistic understanding of the world on the one hand and a fundamentalist understanding of the Bible on the other, each of them foundationalist, in order to elevate the latter. Rather I appeal to the distinction we have begun to discuss between *res* and *revelabilia*. *Revelabilia* are not the same as *revelata*. *Revelata* make a sharp distinction between the world of our experience and the world of the Bible—the latter is revealed and the former is not. *Revelata* set up two domains, one accessible and the other inaccessible. *Revelabilia* do not. Nor do they simply erase the distinction and render all things revealed. They sublate it. They remind us that "all things whatsoever [*omnia quaecumque*]" are reveal*able*: that is, they place *omnia quaecumque* under God's providence; all things whatsoever, and not just the revealed ones, form part of the great salvation history of which the Bible narrates the important parts; all things whatsoever might, in principle, show up in those pages. Our world and the world of the Bible are again one unitary world, and they are one on God's terms, one under providence. The text does not confine God, but God wills infallibly that human beings contingently and freely produce the text, each a total cause,[52] in simple consequence of God's providence over *omnia quaecumque*. Thomas rejects the modern dichotomy implicitly in I.1.3 when he rejects a distinction of *res* versus *revelata*. Thus elsewhere he insists that we ought to interpret the Bible in accord with the best deliverances so far of (relatively independent) natural science that prove adaptable to the text, "preserving the literal sense [*salva litterae circumstantia*]."[53]

If the *inquiry* of sacred doctrine leads to no fundamentalist certainty, that is among other things because the completed form of the science awaits us only in heaven. Thomas would regard some versions of fundamentalism as claiming *scientia Dei* here below. Here below we have only a *praecognitio* of the end (I.1.1), and we interpret it painstakingly with error and dispute: hence the *Summa*'s *quaestio*-format. A very large gap has opened up between the first principles of sacred doctrine as *scientia* and human inquiry into sacred doctrine as *scientia*—a gap as wide as that between Creator and creature.

Not only is there a problem about human *scientia* of divine things, so that in sacred doctrine Thomas presents the paradox of a science with only believers here below. Thomas has inherited a different problem about the residence of forms of any sort in the human mind—the philosophical problem of intentional (mental) forms. It, too, opens up a gap as wide as that between Creator and creature. So far I have ignored it. I have tended to speak as if extramental, worldly, so-called extensional forms could simply impress themselves on the mind. That is an oversimplification. It serves to recover a realistic aspect of Thomas's Aristotelianism, an aspect, after Kant, less controversial than overlooked. Yet Thomas states flatly that "nothing corporeal can make an impression on the noncorporeal" (I.84.6).

To understand the mechanism for overcoming that problem, we need an account of intentionality. In the relevant sense "intentionality" does not mislead us should we hear overtones of psychology rather than epistemology in the word, although matters of volition are involved at a distance.

The medieval problem of human knowing has to do with the human soul and its relation to God, and not with a Cartesian doubt or Kantian security historically abstracted from that context, so that (Aristotelian) psychology, even moral psychology, provides the place where matters of knowing find themselves properly at home. Here I can only refer to—I cannot even sketch—a full account of that complicated subject, which would include the relation of intentionality to the phantasms and the agent intellect.[54] Instead, I offer a brief account of the claim by which Thomas undertakes to save from inappropriateness the Aristotelian notion we have been trying to recover, apparently false or seriously abbreviated, that somehow the corporeal does make an impression on the noncorporeal. It is the proposition that "being is the first concept in the intellect." I follow Victor Preller.

> To have the concept 'being' is to be naturally disposed to use one's conceptual system to refer to the objects of experience.... To have the dispositional concept of 'being' is naturally to construct an intentional [mental] and analogical representation of the world and to judge it to be a mode of knowing objective reality.... That judgment is not a factor *in* our conscious experience, but a presupposition *of* our conscious experience.[55]

(This dispositional tendency or presupposition of all experience now sometimes goes under the name of "preapprehension of being," or, more festively, "*Vorgriff auf esse.*"[56])

> Aquinas holds that all [human beings] possess the kind of conceptual powers they do because God willed it so, and...God willed it so because such conceptual powers result in a mode of conceiving reality that is *appropriate* to the status of [the human being] *in via*—'on the way' to God. Aquinas would not say that we *falsely* conceive the world. For a [human being] 'on the way' correctly to conceive the world is for [that one] to conceive it in the way that we do. Aquinas does not maintain, however, that we directly or nonanalogically *know* the true natures of things [I.16.2]....
> The only way to know things *as they truly are* is to know them in God—by what Aquinas calls 'morning knowledge.' The 'intentional' existence that things have for God is a true, ideal, and completely adequate expression of what things really are in their own being.... The real nature of things is intentionally expressed only in the language or 'Word' of God.[57]

So a small-"r" revelation of what is (an immanent Aristotelian explanation ending with the existence of some thing, and reaching its summit in metaphysics) does give rise to a radically different, if analogical, sort of science from a Revelation of the Word. The latter is strictly beyond us. Should we "hear" God's "Word," it must shed for us a different formal light and create for us a different dispositional tendency in the human soul. Or, in biblical terms, Jesus Christ leaves his Spirit, who excites faith. Even with faith we do not come to share God's intentionality, at least in this life (I.12.13 *ad* 1). And even to begin[58]—that is, causally and not intrinsically[59]—to share God's intentionality could only be to begin to share God's life (I–II.110.3). Should God favor us with that destiny, it could only begin by God's own agency working, or indeed, the whole Trinity's dwelling in us;[60] that is, God's life begins only with God's life.

This is how Thomas's baptism of Aristotle[61] has taken the unity of *scientia* apart. In this case the human *inquiry* that normally leads to *scientia* fails radically. In this case we have a *scientia* without scientists, or whose "scientist" is God. We are dealing with a science that results rather from the *subject's* inquiry after *us*. The effective structuring or habituating of the *soul* that marks other cases of actual *scientia* is reserved by scripture and tradition for the Holy Spirit, infusing the theological virtues of faith, hope, and charity. The academic *discipline* or logic-informed study that usually instantiates *scientia* must borrow rather than possess its first principles, believing them revealed from a higher science (I.1.2). And the *reality* to which the revelation corresponds is no naturally comprehensible form, but God become human.

Thus terminological and material distinctions: the demand of the human being for intelligibility, the natural desire to know, is answered provisionally, in this life, by a *praecognitum finis* (I.1.1) and finally, in the next, by the *scientia Dei et beatorum* (I.1.2); the effective structure of the soul that results from revelation is the infused habit of *formed faith*; the academic discipline or logic-informed study that embodies that intelligibility in propositions is *sacred doctrine*, a science in virtue not of noting but of believing its first principles; and the intelligible structure of reality to which the science's intelligibility corresponds remains altogether unknown to us in this life even as faith unites us to it (I.12.13 *ad* 1) by a self-revelation of God—climaxing in the Word become flesh—to which we now enjoy only textual access.[62] The end of inquiry, the habits of the soul, the axioms of deduction, the forms of things in the world and our access to them have all come *radically* apart. The beatific vision, the habit of faith, the articles of faith, and the events of the incarnation, *ought*, if this is Aristotelian *scientia*, to be clearly one thing. But the circumstances of this life force them apart.

The more scriptural

It takes the *theological* concept of revelation (as it were with an arch, capital "R"), in several aspects, to put the features of *Aristotelian* science back together again. By returning to revelation, in several aspects, *as to its first principles,* sacred doctrine regains and restores Aristotelian scientific character (I.1.3). It does *not* do so, as Thomas sets it up, in such a way as to render sacred doctrine a case of an Aristotelian science that, on account of having borrowed first principles not *per se nota* by the light of their own science, should be accounted deficient. *On the contrary, it does so in such a way as to render other Aristotelian sciences deficient cases of itself.* They have all now come to depend upon as many revelations as formal rationales. It is a move of reversal. Better, it is a move of embedding or sublation. Sacred doctrine takes Aristotelian science up into itself. The latter boasts only revelations immanent in the world. Sacred doctrine considers revelation that transcends creation without therefore ceasing to inform it, or *scientia* whose first principles begin to move the world from without. *Sacred doctrine assumes* scientia *as Christ assumes flesh.*[63] It subordinates Aristotelian science, too, to the principle of creation borrowed from God's *scientia* and recorded in the scriptures. Properly understood, even natural science comes to explicate the doctrine of creation. In the Prologue to his John commentary, Thomas writes: "Natural science...considers things that proceed from God.... The Gospel of John contains all at once what the aforesaid [moral, natural, and metaphysical] sciences treat separately, and is therefore the most perfect."[64]

Alasdair MacIntyre writes that "Aquinas introduce[s] his commentary on the *Posterior Analytics* by distinguishing the task of analyzing judgments within a science, with a view to explaining their warrant and the kind of certitude to which we are entitled by that warrant, from the task of giving an account of investigation." He argues that it falls to the *Physics* and Aristotle's biological treatises to give an account of investigations under way, and to the *Posterior Analytics,* on the other hand, to describe not Aristotle's scientific method, but "what it would be to possess, to have already achieved, a perfected science, a perfected type of understanding, in which every movement of a mind within the structures of that type of understanding gives expression to the adequacy of that mind to its objects."[65] If MacIntyre is right, it is then no accident that Thomas refers to the *Posterior Analytics* in defining sacred doctine's unity, and that, according to

Corbin, he commented upon the *Posterior Analytics* during his redaction of the *Summa*.[66]

Sacred doctrine's character as unified, like its character as scientific at all, derives from the first principles it borrows from a science perfected rather than a science in the process of investigation. The very business of *borrowing*—rather than discovering—first principles alerts us to the fact that we are pursuing a perfected rather than investigative science. Principles stated in language, to be sure, will always need interpretation: that truth lies at a different level. *Scientia Dei et beatorum* is the complete and perfect form of a science, original and intuited in the mind of God, which would match the deductive and achieved form of a science described in the *Posterior Analytics*, were it subject (which it is not) to this-worldly human discursivity and achievement. When Thomas pursues a science that proceeds from principles that lie outside the world, he locates the completed, perfect science of the *Posterior Analytics* also outside the world. Under those circumstances, to proceed from first principles must therefore mean to proceed from borrowed, that is, *revealed* first principles—no longer in the straightforward sense in which all science proceeds from the revelations of existing things, but now in the radically theological sense in which a revelation sheds a light that goes beyond the created tendency to associate being with the deliverances of our natural conceptual scheme and requires an intentionality empowered by God's elevating agency.

As a matter of human interpretation, to be sure, sacred doctrine *does* resemble an investigative science, as MacIntyre also describes elsewhere:

> In the reading of texts there is a movement both towards apprehending what the text says and towards apprehending that of which the text speaks. Because obscurities, discrepancies, and inconsistencies were found both within and between texts obstacles to those movements were identified. So the development of a tradition of commentary and interpretation was required, a tradition which took as its models the commentaries on scripture of Augustine and Jerome. Within that tradition there were elaborated large agreements in interpretation, so that the onus placed upon dissenting interpretations became progressively more difficult to discharge. But there developed also against this background of agreement a set of more or less systematically disputed and debated issues in which problems of perhaps apparent, perhaps real disagreement within the texts commented upon were multiplied by problems of real disagreement between rival commentators and interpreters. So certain issues emerged as *quaestiones*, the formulation and discussion of which

became in time incorporated into the methods of formal teaching, supplementing exegetical exposition by affording opportunity for what became increasingly stylized forms of disputation.[67]

In that respect, therefore, sacred doctrine is *not* a perfect science. The respect in which it is, it owes entirely to the *scientia Dei* from which it takes its first principles. Thomas makes a variety of claims expressing sacred doctrine's perfection, and he defends them by a technical means.

Sacred doctrine's perfection seems to arise from its close association with the revelation in sacred scripture. At I.1.2 *ad* 2 Thomas even seems to identify sacred scripture and sacred doctrine, when he mentions "the divine revelation, upon which is founded sacred scripture or doctrine" (*sacra Scriptura seu doctrina*). It is not that the two are *simply* the same thing; the question is, in what *respect* are they the same? Objectively (*ex parte ipsius rei*), the revelation is of very God as the First Truth (II–II.1.1). Subjectively (*ex parte nostra*), faith by grace recognizes the first truth in propositions whose linguistic character and complexity are inalienable from them in this life (II–II.1.2)—and which are always, for those reasons, subject to interpretation. In "revelation" Thomas is naming the object of faith, objective and subjective, which elsewhere he calls not just "revelation" but "revealed *God*" (II–II.1.1 *in med.*). God's self-revelation to us human beings occurs externally through providentially arranged things or events (I.1.10)—by analogy to the way in which for Aristotle the world's self-revelation occurred through teleologically arranged things or events—only here the events in question are the incarnation, passion, and resurrection of Christ (II–II.2.7). That self-revelation is God's own *teaching* of us, or doctrine, which Thomas defines in his commentary on the *Posterior Analytics* in personal terms: *doctrina* is "the action of one who makes something recognized [*actio eius qui aliquid cognoscere facit*]." Sacred doctrine, as Preller puts it, is the action of God's self-revelation, or better, an "extension of the eternal procession of the Word...[in] the temporal mission of the eternal Person."[68] Corbin calls sacred doctrine "the completed suit [*procès fini*] of the Word of God."[69] By an authorship fittingly ascribed both to God (I.1.10) and to free human beings,[70] we now have access to those events in linguistic form.

The "access" that we enjoy to this science, to be sure, is not the same as our access to other sciences through their linguistic forms. Scriptural first principles do not befit our understanding more or less directly (by our pre-apprehension of being), as worldly first principles do—or if they act as

worldly first principles, they yield only dead faith. In the sciences that cul-
minate in metaphysics, we human beings operate by a dispositional tendency—the light of natural reason—to "take" the objects of experience to
"be" the referents of our conceptual scheme. That conceptual scheme is appropriate to the human being related to the *terminus a quo* of life *in via*, that
is, appropriate to one who begins as God's material creature. In the science
possessed by God and the blessed, we human beings will operate by a dispositional tendency—the light of glory—receptive of "the very form of God's
own self-knowledge," "the final saturation of [the human being's] natural
longing for total intelligibility and volitional fruition."[71] That language—the
Word of God—is appropriate to the human being arrived at the *terminus ad
quem* of life *in via*, that is, appropriate to one become God's friend, participant in God's nature. In the science of sacred doctrine, however, we human
beings operate by a dispositional tendency the efficient and final cause of
which is *not* intrinsic to us—we are not its scientists—but intrinsic to God
and the blessed. The *scientia* that sacred doctrine borrows is borrowed from,
or caused by the *scientia* that God and the blessed possess. But here below
we precisely *lack* the dispositional tendency, the light of glory, that would
make it our own. Thus we cannot comprehend what we borrow. We "only"
(but appropriately) believe it. "In place of an intelligible science, [believers
possess] only nonintelligible 'articles' of faith, which [they believe] to be created analogues of the knowledge shared by God and the blessed."[72]

Such an infused rather than intrinsic dispositional tendency is appropriate to the human being *in via* as a foretaste (*praecognitum*) of the *finis* toward which we move—appropriate not, like the light of reason, in virtue of
our creation, but appropriate as a "inchoate"[73] beginning or "proleptic"[74]
anticipation of our elevation. It is the light of grace. It is the light that ac-
companies the gift of a new, integral end for human beings. It is the eschaton working itself out in us in advance. "Although [believers] cannot [them-
selves] see how the articles of faith are true of God [I.12], [they believe] that
they express the proper intentional state of one whose mind has been directed to God [by God's own agency!], and in some fashion conformed to
[God's] nature."[75] For "God...must conceive in the human soul the forms
that are intended by the language of scripture. This is not done by the
communication of intelligible forms but by the ordination of the whole
soul, intellect and will, to the Word or Image of God—by the creation in
[the human being] of the dispositional tendency [habit of faith] to 'take' the
agency of Christ to be the soteriological agency of God."[76] That dispositional tendency is not a seizing by us of Christ as God, but a seizing of us by

God in such a way as so to dispose us.[77] Otherwise the light of grace would no longer count as grace, or as gratuitous. It is only so that sacred scripture furnishes the enunciable first principles (II–II.1.2) in which the discipline of sacred doctrine (I.1.3) is virtually contained (I.1.7), or elaborates.

Thomas goes on to articulate the dependence of sacred doctrine upon sacred scripture in terms that should embarrass those who are used to thinking of him as doing such a thing as philosophy of religion, or the "theology that pertains to metaphysics," as I.1.1 *ad* 2 calls it, anywhere in the *Summa.* Sacred doctrine "uses the authorities of canonical scripture properly, arguing from necessity" (I.1.8 *ad* 2 *post med.*), and in sacred doctrine scripture "has no superior" (I.1.8c *ca. med.*). Scripture enunciates the revelation mentioned or presupposed in each of the articles (listed shortly), and, when interpreted in accord with the creed, the community, and the best deliverances of human inquiry so far that are adaptable to its literal sense, scripture supplies the articles of faith that Thomas explicitly names sacred doctrine's *"principia."* "The first principles of this science...are the articles of faith" (I.1.7), and "faith inheres in all the articles of faith by one means, namely by the first truth proposed to us in the scriptures well interpreted according to the sense of the believing community."[78] Even Jesus Christ, when he mounts propositional arguments, does so only on the authority of scripture: "He proved his resurrection to [his disciples] by the authority of sacred Scripture, which is the foundation of faith" (III.55.5).[79] Without the formal rationale of believing God supplied by the scriptures even the resurrection is just a brute fact, or to put it more Thomistically, bare matter—both of which are mere abstractions from concrete, interpreted reality.

Those are certainly devout commendations of scripture. Unless we can show that they actually fulfill the office of Aristotelian first principles, however, critics will reduce them to so many expressions of piety, or confine them to the upper story of a two-story system, so above reason that they never touch ground. If so, then Thomas has betrayed the other three aspects of Aristotelian first principles and has remained Aristotelian only in the most flat-footed way. We need the *account* of how the more Aristotelian Thomas is, the more scriptural he is.

In Question 1 Thomas is not so much out to display a theological methodology, as he is to display the logic internal to revelation. It is revelation that guarantees, by its dependence upon the unity in the mind of God, the unity of the four aspects of Aristotelian first principles. It is revelation that answers the demand of the human being for intelligibility, both as a preliminary guide (*praecognitum*) to ordering intentions and actions toward an end that outlies us (article 1), and as a participation in the final perfection of that desire which we will enjoy in the science possessed by God and the blessed, and from which sacred doctrine takes its first principles (article 2). It is revelation that provides the material content of the faith that may, should God grant it, form the soul (articles 1, 4, and 6). It is revelation that gives the axiomatic first principles from which sacred doctrine argues (article 8). And it is revelation that shows forth the reality to which the structure corresponds (articles 7 and 10). Revelation guarantees the discipline's integrity (article 3) and accords it dignity (article 5), securing its real relation to its subject (article 7) and its propositional relations in arguments (article 8). If the *Summa* causes revelation, rather than discursivity in the abstract, to furnish the key to sacred doctrine's principled nature, then the question no longer appears to exhaust itself in its articles on scripture, as if Thomas could find no place where they really belonged. Rather in the articles on scripture a question on revelation reaches its climax.[80] There we learn about the radius or scope of divine revelation, which is truth itself (I.1.9 *ad* 2), and that the author of sacred scripture is none other than God. In his preoccupation with revelation and its objectivity just in the place where moderns would rather expect methodology, Thomas Aquinas comes to resemble Karl Barth.

Already in the *Summa*'s opening article, I.1.1, Thomas explicates revelation's ability to do those things for sacred doctrine in soteriological terms, in terms of God's grant to human beings of a single, unitary end that surpasses or transforms their powers. To reach that end, a foretaste (*praecognitum*) of it is necessary, a foretaste granted in revelation. It may look as if Thomas has already impugned God's freedom, in that human beings could extort the revelation as necessary for their fulfillment, rendering it no longer gratuitous. But the complaint misunderstands the sort of necessity involved. The grant of a supernatural end and of a revelation are not two separate gifts,[81] the second extorted on the basis of the first, by a necessity of obligation. End and revelation are one gift analyzed into two aspects to reveal a unitary necessity *internal to the one gift*. The one gift is first of all internal to God the giver. For it is God's own, free purpose that God is fulfilling in the grant of revelation and end alike. It is God's self-determination for us that establishes the gift, our unexacted determination for God that results from it. Here too end and revelation correspond, Thomas might say, as final and first principles of an inner necessity or form.[82] Karl Barth would say: the creation is the external ground of the covenant, the covenant the external ground of the creation. Just if we human beings are to be granted union with a source of intelligibility outside the world, we also, by the very character of the gift of union, receive a form (as that by which an Aristotelian science accounts for the unity of the knower and the known) "from outside," which is grace. To bestow that gift upon temporal creatures is the end of the mission of the divine persons. And in virtue of the form's appearance from outside the world, we may call it "new," not in the sense of temporally recent, but in the sense of "unlooked for." It is in the second sense, one evocative of wonder and gratitude, that Thomas regards the mission of the divine persons for rendering nature graced as "new." "It befits a divine person to be sent, according as that person exists in something in a new way (*novo modo*)... which befits a rational creature as the thing known in a knower [*cognitum in cognoscente*] or loved in a lover" (I.43.3). The *cognitum* that results within a human being as the result of the projection of the Trinity into creation is the same as the *praecognitum finis* with which Thomas opens the *Summa*. It is thoroughly if quietly trinitarian from the very beginning. "And since, knowing and loving, the rational creature reaches God by [God's engaging] its own operation [as the known in the knowing or the loved in the loving], ... God [in I.43.5, the whole Trinity] ... is said to dwell in the creature as in God's temple.... According alone to grace making graced is a divine person sent and proceeds in time" (I.43.3).[83]

That indwelling bestows upon the creature a new form that absorbs ("perfects") the old.[84] Thomas thereby proposes a thought-experiment that swallows up the Aristotelian scheme from within. The *Metaphysics* contemplates no such thing; it conceives of no "new forms" in that sense; forms do not come to be.[85] Thomas elsewhere describes the sublating function of the new form in terms of "subalternation of formal rationales," unknown to the *Posterior Analytics*.[86] The mission of the divine persons is new in the sense of "unlooked-for" not only in the world, but to Aristotle above all. Suppose, then, that something new should appear under the sun, a radically unlooked-for principle of change. New first principles would become active, and they would ground a new science, whether anyone studied it or not. New forms would give things new trajectories to trace, and thus they would not just add examples to old structures, but structure everything differently, whether or not anyone noticed. New ends would complete things differently, and entirely new effects would demand new disciplines, whether or not they actually arose. New natures, in short, would give a new something to be of to a new science.

New natures apply especially to us human beings, since we are the ratio-nal creatures that God wills to dwell in. The newness applies not to any change in God's plan (since Thomas says nothing about sin and Fall when he explicates the missions of the persons) but to the difference between cre-ation and elevation. But that is also an odd way to talk. Aristotle has as lit-tle room for that distinction as for newness of nature. That talk too comes of an attempt to account for proceeding from first principles in the presence of a doctrine of creation. Thomas resorts to the language of "newness" be-cause as creation takes conceptual priority over things, so creatureliness takes conceptual priority over nature. For Aristotle has no notion of the changes that a *nature* undergoes in a Christian theological scheme, while the creatures that possess natures remain unalterably creatures. Creatures, in short, may alter their natures or find their natures altered. Natures in Aristotle are not subject to creation and elevation, let alone fall and re-demption, in the relevant senses. Human beings in Thomas's scheme were created for elevation to friendship with God, created for their very natures to be moved, or elevated. The elevation, like the creation, is a gift prior to nature and end, for it sets or moves our nature and end. We need a prelimi-nary knowledge of the gift to recognize and reach it as end. God makes the end ours by involving us in its pursuit, by engaging our natures toward it.[87] The elevation of human beings befits—and does not violate—their crea-tureliness. For it marks the human creature, as I will have occasion to re-peat, to lean by nature on grace—if nature is in good order, that is, just if it is shot through with grace. Leaning upon revelation is a special case of lean-ing upon grace (the presence of the known to the knower), one that restores and elevates nothing other than nature. For Thomas it would always be a moot point to describe the human subject of the leaning as *ungraced* na-ture.[88] For Aristotle it would always be nonsense to make the distinction.

Just because human beings were created for elevation to friendship (*ami-citia*) with God (I–II.99.2), sacred doctrine must also treat of God as Creator and elevator, beginning and end. Yet it may not do so as if God were a mem-ber of a common genus with created things, but only and precisely as that to which they are ordered *beyond* creation (I.1.7 *ad* 2), as that *sub cuius ra-tione* it considers them (I.1.7c), and thus principally. That is another way of motivating the move from *intelligibilia* to *revelabilia*, since God is pre-cisely *not* intelligible to us in this life, but has chosen to become revealable. God's (eternal, intratrinitarian) choosing to be revealable does not, as I said, trap God into the same genus with us—as Barth, say, interpreted the *analo-gia entis* to do—but it grants precisely a *formal* relation in which *we relate*

to all things by believing God. For the formal relation under which we consider things in sacred doctrine is "by the sight of the One who is believed [*a*
visione eius cui creditur]" (I.12.13 *ad* 3). Since the sight or vision is precisely the *scientia Dei,* from which sacred doctrine's first principles come
when they are revealed, Thomas comes to state the formal rationale this
way: according as they are divinely revealables [*divinitus revelabilia*]" or
things susceptible of being revealed by God (I.1.3). Just because according to
sacred doctrine human beings properly relate to all things by the God-
bestowed disposition to believe God, the *scientia Dei* works the change in
the soul through a formal rationale analogous to ones Aristotle accords
other sciences. In that case Thomas calls the formal rationale "faith." And
because in sacred doctrine we relate to all things by believing God, what we
have here is a description of what Barth and others would call the *analogia*
fidei. With that we have one way of stating the technical, *theological*
means by which Thomas engulfs Aristotle. Thomas engulfs Aristotle first
of all by subordinating him to a version of the *analogia fidei,* and the phrase
"the more Aristotelian, the more scriptural" simply acknowledges
Thomas's application of the analogy of faith to him.

Since God is the first principle of all things, and all things may be considered therefore *sub ratione Dei*—that is, relating to God as beginning and
end (I.1.7)—Thomas presents the form of revelation in I.1.3 as illuminating
and therefore inhering in "*omnia quaecumque.*" Sacred doctrine, that is,
treats "all things whatsoever" under the formal aspect of *revelabilia.* It
is hard to overstate the authoritative daring of that move. It is not the grant
by a pope of a whole or half-continent to a discovering power. It is a grant to
a scientific discipline of *omnia quaecumque.* For with that, *contra* Aristotle, *res* gain something other to be than *intelligibilia.* The claim, Aristotle could only say, is unintelligible. But it is, Thomas would reply, revealable. Thomas posits a science beyond (I.1.1), higher (I.1.5), and more
universal than metaphysics: "a superior power...regards its object under a
more universal formal rationale [*sub universaliori ratione formali*]" (I.1.3
ad 2).[89] That is the "scientific" means—the technical, Aristotelian means—
by which Aristotle has been subsumed, *aufgehoben,* made to engulf himself. Thomas engulfs Aristotle by subordinating metaphysics to a higher
formal rationale. The phrase "the more Aristotelian, the more scriptural"
simply acknowledges the subordination of Aristotle the inventor of metaphysics to Aristotle the student of real forms—of whatever provenance.

Recall that we are not talking about things that *have been revealed,*
"*revelata,*" or even things that *could have been revealed, whether they*

were or not, possible *"revelata."*[90] *Revelabilia* are things trans*formed*—that was the point of the thought-experiment about a new form—things that not *only* could have been revealed, but things that contain within themselves the form of revealability. They possess an intrinsic under-God-ness, they enjoy natural citizenship in the world that revelation depicts, they already belong to and comprise that world, quite apart from whether scripture comes to *mention* them or not. They are revealable as God-created and God-ordered. And that under-God-ness is theirs and ours and the whole world's, patient of discovery, just as the Aristotelian forms of natural things remain their own apart from study. To treat a form otherwise—as something additional or accidental to things, as something that belonged only to study and not to reality, as dependent upon the interpreter or observer *alone*—would be to leave Aristotelian realism thoughtlessly behind, and to belie the notion of an Aristotelian science in the very act of claiming it.

Just because sacred doctrine gives *res* something to be other than *intelligibilia*, metaphysics, which treats of things as *intelligibilia*, is precisely what sacred doctrine must *distinguish* itself from (I.1.1 *ad* 2 *in fin.*). Sacred doctrine never denies, rather affirms the intelligibility of things. But the very first article of Question 1, when it asks whether a discipline exists beyond (*praeter*) and not among (*inter*) philosophical disciplines, leaves the consideration of *res* as *intelligibilia* behind. It replaces metaphysics with or subsumes it under another genre, in which *omnia res quaecumque* are *revelabilia*. Beside (or better, below) it, therefore, other sciences, including the theology that pertains to metaphysics (I.1.1 *ad* 2) take on the aspect of the provisional and penultimate investigations that Aristotle describes in the *Physics*. Thus it is that according to the John commentary (cited above), physics, ethics, and metaphysics derive their cogency from their participation (where participation short of intuition implies a greater or lesser remove) in sacred doctrine.

Thomas opens the *Summa* with the example of the astronomer and the physicist reaching the same conclusion about the shape of the earth (I.1.1 *ad* 2). The astronomer supplies a first principle about heavenly bodies, treats the earth as a heavenly body, and concludes to its roundness. The physicist supplies a first principle about things sinking to the earth as a center, treats the earth as a center of sinking, and concludes to its roundness. Independent first principles impose different formalities on the earth (heavenly body, center of sinking) in the second step. In fact, it already abstracts the matter from the form to observe that the conclusions are "the same." For the two arguments describe the earth differently, so that roundness is predicated in the one case of a heavenly body, and in the other case of a center of sinking. The result would not transfer from one discipline to the other without additional premises. For the science of things whose natural motion is down, as Thomas conceives of physics, has no first principles for treating heavenly bodies, whose natural motion is circular; and the science of bodies that move along the heavenly spheres, as Thomas conceives of astronomy, has no first principles for treating things that sink. In the absence of a higher science, the earth provides a special, as it were accidental case of overlap, and the comparison needs a new context in which to take place.

Since independent, distinctive first principles grant a discipline its integrity, disciplines proceeding according to a different first principles ordinarily enjoy equality with one another, as Thomas assumes in I.1.1 *ad* 2. One discipline may also make use of another's results as "extraneous and probable" (I.1.8 *ad* 2 *in med.*). To be used by an independent discipline, however, is precisely to come under another, independent set of first principles. The usual equality of the subordinate discipline must yield (hence metaphors of servitude), just so that its integrity can be restored ("led back") in the new ordering. Because any particular draft upon another discipline, however rigorously carried out, occurs in response to a particular demand of sacred doctrine, and thus strictly *ad hoc*, the metaphors vary. Sacred doctrine enjoys a superior light (I.1.2); it possesses a greater dignity (I.1.5); it acts as a judge (I.1.6), orders as an architect, commands as civil authority (I.1.5 *ad* 2); it transcends (I.1.5), it perfects, and it leads back captive (I.1.8 *ad* 2). Accordingly it treats other disciplines as subcontractors, foot-soldiers, captives, slaves (I.1.5 *ad* 2, I.1.8 *ad* 2).

In the citation of 2 Corinthians, therefore, Thomas offers no mere rhetorical ornament. He uses it to accomplish real conceptual work: it furnishes him with a formal rationale. It specifies the *sort* of subordination involved. It does not allow sacred doctrine to treat its inferiors as free agents. It takes them captive. In interpreting the same verse elsewhere, Thomas pushes the significance of a change in formal rationale to its limits, explicating it as one that trans*forms* the matter: "Those who use philosophical arguments in sacred doctrine by 'leading them back into obedience' to faith (*redigendo in obsequium fidei*) do not mix water with wine, but *convert* water into wine"(*De Trin.* 2.3 *ad* 5). Thus the more water, the more wine. Thus too the more Aristotelian, the more christoform.

Aristotle's account of a science then proves itself useful precisely not as something intelligible, but as a *revelabilium*. Even *Aristotle* becomes something that can be made to exhibit not its innate reasonableness, but its innate under-God-ness. *Aristotle* is *nolens-volens* revealed as something that can be rendered of a piece with, assumed or subsumed into the world of the scriptures. That this particular *revelabilium* appears also in relative or apparent independence from the revelation of scripture and that it enjoys resources that can be put, as footsoldiers or subcontractors, to good use, together qualify it for *manuductio,* the name that Thomas gives to the process of leading learners—the *parvuli in Christo* of the *Summa*'s prologue—by the hand, in an *ad hoc* way (I.1.5 *ad* 2 *in fin.*). "Briefly, rather than constituting a special part of theology as demonstrations, philosophical arguments used in sacred doctrine are no more than *manuductions,* or arguments external and probable, as Thomas puts it in article 8."[91] Think of Aristotle's account of science, then, as ready to hand in two ways. It is ready to hand first because it is assimilable to scripture, "lest anyone limit scripture so to one sense that other senses are completely excluded, that in themselves contain truth, and can, saving the circumstances of the literal sense, be adapted to scripture."[92] It is ready to hand second because it is able to meet learners where they are, just as our temporally primary and logically secondary appreciations of parental love and justice provide temporal starting places for the love and justice that exist primarily in God, and in which the imperfect love and justice of human beings are wittingly or unwittingly participant.[93]

The sublation of other sciences in sacred doctrine means not only that it may use them as manuductions. It also means that they are deficient until taken up into it. The move to *revelabilia* tells us that things are intelligible *just as* they are under God; they are not under God in virtue of being intelligible. When we read in I.1.6 *ad* 1 that *"omnis nostra cognitio"* is ordered to the highest wisdom, which is *scientia Dei* (I.1.6),[94] we must not think that the ordering is merely immanent to the discipline recorded in the *Summa.* That ordering too is a feature of reality. Pesch calls attention to "the programmatic remarks of St. Thomas about the christocentric [!] orientation of *all* sciences in the commentary on the John prologue."[95]

Thomas's use of Aristotle's account of a science puts us in a position to understand a troublesome passage in article 1 where Thomas mentions other Aristotelian disciplines: "Even in those things about God that human reason is able to investigate [*ad ea etiam quae de Deo ratione humana investigari possunt*], it was necessary that the human being be instructed by divine revelation" (I.1.1 *in med.*). Article 1 is sometimes read as if the *etiam* were comparative, as if it were replicating the two domains of the beginning of the *Contra gentiles,* according to which there are two modes of truth, one accessible and one inaccessible to human reason.[96] It is not. As Corbin says, "the projection of the problematic of the *Summa contra gentiles* onto this first text of the *Summa theologiae* is strictly forbidden."[97]

The move to *revelabilia* subsumes those two possibilities into a unified domain *rendered accessible* as a singular whole. Thomas makes revelation now, among other things, a grant of unimpaired integrity to the scriptural and extrascriptural or Aristotelian domains. The formal rationale of sacred doctrine treats them as one; it rejects the division *revelata*/non-*revelata* in favor of seeing under God "all things whatsoever" as "*divinitus revelabilia*"—which is simply universal providence ("under-God-ness") applied to cognition.

The *Contra gentiles* actually anticipates this move, so that Thomas leaves its opening distinction behind, and its scheme becomes a self-consuming one.[98] The "*etiam*" of the opening of the *Contra gentiles* is one that almost stacks two domains in which one is higher, one lower; nothing is subsumed. It is an "*etiam*" of addition. It is an "*etiam*" that establishes something like the notorious two-story Thomism of the handbooks. It is an "*etiam*" which scholars have often mistakenly carried over into the *Summa,* although Thomas was abandoning it already in his progress through the *Contra gentiles,* and although it flies in the face of the *Summa's* move to subordinate formal rationales. Quite apart from textual evidence, which Corbin renders conclusive, the extreme intensity of this stage of Thomas's writing career gave him numerous occasions—including the most important biblical commentaries (Romans and John) and almost all the commentaries on Aristotle—to rethink his positions between the *Summa contra gentiles* and the *Summa theologiae.*[99] False assimilation of the two explains many misreadings of the latter *Summa.* The "*etiam*" of I.1.1 is the "even" that subsumes other Aristotelian disciplines under this one. Even they require the perfection that Thomas finds in the Gospel of John. Even they remain deficient until they come under sacred doctrine's rationale of a "*more* universal" form. Just where Aristotle would have imagined that metaphysics was a universal category, and, with most Latinists, that "universal" was not a concept that would admit of a greater degree, Thomas invents the odd and impressive word "*universalioris*" to stake his claim.

The *etiam* that sets out the problematic of the *Summa theologiae* is the revelation of other disciplines' creatureliness and the charter of their perfection. The *etiam* that sets out the problematic of the *Summa contra gentiles* was an *etiam* of correlation: also. Now it is an *etiam* of inclusion: even. The *Summa theologiae* leaves transformed even metaphysics. It leaves transformed even the scientific itself.

The *"etiam"* paragraph of I.1.1 ends with a comparison of the Aristotelian sciences and sacred doctrine: "So that, therefore, salvation for human beings should more fittingly and more dependably succeed [*et convenientius et certius proveniat*], it was necessary that they be instructed in divine things by divine revelation." The comparative adverbs may make it sound as if human salvation would have succeeded in any case, only less fittingly and less dependably. But we are now able to give a more precise reading of those adverbs. In the light of Thomas's use of Aristotle in the articles to come, we can see that to characterize sacred doctrine as *convenientius* and *certius* by comparison with ordinary Aristotelian sciences is to pay it no mere compliment. It is first of all to relate sacred doctrine to ordinary Aristotelian sciences as the perfect science of the *Posterior Analytics* relates to the investigative sciences of the *Physics* and the biological treatises. Thomas signals that relation when he states the contrast like this: "even in those things about God that human reason is able to *investigate*." Rather the *"certius"* of I.1.1 anticipates another *"certius"* at I.1.5 *ad* 1 (*in init.*). The fact that sacred doctrine is more certain or *"certius"* is one of two features of what renders it higher or *"dignior"* (I.1.5c). Sacred doctrine differs from (other) Aristotelian sciences first of all in that its mode of argument proceeds directly (*immediate*) from things clearer in themselves (*notiora in se*) to things clearer to us (*notiora quoad nos*, I.1.5 *ad* 2 ca. med.), since it has the former by revelation, and it does not have to grasp after the *notiora in se* from the standpoint of fallible and mistaken *notiora quoad nos*. Hence it is absolutely *"certius."*[100] For *certitudo* is a property of the perfected science such as God and the blessed enjoy. Hence too it argues from authority, as I.1.8 says: "Nor does that take away from the dignity of this teaching: for although the argument from authority that is founded upon human reason is of the weakest, nevertheless the argument from authority that is founded upon divine revelation, is of the strongest." It is also because sacred doctrine argues from the *notiora in se* that *scientia Dei* reveals to it, that sometimes it is precisely *not* or not yet *notiora quoad nos*, and Thomas finds himself using Aristotle to remind us that "we blink at the most evident things like bats in the sunshine."[101] The comparative form of the adverb *certius* does not, therefore, mark a *relative* degree of the *same* kind of certainty; it marks an *absolute* superiority of one kind of certainty over *another*.

The second respect in which sacred doctrine relates to Aristotelian physics, ethics, and metaphysics Thomas characterizes with the adverb *"convenientius,"* "more fittingly." Now in Aristotle it befits the completed, perfected science to arise out of human inquiry carried far enough and for the first principles that stand at the end of human inquiry to be the same first principles that stand as axioms at the head of deductive arguments in minds adequated to things. In Aristotle there must be a continuity at least in principle between the way *toward* first principles as ends and the way *from* first principles as axioms. And in Aristotle it is again the forms of things that guarantee and account for that continuity.

Thomas, on the other hand, says nothing to defend *that* kind of continuity, although he offers another. Rather it is the point of the postulation of an *in se* intelligibility that *outstrips* the human powers of investigation to put up a roadblock against the assertion of such continuity. It is the point of depicting sacred doctrine as a science without this-worldly scientists to deny such continuity. And it is the point of a discipline *praeter* rather than *inter* philosophical disciplines (as the title question has it) to get beyond the bounds of such continuity. Rather the continuity comes from sacred doctrine, as it were, down, when Thomas creates a *different* continuity among *"omnia quaecumque"* according as they are *"divinitus revelabilia,"* when Thomas creates a different continuity according to which we relate to all things not, as in standard Aristotelian investigation, by attending to their thingly forms, but by attending to their forms in the first truth, or, as I said, by trusting God. Sacred doctrine treats "more fittingly" of what human reason can investigate because it treats it under the more universal formal rationale; the formal rationale is more universal because it also includes or relates things to the beginning and end that possesses them *outside* the world, which in this life can only be revealed and not understood; and that more universal formal rationale is more fitting because it can do what the investigations of human reason could never do, namely conduce to our salvation; that is, it is absolutely, not relatively fitting.

Thus too the *"convenientius"* of I.1.1 anticipates another way in which I.1.5 explicates sacred doctrine as having dignity over other disciplines: as both speculative and practical at once, sacred doctrine orders the ends of all other sciences to its own.[102] Only from within it can we see, as John indicates, that Aristotelian physics, ethics, and metaphysics might be less fitting by comparison, instead of not fitting at all. Or better: from the standpoint of John we can see that physics, ethics, and metaphysics enjoy their lesser fittingness by participation rather than comparison, as *intelligibilia* receive their intelligibility from participating in the intelligibility of the first truth that is precisely not intelligible to us but only revealable.

Thus sacred doctrine constructs and secures a continuity between Aristotle's *intelligibilia* and its own proper *revelabilia* just as it lays claim to the former as its own. In the chapters on the Romans commentary we will see how Thomas takes Romans 1:19–20 to lay claim to human wisdom so as not to leave it God-forsaken. And thus it is too that the body of article 1 concludes not with the assertion that sacred doctrine is remedial or merely helpful in this second regard, but with a *third* assertion of its *necessity*. Thomas belabors the point. "It was therefore (!) *necessary* that beyond philosophical disciplines, which are investigated by reason, a sacred doctrine be had by revelation." A merely relative reading of *"et convenientius et certius"* would not have supported a "therefore" or a claim of "necessity" and would have led to a qualified, not an identical conclusion in that place.[103]

Question 1 as a whole has a circular structure according to which article 1 demands something foreknown about the end, a *praecognitum finis*, that article 10 supplies, and article 10 sets up a structure of scriptural authority upon which article 1 has already depended. Precisely if a science is the more Aristotelian the more it attends to its real and propositional first principles, sacred doctrine is the more Aristotelian the more it attends to revelation—both as propositional *and* as real.

Interpreters of Question 1 sometimes have trouble seeing what articles 9 and 10, the scriptural ones, are doing there. That is because they imagine, like John of St. Thomas, that the Aristotelian character of a science depends upon its use of logic or syllogism, and mistake the order of Questions 1 and 2.

But just if to be an Aristotelian science is to return also to *real* first principles, then it falls to article 9 (on use of metaphor) to eliminate some mistaken readings of them, and to article 10 (and this is crucial) to specify how sacred doctrine's real and propositional first principles relate to each other (I.1.10c):

> I answer that the author of sacred Scripture is God, in whose power it is that God dispose not only [spoken or written] utterances to signification, which even a human being can do, but also states of affairs themselves [*res ipsas*]. And therefore, whereas in all sciences utterances sig-

nify, this science has this peculiarity, that the very states of affairs signified by the utterances also signify something. Therefore that first signification, by which utterances signify states of affairs, pertains to the first
sense, which is the historical or literal sense. But that sense by which the
states of affairs signified by the utterances in turn signify other states of
affairs is called the spiritual sense; and it is based on the literal sense and
presupposes it. . . .

Now since the literal sense is that which the author intends, and the
author of sacred Scripture is God, who comprehends intellectually all
things at the same time, it comes not amiss, as Augustine says in *Confes-
sions* 12 [ch. 31], that even maintaining accord with the literal sense,
many senses are present in a passage of scripture.

God arranges not just words but *states of affairs* (*res*) to speak. That is,
not just scripture's words, but scripture's very events reflect God's intention.
Recall that it is the intentionality of the divine, the unsearchable prudence
of providence, that, among other things, distinguishes Thomas's *scientia*
from Aristotle's. Thus Thomas calls it peculiar to this science that the things
themselves *signify* something. That is, they do not possess mere, Aristotelian formal teleology: they are rendered participants in God's willing *intentionality*. For it is how things stand *sub ratione Dei*—in the divine ordering from beginning to end, or in God's prudence or providence, or, as the
current article has it, in God's authorial intention—that turns them into *revelabilia*. In short: The intention of God as author arranging states of affairs *to
speak* makes them revelatory, makes them *revelabilia* (Quod.7.6.3c).

God's authorial intention, providence, or plan, infuses our whole world
with a form "new" to fallen nature—better: with a form elevating to nature
and renewing after the Fall—independent of its writing down: it is the *real*
first principle of sacred doctrine, God's *arranging*: it is active, like Aristotelian forms, in the world. And the means by which "*omnia quaecumque,*" including the stories of the church and of human beings' own
lives, are assimilable into the activity of that form, the real story of God's
authoring, the realm of things under God, or *revelabilia*, are the spiritual
senses, which are first of all other states of affairs, other *res*, indeed *all* other
res "*quaecumque,*" as related to the primary *res* of God's story.

For the *omnia* that are *divinitus revelabilia* in I.1.3 are the very same
omnia that appear under the intellect of the author of scripture in I.1.10,
when Thomas writes that "the author of sacred scripture is God, who comprehends all things (*omnia*) intellectually." Thus God becomes author not
only of scripture and of scripture's states of affairs, but of our own states of

affairs as well. For Thomas sets sacred doctrine up as a science in such a way that an earlier characterization of sacred doctrine still holds: "it is necessary too that the mode of this science be narrative (*narrativus*)."[104]

In the well-interpreted *litterae* we have a record of God's providential activity, a record of the real, revelatory states of affairs, a telling of the narrative (often, multiple tellings): the propositional first principles. To proceed from real first principles means to return and attend to the states of affairs in the world as they are *revelabilia*, God-intended; but since God's intention lies beyond our powers of discernment, we cannot simply read providence off from any states of affairs, but only when we have access by means of the propositional first principles in the literal sense of scripture. Thus Thomas admits multiple senses in one passage of scripture only "in accord with the literal sense."[105]

The article relates the spiritual senses both to the propositional first principles in the literal sense, and to the other aspects of an Aristotelian science. The anagogical sense, which considers the life to come, where we actually enjoy the *scientia Dei et beatorum*, bespeaks the postponed Aristotelian end of inquiry. The moral or tropological sense bespeaks that formation of the soul that the grace of charity alone can accomplish. And the allegorical or typological sense bespeaks the central reality, *res*, or state of affairs from which sacred doctrine takes its rise, God's elevating, redeeming, and self-revealing work in Jesus Christ. In the literal sense sacred scripture records, and in the spiritual senses it carries forward the progress of God's own form in the world, or the mission of the persons. For in the spiritual senses—as the following chapter will show for the life of Paul—we find our life in God's, which is a beginning of our friendship.

The event of that revelation, the appearance of that form, goes unmentioned in I.1.1. Although none of Thomas's readers would fail to identify that event and appearance as the incarnation of Jesus Christ, he saves it for the climax of the *Summa*, where he devotes to it the entire *Tertia pars*, the "consummation of the whole theological enterprise" (III, prol.)—as it is the consummation of any lesser Aristotelian science to consider its own formal rationale. And the whole (*"totius"*) of which Thomas comes, in the *Tertia Pars*, to consider the consummation, is the very same whole (*"totius"*) that he mentions in I.1.7 when he speaks of the first principles "of the whole science," or *"totius scientiae."* It is Jesus Christ who stands tacitly as the new light or form that gives rise to this new *scientia*, a *scientia praeter philosophicas disciplinas*. And he is quietly named whenever Thomas uses tell-tale "form" words: *via* and *ratio* and *iter* and *exemplar*.

The more christoform

The implicit logic of the fourfold sense of scripture is to keep together the Christian canon of Hebrew and Greek scriptures by seeing Christ in the law, narrative, poetry, and prophecy of the former. Thomas follows scripture and tradition to see types of Christ in the stories of ancient Israelites and in the Psalms. And Thomas has Jesus himself, as we have seen, argue from "law, psalms, and prophecy" about himself (III.55.5). The allegorical or typological sense alone can stand for *all* the spiritual ones (I.1.10 *ad* 2)—because it is the allegorical sense that performs the work of relating the Hebrew scriptures to Christ. It is that "by which those things are expounded of Christ which had preceded in a figure of him."[106]

The version of I.1.10 that appears in the *Quaestiones quodlibetales* expresses what I.1.10 allows to go without saying: that what all four senses center on is Jesus Christ. "Even those things which [allegories immanent to the Hebrew scriptures] conceal in the truth of the matter [*res*] are ordered to the designation of Christ, as shadow to truth."[107] The passage relates each of the three spiritual senses to Christ. He is the exemplar of the virtues that the moral sense requires; the captain of the church triumphant that anagogy invokes; and the head of the church militant to whom allegory proclaims him as "justifying her and infusing grace." The passages about Christ also according to the letter will bear, indeed, all three of the spiritual senses as well and as a matter of course.[108] And it is to be sure because Christ stands at the center also of the entire literal sense, that is, of the biblical story as a whole, that the prologue to the *Tertia Pars* calls him the "consummation of the whole theological enterprise." Thus too Thomas comes to say that "the *principal* thing in the teaching of the Christian faith is the salvation wrought by the cross of Christ."[109] It would be a correct interpretation to say that the cross of Christ is *the* first principle of sacred doctrine.

So the first sense in which we can call the *Summa* the more christoform, the more Aristotelian it is, is this: It is the more *scriptural*, the more Aristotelian it is, since scripture gives sacred doctrine its axiomatic first principles, and it is for that reason also the more christoform, since scripture centers (as a matter of the interpreted *res ipsas*, and as a matter also of the spiritual senses) upon Jesus Christ. Yet so far that is not a very satisfactory way of putting the matter. So far it might appear to be a mere accident of traditional ways of interpreting scripture that Thomas's Aristotelianism should lead that way. We need to get closer to the internal necessity of the matter. And in the case of Thomas's Aristotelian set-up, that means closer to the forms of things, closer, that is, to the *revelabilia* in the real aspect of their existence *sub ratione Dei*.

Sacred scripture records God's *form in the world*, or God's objective claim through providence to render things God's witnesses, in four ways: in the life of Jesus Christ (principal to the most important part of the literal or historical sense), in the way that God's history with Israel prefigures it (principal to the allegorical or typological sense), in the way that it involves human creatures in the working out of Christ's form indwelling in their hearts through faith (the moral or tropological sense), and in the way that it anticipates for them the life with God, where their searching reaches its appointed end: the life, the searching, the end—one thing—that Christ began in them (the anagogical sense). Thus again in the states of affairs really signified, the four aspects of an Aristotelian science get expressed: the form of God in Christ saving the whole world (history); the form of God in Christ rendering reality intelligible (typology); the form of God in Christ structuring human souls (tropology); and the form of God in Christ achieved as end in the life of glory, which enjoys the *scientia Dei* (anagogy). Thus the fourfold sense of scripture can be read as expressing the four aspects of Aristotelian form not just because they are fluid, but because they are *real*. When Thomas grounds them in the relations of real, historical or existing states of affairs to other real, historical or existing or future states of affairs, and makes them the first principles and formal rationale of an Aristotelian science, he replicates the structure in which it falls to form to account for the relation of real and propositional first principles in all four aspects. In article 1 it is the *praecognitus finis* that holds a place for form's function; in article 10 it is the fourfold reading of scripture that spells it out. And as form grounds the integrity of the four aspects in Aristotle, it is Jesus Christ that grounds it in Thomas.

So far we have moved from a possible accident to a plausible speculation. We still lack a sufficiently grounded account. But fortunately Thomas's thinking about *scientia* and its form does not end with I.1.10. "Word" is the personal and proper name of the second person of the Trinity, where it bears the sense of "a concept of the intellect" (I.34.1 *post med.* and I.34.2). So it represents the divine intention to which the *res* accommodated to signification and recorded in scripture correspond in the mind of scripture's author—or the Form in the mind of God. Thomas relates that name specifically to created things (I.34.3). "As God's *scientia* ... knows and makes creatures, so God's Word ... executes and operates them."[110] Similarly, Thomas

compares the *"ratio"* by which God created and governs the world to the
plan in the mind of an artisan, thereby identifying it with an Aristotelian
form, and appropriates it to the Son (I–II.93.1 *in init.* and *ad* 1 *in fin.*). The
second person of the Trinity has as mission "to render human beings participants in the divine wisdom and knowers of the truth [*ut faciat homines
participes divinae sapientiae, et cognitores veritatis*]," and to bring us
teaching.[111] Now in Aristotle it falls to form to execute and develop what it
falls to science to know and shape. So in short: *scientia Dei* relates to
Christ as Aristotelian science relates to form.

In the Romans commentary, as we will see, Thomas puts forward the
following scheme. Some human reasoning attempts to reduce things to
their first principles: *"reducer[e] omnia in primum principium."* That is
just what Aristotle defines *scientia* to do. That attempt (and its this-
worldly failure) belong to God's power, "according to which things proceed
from God, as from their first principle." Now the power according to which
a thing proceeds from its first principle is nothing other than its form. And
God's power belongs "to the person of the Son, according to 1 Cor. 1:24:
Christ the power of God." The Romans commentary too treats the second
person of the Trinity as God's form, and demonstration of the Aristotelian
sort as befitting the divine Word.[112]

Thomas seems not to relate the Word of God in Christ immediately to
the words of God in scripture as many modern theologians do. He relates
them through the fourfold sense. We can now begin to account for the patterns I noted, possibly accidental or speculative, in the way that Thomas
set up the fourfold reading of scripture. The Word is the form by which God
plans and governs all things (I–II.93.1c and *ad* 1, as we saw above). But
God's plan is just the intention of the author of scripture, and God's gover-
nance is just the providence by which God accommodates states of affairs
multiply to signify what the four senses of scripture express. So the states
of affairs in the world (*res ipsas*) that the literal sense of scripture narrates
become *revelabilia* by participating in God's intention. They express and
develop what God's *scientia* contemplates and shapes. In so doing, the fourfold signification reflects Aristotle's form, and Thomas's Christ.

Thus to sum up so far: In the preceding section we saw how *intelligibilia*
relate to Aristotelian *scientia* as *revelabilia* relate to sacred doctrine. In both
cases the formal rationale specifies the objects. Here we see that form is to
Aristotelian *scientia* as *Verbum Dei* is to *scientia Dei*. Now sacred doctrine
is not simply *scientia Dei*: sacred doctrine only *borrows* its objects from *scientia Dei*. *Scientia Dei* is a form it never enjoys, a source of first principles

that it never possesses, as its own. Therefore it cannot move from its objects directly to the formal rationale that unites them in the mind of God (*Verbum Dei*); it can only take its objects on faith according to the formal rationale that God grants us in revelation (*"secundum sunt divinitus revelabilia"*). One way of stating the relation between *scientia Dei* and sacred doctrine is to say that in subalternation their formal rationales get diversified so that the lower participates in the higher. But to move from the lower level to the higher is just what we cannot do. For the form of *revelabilia* involves an inherent creatureliness proceeding from a radically transcendent first principle. The divinely disposed objects of sacred doctrine can*not* be simply understood: that would be to know the mind of God. Since we do not control but wait upon God, sacred doctrine's objects enjoy a *revealable* rather than an intelligible form. *If* we had them as *intelligibilia*, then we would be able to possess them and see God face to face.[113]

Yet that is not the whole story. We also know that some of the *revelabilia* participate more fully or at least provide better access *to us*. The fourfold sense of scripture has a definite center or tendency to it.

For chief among the *revelabilia* is the form of God made flesh.

Thus Jesus Christ becomes *"as a human being* the way that has to be stretched out for us into God [*secundum quod homo via nobis tendendi in Deum*]"* (I.2 proem.). And as incarnate savior he "has manifested to us *in his very self* the way of truth [*viam veritatis nobis in seipso demonstravit*]" (III prol.).[114] Not only objects participating in and specified by the form are granted to us. Not only bits and pieces, willy-nilly. The form also comes to us, as remedy for sin, in a real, followable structure. As such it is a *via*, an exemplar cause, a "demonstration," as well as a manifestation.[115] The incarnation makes the Word not just a *ratio* of God, but a *via* into God. It makes the word not just the *ratio* of the First Truth, but a rational *demonstration* of the truth that we cannot see. For a demonstration is a rational structure that leads to knowledge, in this case, eventually, the *scientia beatorum*.[116] In fact, Jesus Christ, as a human being, is the demonstration *par excellence*. For *only* through him do human beings reach the *scientia beatorum*. For Thomas, even non-Christians reach *scientia beatorum* only through him.[117] For that *scientia*, after the Fall, no other demonstration suffices except the Word incarnate. Thus after calling Christ "the way that demonstrates," Thomas calls it "necessary" that sacred doctrine consider the Savior as "the consummation of the whole theological enterprise," as a demonstration is the consummation of an Aristotelian science.[118] As such it is no necessity of pious obligation, but a necessity structural to the way in which Question 1 of the *Summa* has set sacred doctrine up.

After he distinguishes natural from propositional first principles in his *Physics* commentary, Thomas continues: "Now those things which it is necessary to recognize first in any science are its subject and the medium by which it demonstrates" (*In phys.*, bk. 1, *lect.* 1, *in init.*). The "subject of this science," according to I.1.7, is God. It is the office of the following articles, I.1.8–10, to specify the "medium by which it demonstrates." They ask respectively whether and how sacred doctrine mounts arguments, and they answer that it does so by God's speaking through states of affairs recorded in sacred scripture. I.2 *proemium* provides a shorter, more programmatic answer to the question of the "*medium, per quod scientia demonstrat*": it is Jesus Christ, "who, as a human being is the way [*via*] that has to be stretched out for us into God." The medium is that *via*. And that *via* is primary analogate to the Five Ways, the *quinque viae*, that follow it.

Granted that is an analogy. A life is not a syllogism. But it is an analogy in a precise way, neither univocal nor equivocal. As Preller puts it, "a great deal of epistemological nonsense has been generated by the failure to see that such analogies are *appropriate* equivocations."[119] Thomas uses analogy to hold together distinct uses of a word that capture something related also about the reality being expressed (I.13.5). Here he needs analogy to hold together the way in which Aristotelian and christological demonstrations work. In fact, Thomas requires a Christ-centered analogy not only to make sense of sacred doctrine as an Aristotelian science, but also to hold together additional usages in sacred doctrine that touch every important point in Jesus's life.

Before Jesus's birth there was "a demonstration of sensible signs, namely by the spirit of prophecy." Among them was the star of Bethlehem. It was no "mere" sign but a "*manifestatio syllogistica*" (III.36.5 *in init.*). A more determined mixing of Aristotelian and biblical categories is hard to imagine. Jesus's nativity was necessary precisely as a "*demonstratio divinitatis*" (III.36.4). The words of God the Father at Jesus's baptism, "This is my beloved Son," were necessary as a "*demonstratio ad suppositum*," i.e., an identification of the subject (*CG* 4.5.12). During his ministry, Jesus became a "demonstration making disciples [*demonstratio fienda discipulis*]" (*In* John 5:20b, §758), referring to his miracles. For miracles are "the demonstrations of faith [*demonstrationes fidei*]." And lest anyone think that those are "mere" ostensive as opposed to scientific demonstrations, Thomas immediately continues: "For all *scientia* becomes clear by demonstrations [*omnis scientia clara per demonstrationes]" (In* 2 Thes. 3:1, §65). Again we have explicit analogous usage. The institution of the eucharist also counts as a *"demonstratio."* Thomas once more rejects the notion that "mere" pointing is in question: the "this" of Jesus's "this is my body" demonstrates "that what before was bread becomes the body of Christ" (III.78.5 as a whole, including replies to objections). Indeed, the commentary on 1 Corinthians implies the following analogy: as an Aristotelian demonstration is a syllogism that effects knowledge by signification of real causes, so in the sacraments we have demonstrations that also effect something by signifying: *"significando enim faciunt" (In* 1 Cor. 11:24, §669). Finally it falls to Pilate to set in motion Jesus's passion by making a "demonstrative explication" (*"explicatio demonstrationis"*) when he says *"Ecce homo" (In* John 19:5). Such pointing has "the force of demonstration" (*"vis demonstrationis"*) in important sentences like "this human being is God" (*In III Sent.* 10.1.1.ii) that tell who if not what God is.[120] Finally, "in Christ is the demonstrated way for us" to the final *scientia* of the blessed [*in Christo est nobis iter gloriae demonstratum]" (Quod.* 7.6.2 *ad* 5). Those cases are not all identical, and they are not entirely disparate. Thomas has the resources for picking out that in virtue of which they have something in common. For in all those cases—the syllogistic, the ostensively identifying, the miraculous, the sacramental, and the semantically identifying—"a word comes between the one demonstrating and what the demonstration is of [*verbo est inter demonstrantem et cui fit demonstratio]" (In* John 5:20a, §754).

But the place where all the demonstrations reveal what they have in common is not a commentary upon the *Metaphysics* or the *Posterior Analytics.* It is in the commentary upon the Gospel of John. For "the one demonstrating" is God the Father, and the phrase refers to the Word as the *"demonstratio Patris"* of I.42.6 *ad* 22. Just because the text of John has the Father showing *to the Son* (rather than to us directly) everything that God does, Thomas makes some qualifications there and in I.42.6 *ad* 2 that improve the case. Thomas denies that there should be some additional word between Father and Son, since the Son just *is* the Word. That makes the Word not only the medium of demonstration, but the demonstration itself. Nor should anyone assume that here the second person of the Trinity is in question in abstraction from the incarnation. For that the Father demonstrates everything to the Son (v. 5:20) appears as an *explanation* for the reliablity of the revelation in Jesus: the Father demonstrates everything to the Son *just so* that, in his life on earth, "whatever the Father does, the

Son does likewise" (v. 5:19, §754 *in fin.*): just so that Jesus Christ may be a demonstration of the Father also to us.

It is therefore just because the Word is "demonstration of the Father" that it can become "as a human being a way for us." And it is similarly just because the Word is *demonstratio Patris* that as *Salvator noster* it "has demonstrated to us the way of truth" not by another but "in his very self." That is the analogical relationship. It falls to the Word as *demonstratio Patris* to both *be* the First Truth and that by which the First Truth is known, the *ratio formalis* or *medium demonstrationis* in which particular conclusions, or plural *media demonstrationis,* participate, as II–II.1.1 has it.

Thus we have exactly fulfilled the conditions of analogy that Thomas sets forth in I.13.5:

> [S]ome things are said of God and of creatures analogically, and not merely univocally, nor equivocally....And so, whatever is said of God and creatures is said according as there is some order of the creature to God, as principle and cause, in which all perfections of things excellently preexist....For in those things that are said analogically, there is neither a single rationale, as in univocal things, nor an entirely diverse one, as in equivocation; but a name which is applied in many ways signifies diverse proportions to some one thing [the "primary analogate"].

Here the word "demonstration" is used in diverse ways because demonstrations come in varying proportions to the Word or *demonstratio Patris* as *the* first principle and cause in which their perfection preexists. Thus it is only by being taken up into sacred doctrine which depends upon the various identifying, miraculous, and sacramental demonstrations in the life of Jesus, and which uses the *demonstratio Patris* as its own *medium demonstrationis* or formal rationale, that Aristotelian demonstrations can come to perfection.

It is a special case of the analogical relationship that Jesus Christ is to Aristotelian demonstrations as sacred doctrine is to Aristotelian sciences. We also find evidence that the reasoning applies to Aristotelian demonstrations. The article on analogy denies that words are used of God equivocally *just because* analogy is necessary to hold Paul and Aristotle together. "For this [the claim of equivocation] is *both* against the philosophers, who prove many things demonstratively of God, *and* against the Apostle speaking in Romans 1:20" (I.13.5 *in med.*). Thus when Thomas comes to assert the Aristotelian demonstrability of the proposition "God exists," he cites Romans 1:20 as his warrant (I.2.2 *s.c.*). The demonstrability of God's existence depends, in sacred doctrine, on sacred scripture. But the same warrant, Romans 1:20, grounds the fittingness of the incarnation of Jesus Christ (III.1.1 *s.c.*). *So the Aristotelian demonstrability within sacred doctrine of God's existence, and the demonstration in himself of the truth in Jesus Christ, have the same warrant and derive, as a matter of sacred doctrine, from the same christological insight.* They both derive from God's Word as God's form: the one by participation (by being taken up) as metaphysics into sacred doctrine, as the prologue to John told us and as the subordination of *intelligibilia* to *revelabilia* accounted for; and the other by incarnation. It is clear which is the paradigm form, which the primary analogate (the *"per prius"* of I.13.3). Jesus Christ is the "one thing" to which other demonstrations "signify diverse proportions."

For as Thomas is willing both to call the Word the *demonstratio Patris* and to use the word *"demonstratio"* analogously to describe incidents in Jesus's life, so too he is willing to call not only the Word, but also the human being, the truth itself. Thus in the John commentary we find him writing, "This human being is the divine truth itself [*Ille homo esset ipsa divina veritas*]: for many truths have been imparted [*participatae*] in other human beings, according as the first truth reflects in their minds by many similitudes, but Christ is truth itself."[121]

If the reflected truths of the Five Ways[122] look more like demonstrations to us than Christ does, the misprision should come as no surprise. In the same way human justice looks more familiar to us than God's justice because we have learned it first temporally, and not as if human justice stood first logically.

Thomas pursues a similar train of thought when he treats Jesus Christ as true light. The principles of demonstration and the light of bodies are both that by which something becomes "maximally manifest."[123] Thomas contrasts "true" light to other light in three ways: versus false light, versus symbolic light, and versus participating light. Participating light is the light that "the holy" have by grace; those who regard all things by trusting God participate in God's light by grace. That sets things up in the same way as sacred doctrine does, since I.1.1 *ad* 2 uses "cognoscibles by the light of divine revelation," and I.1.4 "cognoscibles by the divine light" as synonyms for the *"divinitus revelabilia"* of I.1.3. But "the philosophers" (as opposed to the faithful, instead of as included among them) had, "before the Word came," i.e., before the incarnation, a false light! That is, it was false precisely as not participating in the true light which has actually come into the world.[124] Thus it is that the arguments of the philosophers become only "extraneous and probable" (I.1.8 *ad* 2 *post med.*) in the genre of theology that pertains to sacred doctrine (I.1.1 *ad* 2 *in fin.*), for they proceed only "with the admixture of many errors" (I.1.1 *post med.*).

We can observe an appeal to Jesus as Savior (rather than as Word) not only *ex parte ipsius rei* but also *ex parte nostra*, in the long consideration of the human being in the *Secunda* that the proemium to I.2 anticipates and the prologue to the *Tertia* looks back on.

Because the end does not just complete but also elevates us, and lies therefore beyond the powers that we would have were it not granted us— beyond, that is, the powers that we would possess as creatures *not* destined for elevation—the common form or isomorphism with divine things begins not in discursive reasoning from sense data but from *faith* (II–II.2.3), through which we already begin to be united to God in this life as to One Unknown (I.12.13 *ad* 1). In addition to the way in which the object of beatitude lies beyond the powers of the mind, the proper motion of discursive reasoning is also frustrated on its *own* account, because of finitude and sin; discursivity becomes itself restlessness. It needs faith also just so that it can *pay attention* even to what God has revealed to it;[125] the mind could not attend to the first principles to which sacred doctrine as *scientia* must ever and again return unless faith should settle it from outside. It could not muster the courage and fortitude. That settlement of the mind by faith is an aspect of the taking of all understanding into captivity to Christ, and marks another way, *ex parte nostra*, in which sacred doctrine becomes more christoform, the more Aristotelian it is.[126] The form by which God is true to God (the form *ex parte ispsius rei*), by which and to which and through which human beings, in faith, return to God, is also the form (*ex parte nostra*) by which human beings know God. That form (*via nobis tendendi in Deum*) is, in both senses, Jesus Christ. Through knowing Jesus Christ we get a foretaste (the *praecognitum finis* of I.1.1) of what friendship with God is like. So it is that Jesus Christ is that to which sacred doctrine returns and attends as to its first principle. It too is no equivocation, but primary analogate, that the paradigm case of deduction is God's leading us into truth through Jesus Christ, *via veritatis*, as Thomas reads the Psalmist's prayer: "Teach me your way, O Lord, and I will walk in your truth," where "teach me" is *deduc me*, "way" is *via*, and "Lord," (*"Domine"*) is Jesus Christ.[127] Jesus Christ, in short, is no less first deduction than God is first truth.

Thomas does not, therefore, simply throw off remarks about Jesus Christ as demonstration as so many *obiter dicta*. He articulates several interrelated rationales for a strict and appropriate usage, among them: the definition of demonstration as "medium," the doctrine of analogy as governing the word's proper semantic range, biblical (trinitarian) usages of the word, a complementary deployment of light metaphors, the discursive movements of the human mind, and the christological interpretation of the Psalms. I close the discussion with reference to another, stricter reading of the definition.

Earlier we saw that the medium by which a discipline demonstrates varies according to the discipline, and that in sacred doctrine Thomas counts all sorts of things, from the star of Bethlehem to the bread of the eucharist, as demonstrations appropriate to it. It was necessary, therefore, to take in a broad and appropriately rule-governed or analogous sense the definition that a demonstration is a rational structure leading to knowledge. I prescinded from discussing how the theological modifications of Aristotle's concept of *scientia* cause modifications also in the matter of demonstration. We find a similar pattern. The demonstration that is the humanity of God in Jesus Christ both leads and does not lead to *scientia*, depending on which of its fourfold senses one has in mind. As before, it does not lead to complete conformity of the human being to the first truth, the fully adequate conformity that only God and the *beati* possess by the light of glory, and in that sense demonstration is *denied:* Jesus Christ, in offering arguments from scripture about his own resurrection, does not offer the sort of reason (*ratio demonstrativa*) that would so compel the mind to assent as to exclude the merit of believing (III.55.5 *ad* 2). Jesus Christ does not offer, and is not in himself, the sort of demonstration that would provide an exception to the rule that human beings do not see God in this life, the sort of demonstration that causes a human being to see or possess *scientia*. Or more precisely, they do, sensibly, see God's body, but seeing that it is God's remains for faith, and seeing God's essence remains for glory. The demonstration that God's humanity provides does not make us scientists like God and the blessed. And yet the exception proves the rule. For Jesus Christ, as God, *is* such a scientist, does possess the beatific vision, does enjoy the fruits of the demonstration his humanity provides, even in the strictest sense: and he does so *for us. In that case too Jesus Christ is a demonstration for us, in the very strictest sense, in the sense of leading to actual, adequate, beatific* scientia *of how things are in the mind of God*—even if we do not enjoy that demonstration in this life. So Thomas writes:

That which is in potentiality is reduced to act by that which is in act ....
Now the human being is in potentiality to the *scientia* of the blessed,
which consists in the vision of God, and is ordered to that *scientia* as end.
For the human being is a rational creature capable of that beatific cognition, insofar as the human being is [ordered] to the image of God [which
in Jesus Christ exists in act.] *But human beings are reduced to that end
by the humanity of Christ....* And therefore it was necessary that the
very cognition that consists in the vision of God should befit Christ most
excellently among human beings.[128]

As an Aristotelian demonstration, therefore, reduces the potential *scientia*
contained virtually in first principles to act, i.e., to an actual structuring of
the human soul, so Thomas causes the humanity of Christ to fulfill that
function even when, as we have seen, he reserves the *scientia* in question for
the next life. Christ as demonstration does not undermine but becomes the
linchpin of this system. In the use of the concept of demonstration, Thomas
reaches the height of Aristotelian rigor, recovering *scientia* as the actual
structuring of the soul, precisely where he is most uncompromisingly christological. Christ is a *via demonstrationis* to us in that when we human beings are "reduced" to *scientia Dei* in the next life, it will have been by his
humanity. Because it is the demonstration provided by the humanity of
Christ that will have caused in us the *scientia* of the blessed, we may say
that it is at his most christocentric that Thomas is most Aristotelian.

It is fitting that God's existence should be demonstrable, I.2.2 tells us, because, as Paul says, "The invisible things of God have been clearly perceived
in the things that have been made" (Rom. 1:20 as in the Vulgate). The first
article of the *Tertia* interprets that verse as follows: "It seems to be *most* fitting [*convenientissimum*] that by visible things should be demonstrated
[*monstrentur*] the invisible things of God: since for that reason the whole
world was made." And for the same reason, "nothing is greater than that
God should become human" (III.1.1 *s.c.*). We have, that is, a God who created the world for God's self-revelation, even if the scriptures confine talk of
incarnation to the remedy for sin (III.1.3), and to whom it is therefore most
fitting to become flesh (III.1.1). Jesus Christ is God's own reasoning, accommodated to us by God's will to self-revelation. III.1.2 gives many reasons for
the incarnation, first among them that "faith gains a greater certainty
[*magis certificatur*] in believing very God speaking," and last that we attain
to the "full participation of divinity [*plenam participationem divinitatis*],
which truly is a human being's happiness, and the end of human life"
(III.1.2). But *mutatis mutandis* those are goals—happiness and participation

in divinity—of Aristotle's *Metaphysics*. Here however they are not achieved by metaphysics; rather, beatitude and participation in divinity are "conferred on us by the humanity of Christ" (III.1.2). In sacred doctrine Jesus Christ replaces—or better: *assumes* metaphysics. Jesus Christ exemplifies demonstration in sacred doctrine not as some vague *logos* or disembodied argument, but, Thomas is careful to specify, as God's argument embodied, "*secundum quod homo*" and as "*Salvator noster,*" than which "nothing is greater," and which is thus "*convenientissimum.*" The *scientia* of sacred doctrine renders Jesus Christ demonstration not just ornamentally but with supreme fittingness.

In the last section we saw that the reality of God's form inheres in the things that God has arranged to speak. In this section we see that the reality of God's form becomes a demonstration for us in the humanity of Jesus Christ. The various senses of "demonstration" are held together by their reference to the demonstration as primary analogate ("*per prius*") in the divine Word, and it is therefore most fitting (as a cause of the Incarnation) that it should be by that Word as a human being that a way should be stretched out for us into God. Furthermore, it is by reference to that Word precisely as a demonstration that the other *revelabilia* relate to the providential ordering that transforms them from *res* into *revelabilia* at all.[129] "[W]e immediately know-by-faith that Christ's humanity is expressing the agency [proper to God]. In the act of faith, one sees or knows the humanity of Christ, and believes the divinity.... It is the given function of the light of faith to recognize in any ordering—intentional or existential—of [the human being] to God, the agency [proper to God]."[130] For as the John commentary also puts it: "This governing authority"—the same governing authority that arranges states of affairs to speak as narrated in the scriptures—"is demonstrated in the Word of God."[131]

It is no accident, therefore, and no mere piety, that the article that engages in detail the Aristotelian charge to "proceed from first principles" (namely the article on how sacred doctrine argues, I.1.8) engages also the scriptural charge to "take all understanding captive into obedience to Christ." For to set up sacred doctrine as *scientia* means that to "proceed from first principles" just is to "take all understanding captive into obedience to Christ."

So far Question 1 of the *Summa*. Does question 2 change the rules? Do the Five Ways make an exception to the *scientia* of sacred doctrine? Does Thomas, as Pesch denies, "backslide" into philosophy?[132] Or do the Five Ways count as "strictly metaphysical knowledge" that, as Gilson insists, "can be included in a strictly philosophical structure without losing its purely philosophical nature"?[133] Does Thomas there modify his scriptural-ism, or abandon the analogy of all demonstrations to that provided by the humanity of Christ?

To answer those questions we turn now to the text that Thomas adduces as a warrant for the appropriateness in sacred doctrine of God's demonstra-bility both in the Five Ways (*sed contra* to I.2.2) and in the humanity of Christ (*sed contra* to III.1.1). It is Romans 1:20: "the invisible things of God are known from the things God has made." As a test and extension of the argument offered in Part I of this essay, I now devote Part II to the place where the verse is at home, Thomas's commentary on Romans, where Thomas treats Christ and cosmology in the same context.

II

A Partial Test:
The Theological Context
of the Natural Knowledge of God
in Thomas's Commentary on Romans

3

The Identity of Paul in the Prologue to Thomas's Commentaries on His Epistles: Election, Vocation, Inspiration

---

Barth's question

Consider the following, characteristically provocative, reading of Paul from Barth's *Shorter Commentary on Romans:*

> Let us admit at once: if [Rom.] 1.19–21 had come to us by themselves, say as fragments of an unknown text by an unknown author, then one might possibly conjecture that all these words referred to the existence of a "natural" knowledge of God by the Gentiles, prior to and independent of God's revelation in Jesus Christ. Time and again these words have been read as though they were such a fragment and they have in fact been interpreted and ever and again quoted as evidence of a general doctrine of such a natural knowledge of God. Even on that strange presupposition too much has been read into these words. It does not say in these verses, in which the Gentile religions as such are as yet not even mentioned, that the Gentile religions witness to a relationship to God which is indispensable to human existence and that they should be interpreted as the result of God's revelation and the human being's sin. But even this presupposition is wrong. These verses happen not to be a loose fragment. They occur as the words of the Apostle Paul in a definite context in the Epistle to the Romans and in the whole body of Pauline literature....Paul does something which is done by no student of comparative religion or philosophy of religion: he sees the Gentiles as well as the Jews in the reflected light of that fire of God's wrath which is the fire of [God's] love.[1]

Of course Barth would expect to find Thomas on the wrong side of that divide. And Barthians might seem to have some *prima facie* evidence for the conclusion. For if we look at Thomas's commentary on the same passage, on Romans 1:19–21 (that the invisible things of God can be known from the things God has made), what do we find? Proofs. Proofs for the existence of God (*In Rom.* 1:19, §115). Or so it seems. The odd thing is, it turns out that each of the arguments—this time there are three—gets assimilated to a person of the Trinity (*In Rom.* 1:19–20, §§115–122). But that is a chapter for another day. Let us see now whether Thomas comes closer to treating Paul as a philosopher of religion or to treating him as an apostle.[2]

The answer to that question will be important not just in order to assess the reception of Thomas by friend and foe in the nineteenth and twentieth centuries. It will also provide important background for how we come to articulate the paradigm form of human cognition[3] of God as Thomas presents it. For Thomas is Aristotelian enough to think that we learn an excellence or virtue from a person who has it (I.1.6 *ad* 3 *in med.*). If the reasoning is circular, an Aristotelian would say, the circle is not a vicious but precisely a virtuous one. In the case of the virtues or excellence characteristic of sacred doctrine Thomas refers us to the person whose virtue it is to be "spiritual." Since "spiritual" here picks out someone who has received wisdom as a gift from the *Holy* Spirit (I.1.6 *ad* 3 *ca. fin.*), the result is that cognition of God comes from none other than God. In accord with Aristotle's circle of virtue we will see Paul described as one whose calling it is both to teach and to *exemplify* virtue. *Cognitio Dei* will sometimes turn out, I shall be arguing, to involve moral virtues that Paul exemplifies, primarily faith, which is a form of *cognitio Dei.* Meanwhile, Thomas will take Paul as exemplary to the point of using certain virtues ascribed to him, such as justice and gratitude, as *tests* for *cognitio Dei* in its effective form. But that is to get chapters ahead of the exposition.

Election as introduction

Thomas begins his commentary on the Pauline epistles by putting them into the context of scripture as a whole and its picture of Paul's life. He titles the opening section, three pages in the Marietti edition, *Super epistolas sancti Pauli lectura: Prologus*, "A reading of the letters of St. Paul: Prologue." Unlike modern prologues to scriptural commentaries, Thomas's sets out no hermeneutical manifesto. Nor does Thomas attempt to find or make a text about texts. The Prologue too, and not only the commentary to follow, simply interprets a text, a scriptural text. It sets up interpretation by interpreting, by doing it. *In* so doing, rather than before it, Thomas will develop a theory about the relation of divine and human authorship that will tacitly rather than explicitly defend his approach.[4] He begins with a text that relates the authorship of Paul to the rest of the scriptures. He

takes scripture to hold the key to scripture, with no general theory of interpretation, no universal anthropology, no hermeneutics, in short, as we late
twentieth-century academics would recognize the term. No self-absorbed
reflection upon one's own project, no attempts to guarantee in any strong
sense of the term either the avoidance of mistakes or (more ambitious) the
discovery of the text's one meaning. *Nor even any polemic against such
approaches.* Rather Thomas proceeds with an apparent naiveté that must
seem remarkable to us, an immediate concern with the matter. For the interpretation provides its own defense.

And what a surprising matter it is: the doctrine of election. A theological locus more remote from the science of interpretation as the Enlightenment would understand it, more potentially offensive to Enlightenment
canons of universality, or more outspokenly theological as apparently
opposed to the philosophy of Aristotle scarcely bears imagining: "'*Vas
electionis*,'" he quotes from the Vulgate of Acts 9:15, "'*est mihi iste*,'
etc.": "'A vessel of election is this one to me.'" "*Vas electionis*": what a
way to begin!

Thomas allows that beginning to stand on its own authority: he offers
no defense that might, despite itself, undermine the standing of the line
from that scriptural continuation of the gospel story. Evidently it requires
no shoring up. It is as if Thomas expected scripture itself to prove sufficient: as if the context that the one verse will provide—indeed that the
opening word pair *vas electionis* will provide—could replace prole-
gomenon, methodology, hermeneutics, foundation, and everything else
necessary to the world of scriptural commentary and *wissenschaftlich* theological work: as if reader and writer could find themselves, in short, immediately within a different, biblical world, a world in which the relevant way
to begin a commentary upon the letters of Paul is with a reflection upon the
way in which Paul and his letters serve as a vessel of *election.*

The phrase comes from God's command to Ananias. The Greek has
"*skeuos eklogês.*" The RSV has "chosen instrument." The whole quotation
reads there (vv. 15–16, RSV): "But the Lord said to him [Ananias], 'Go, for he
is a chosen instrument of mine to carry my name before the Gentiles and
kings and the sons of Israel; for I will show him how much he must suffer
for the sake of my name.'"

Thomas proceeds with a fourfold analysis of the way in which the
phrase from Acts functions in and evokes the biblical world into which he
has catapulted his readers and himself:[5]

1. Human beings in sacred scripture are found compared to vessels in four respects, namely: with respect to make, fill, use, and fruit [*constitutionem, repletionem, ususm, fructum*].

Each of the four aspects arises, as Thomas announces, from a comparison found in sacred scripture. I will be calling *"constitutio," "repletio," "usus,"* and *"fructus"* the formation or the make, the filling up or the fill, the use, and the fruit or enjoyment of a vessel, and I will be deploying the more familiar Aristotelian scheme of form, matter, end, and effectiveness as a heuristic device to explicate them. Thomas does not himself mention the Aristotelian scheme anywhere in the Prologue. The danger is not that the Aristotelian categories will take over, for the commentary is a virtual catena of biblical passages; the danger is that Thomas's biblical words "formation," "filling up," "use," and "fruit" will sound merely picturesque, so that we will miss the logical work that they do. Aristotle's words have the *ad hoc* advantage that we expect them to do logical work.

The formation

"A vessel...falls under the authority [*arbitrium*] of an artisan....So also the formation [*constitutio*] of a human being falls under the authority of God.... Paul therefore, since his is called a vessel of election in the words under discussion, was such a vessel" (*Prol.*, §1). Paul counts then as a vessel of election first of all just as he enjoys his constitution as God's work; as God's work Paul possesses "all virtues," of which Thomas, by scriptural catena, singles out wisdom and charity. It pertains to Paul's determination (*"constitutio"* again) as one of the elect secondly not only to enjoy those virtues but also to deploy them: "he therefore most excellently taught the mysteries of divinity, which pertains to wisdom, I Cor. 2:6 shows; he also most excellently commended charity, I. Cor. 13; he instructed human beings about various virtues, as appears from Col. 3:12" (*Prol.*, §§1–2). Thus we have Thomas's first description of the apostle Paul: he is formed by God's work as a possessor of virtues and determined by God's purpose as their teacher. Paul's God-formed-ness or *constitutio* renders him native to the world of *revelabilia*.

Although he does not use the word *"forma,"* Thomas uses election to define Paul according to a form in two ways. The artisanship of God to which Thomas refers functions here not so much as an efficient fashioning as a fashioning of formation. For it marks a form both to be and to show

how a thing is made; it provides matter with structure, and it renders that structure visible.[6] So it is that Paul both possesses and exhibits virtue; his particular virtues, christoform and idiosyncratic, provide his character with structure and render him visibly the figure that he plays. It marks form not to hide but to show itself precisely through its development, as it is the office of the form of an oak to develop and show itself out of an acorn. Thomas finds the notion of "nature as an inner principle of change"[7] already ripe for talk about *graced* nature, where the indwelling of Jesus Christ trans*forms* nature without violating it, or applying an exterior principle of change.[8] Thomas will recur to the matter of Paul's particular development, which is his story, and specifically the story of his transformation from Saul into Paul, when he comes later to discuss Paul's vocation. Here he treats the make of Paul as something that drives rather than attracts his story, as it belongs to the form to drive, the end to attract the development of a thing. The two are, as we saw in Chapter 1, closely related, form and end, what drives and what attracts a thing in its development according to God's purpose. We separate them only as points in an analysis. Thus when Thomas talks about God's determination of human beings generally in the *Summa* he does so under the rubric of their end. When Thomas comes later in this text to talk about Paul's end he will turn to the end as peculiar to Paul in a less easily generalizable way. It is illuminating therefore to talk here about how the determination by human beings by their form in the Prologue to the Pauline epistles relates to the determination of human beings by their end in the *Summa*. The one way of dividing up the exposition appears to complement and enrich the other.

The remarks about Paul suggest that we may think of human beings generally in Thomas as being formed by virtue (infused virtue, and particularly, for the question of the cognition of God, faith) toward the end which is beatitude, so that virtue is the driving form: It is not the moral prerequisite, but the logical accompaniment; it is not the efficient agency, but that in which God's pressings and urgings-on of us come to structure us; it is the driving form of God's befitting human beings for divine friendship. Relating virtue and beatitude as form and end has the advantage too of forestalling the way of thinking that would take beatitude as a reward external to virtue; rather, as for Aristotle's *eudaimonia*, beatitude no more adds to the developed structure than an oak tree adds to its leaves and branches; it emerges in and through the structure. If that is so about the way that beatitude relates to human beings, then the end of friendship with God cannot be a supernatural end as *opposed* or even *additional* to another, separable natural human end. Rather virtue is itself so transformed that grace always already shoots through nature: so, namely, that beatitude may remain internal to the human being whose formation is precisely God's transforming.

Thomas's exposition of the material aspect of election will make it clear that grace, indeed the grace of Christ, is inalienable in the entire fourfold characterization. Thomas's exposition of the end peculiar to Paul, in which Paul's emergence out of Saul prominently figures, instantiates the formation by transformation that an integral (as opposed to alien) supernatural end requires. Neither is the end internal to us in a way that would render us our own creatures, instead of the creatures of the Creator. Rather the lack of opposition between nature and grace has two aspects: 1) the end is "new" to nature (in the sense of the distinct, *"novum modus"* of the mission of the Persons) as elevating it, and yet it is or "becomes" 2) internal to nature so as to elevate it as *itself*, that is, as an *inner* rather than violent principle of change. So the famous dictum "grace does not take away nature, but perfects it" (e.g., I.1.8 *ad* 2 *ca. med.*, I.2.2 *ad* 1). The matter will be a theme of this Part, since Thomas notes already at the second place cited—in the context of the demonstrability of the proposition "God exists"—that the knowledge of God works according to the same pattern.[9] The argument for the interpretation will gain force, clarity, and nuance, I hope, by accretion. In the case of the apostle, it is none other than Saul whom God transforms into Paul; it is none other than Paul whom God always meant Saul to become; and it is therefore for no other reason than that, that the transformation is "natural" to his life. That is, it accords with God's plan for him. It has a storied rather than a static naturalness.

Thomas gives Paul a general and a special determination. The general he shares with all the elect. In the first question of the *Summa,* as we have seen, Thomas defines or redefines human beings according to God's gracious granting to us of God's own self as our end. That single, integrated end then elects and constitutes us not otherwise than through our nature, and makes us like Paul vessels of election. It is furthermore the purpose of such revelation as we find in the letters of Paul to give us some foreknowledge of that end, *praecognitum finis,* so that we may seek it. Paul's special determination, that of teaching the general determination in turn to us, belongs especially to Paul as a vessel elected for the teaching, commending, and instructing of other human beings about their end. Thomas here sets up Paul's role in the passing on of the revelation formally defined at the beginning of Question 1 by the casting of things as *revelabilia,* and materially at the end of Question 1 by the article on scripture (I.1.10). The material of the *praecognitum finis* specified by the mention of scripture becomes concrete and detailed when the Romans commentary comes to consider human *cognitio Dei*. And when it does so, true to the promise of the Prologue, it takes Paul as both explicit teacher and implicit exemplar of *cognitio Dei* in its effective or paradigm form—in the form (namely faith), that is, that drives us toward the end of which it tells us. As exemplar Paul serves as no mere ornament: Thomas will draw positive conclusions about the right cognition of God from Paul's expressions of attitudes like piety and gratitude. All that is involved in Thomas's first specification of the way in which Paul counts as an apostle, the specification of his determination or constitution, the "make" of Paul.

Note too, by the way, that Thomas's procedure here exposes the way in which his use of Aristotle remains relative to his specific purpose. The reference to the human end that Thomas in the *Summa* warrants with scripture and explicates with Aristotle he here explicates with a doctrine of *election*; the doctrine of revelation that Thomas there warrants with scripture and explicates with an Aristotelian formal rationale he here explicates with a reference to the purpose of Paul's election or calling: a reference, that is, to *Paul's particular story*. The difference in procedure calls attention to the way in which *also in practice* Thomas regards the use of Aristotle as optional and the use of scripture as obligatory: or to the way in which, in the words of the article about the structure of argument in sacred doctrine (I.1.8 *ad 2 ante fin.*), Thomas characterizes the authority of sacred scripture as "proper" and "necessary," and that of philosophers as "extraneous" and "probable."

But Thomas goes on to flesh out Paul's office as a vessel of election in a second respect.

The filling up: The matter of election is Jesus Christ

One might expect Thomas to return to virtue as the liquid that fills a vessel of election. At first he does:

> 3. ...So also human beings too are filled by divine power with different gifts as with different liquids, as in I Cor. 12:8: *To some are given by the Spirit the utterance of wisdom, to others*, and so on.

Immediately however Thomas returns to the text from Acts that supplied the phrase he continues to explicate. Acts adds the phrase "in order that he carry my name." That requires a more specific sort of filling up of the elect, namely a christological one.

But this vessel, of which it is now treated, was full of a precious liquid, namely the name of Christ, of which it is said in Cant. 1:3: *Your name is oil poured out.* Indeed he seems to have been full of this name.

He had this name in the cognition [*cognitio*] of his intellect, according to I Cor. 2:2: *For I have not judged myself to know [scire] anything among you except Christ.* He had this name also in the love of the affections, according to Rom. 7:35: *Who will separate us from the love of Christ?*—I Cor. toward the end [16:22]: *If anyone does not love our Lord Jesus Christ, let that one be anathema.*

He had it also in the entire manner of his life, whence he said at Gal. 2:20: *For it is no longer I who live, but Christ who lives in me.*

3. It seems secondly to pertain to vessels that they be filled with some liquid, according to II Kings. 4:5: *They brought vessels and she poured.*

The fourfold analysis acts as a heuristic device here to show up the significance of a particular christological turn in Thomas. It makes the scripturally inspired phrase "full of a precious liquid" into more than a suggestive or programmatic metaphor. Thomas regards and presents Christ as election's very matter. In that way he need not choose as Calvin[10] so notoriously seemed to have to do between possible subjects of election, God *in se* or God in Christ. The fourfold analysis drives no wedge between such false alternatives—its beauty is not to permit them. Rather it holds the two moments together in order to unfold them one at a time. Thomas has found a way to build a christological reference into both this treatment of election and this Prologue to the letters of Paul. He does so, furthermore, in a way that renders Christ constitutive. Unlike the somewhat helpful, perhaps dispensable metaphors for Christ's role in election that Karl Barth lists, judges, and discards—Augustine's *lumen,* Calvin's *speculum electionis*—Thomas's analysis builds Christ inalienably in. It seems in that way as Christ-informed an account as any Barth praises, and one more secure than any he rejects.[11]

Nor do the scriptural quotations that elaborate upon Christ as election's matter appear as mere ornaments to the exposition. As elect in Christ Paul refers to him all his knowledge: "For I have not judged myself to know anything among you except Christ."[12] The citation serves Thomas's characterization of theology as a genre. Ordinarily Thomas deploys the even stronger phrase "taking all understanding captive into obedience to Christ" to make that point. Here he finds Paul's first-person statement of intention more appropriate. The words *"omnem"* ("all") and *"non aliquid nisi"* ("not anything without") agree in their exclusive force. They assert and warrant a principle in sacred doctrine of *sola fide.*[13] Or better, *solo Christo.* By deploying it already here Thomas marks off Romans for sacred doctrine as one of two distinct theological genres: it is "the theology that pertains to sacred doctrine," which despite some overlap in material content *"differs from"* "the theology that pertains to metaphysics" according to its very form (I.1.1 *ad* 2 *in fin.*). It is that also as a whole: *"non aliquid nisi."* And by deploying it already here Thomas sets Paul apart for the theological office of *apostolus*: Paul speaks with salvific intent conforming, as we have seen, to his determination as *electionis vas.* Thus Thomas claims both the intent of the author and the genre of the text for a purpose he takes Christ to define: with the words of exclusion he forecloses, for *his* purpose at least, the possibility of readings that would take Romans as a license for philosophizing also without Christ, or, to borrow a phrase the Reformation would use differently, *etiam extra Christum.* He forecloses for his purposes the possibility of a reading that would take Romans as a license for what the *Summa* calls the theology that pertains to metaphysics; he forecloses the possibility for his purposes of using Romans as a license for impersonations of Paul that would present him *etiam extra Christum* as a metaphysician, or as (the Enlightenment might have it) a philosopher of religion, or as exercising any office other than that of *apostolus*, pursuing any purpose excluded by his wish "not to know anything among you except Christ."

The verses that follow pursue the principle of *solo Christo* into the will. For the goal of determining Paul, and through him others, for the virtue that Thomas has specified as election's final cause, it will prove insufficient for the mind alone to hold certain views, however Christ-informed. It will be necessary as well for the will to be replete with Christ. Thomas adduces three verses, which I repeat here from the beginning of this section:

> Rom. 8:35: Who will separate us from the love of Christ?—I Cor. toward the end [16:22]: If anyone does not love our Lord Jesus Christ, let that one be anathema.
> ...Gal. 2:20: For it is no longer I who live, but Christ who lives in me.

If we consider each verse also in the context of the commentary Thomas makes in the proper place upon *it*, each one contains a meaning that considerably fleshes out the christological doctrine of election that Thomas is here developing. I take each verse separately.

"What will separate us from the love of Christ" ascribes the perseverance of God's election to Christ as its matter somewhat as one ascribes the persistence of an agent to its substantiality. That is, the verse knows an electing and loving that does not simply sometimes happen, and sometimes not, punctiliar and occasional, but it has a continuous location and agency; it belongs not to acts that are isolated, but to acts that belong together as of a person. And it ascribes to Christ as its matter, or its persistent location, also the love of God and neighbor—a love with which the scriptures' text and Christ's example specify material content for the very virtues to which God's election determines us. For God's election does not leave us disengaged, but inflames our hearts in such a way as cannot be extinguished.[14]

"If anyone does not love our Lord Jesus Christ, let that one be anathema" might well be explicated so that "anathema" is taken literally, or at least, not *in malam partem*, as a remanding to God[15]—root meaning, to devote to God, as an offering—because the will to adhere to Christ is *God's* will and work: it too refers us back to God's election, and need not lead to a doctrine of reprobation. For an anathema can be less a reliance upon the judgment of the church than a demurrer in the face of the church's judgment. Rather it is an appeal, result unknown, to the judgment of God. And that is a return, as I noted, to God's election.

The third verse that Thomas quotes intensifies the christological concentration, wherein Paul in effect calls no part of himself Christ-free: "For it is no longer I that live, but Christ that lives in me." What we have called an *etiam extra Christum* is here again denied, or the possibility of doing theology also outside of Christ. Paul does not intend to represent or perform or speak anything (in Anselm's phrase) *remoto Christo*, Christ having been put aside; he ascribes his entire agency and being to Christ, excluding the possibility of any exception. Thomas will have little use therefore, for the reading of Romans that takes Paul as speaking at first in the person, for example, of Saul. Thomas could choose no verse to intensify more effectively a principle of *solo Christo* than the one he here has chosen: "For it is no longer I that live but in me Christ."

The logic of the passage is thus triply Christ-informed. It refers God's election as cause and context to Christ as its material content: Christ becomes the location, the accessibility, the story, the Aristotelian material cause, in several senses, *in which* election takes place. It refers to God's election also the apparent absence of Christ as matter, that virtue or love, since it has described election so far only in terms of God's positive will in Christ to love and to inspire love in human beings. A lack thereof receives no characterization of its own, only an anathema, and the anathema in turn receives no characterization of its own; it only executes a return to the will of God described in terms of the good end God elects for human beings. And it makes Christ's matter exhaustive, unalloyed, in specifying what it calls the repletion of Paul. It refers therefore the presence and the apparent absence and the fullness of God's election to Christ, the presence and the apparent absence and the fullness of Christ's material presence to God's election.[16]

In other words, *this* passage at least presents only the positive will of God to save, and mentions no will of God, positive or negative, to condemn to reprobation, and it supports those who interpret Thomas as holding only single predestination.[17] Thomas has the resources—which this passage displays—to affirm only God's justice in judging, and will to save. He sees no need to affirm the case of a negative outcome, unless he regards himself as otherwise constrained by scripture. In this passage he is free from such a constraint. To take sin seriously does not require him to affirm that God damns, but that God alone can save.

The use: Election as providence and vocation

That brings us to the third moment of Thomas's four-cause analysis. He speaks of a vessel's possible noble or humble use. It receives in this case the noble use of bearing the divine name from afar. The divine name comes to us from *afar* on account of the sin of human wills and the obscurity of human minds.

The passage begins like this:

> 4. Third, with respect to use it is to be considered that all vessels are deputed to some use, but some to a more honorable, some to a meaner use, according to Rom. 9:21: *Does not the potter have the power to make of the same lump one vessel into one of honor, but another into one of dishonor?* So also human beings, according to divine ordination, are deputed to diverse uses, according to Eccl. 33:10–11 . . .

Doctrines of election and providence tend to get widely separated, so that the doctrine of election treats only what happens after death and the doctrine of providence only what happens in this life. Perhaps the separation owes something to Kant's division of the noumenal from the phenomenal realm. In any case it serves the good purpose of preventing people from trying to read off from the facts of their lives the state of their souls before God, of denying the practical syllogism, and of asserting the power of grace to save anyone, beginning, as the parable has it, at any hour of the day for the same wage. But such abuses as the practical syllogism do not take away a proper use, and Thomas here treats providence and election as belonging together in this way: those whom God elects, God elects to serve God's purposes, however transparent or opaque to us. The God who elects and the God who disposes events remain the same God.

It befits the broad lines of the biblical story, of course, that this should be so. In the Old Testament it is Israel that bears God's election and Israel whose story is told as one in which God providentially arranges states of affairs to speak. In the New Testament, similarly, it is Jesus Christ who bears God's election and Jesus Christ whose story is told as a story in which God providentially arranges states of affairs to speak. Thus it is, too, that Paul's election and Paul's life do not run independently for Thomas as noumenal and phenomenal, but together as two aspects of what God sees and plans, intuits and intends, as one.

So in the following paragraph Thomas goes on to specify Paul's calling. It is to bear the divine name from afar.

> Now this vessel has been deputed to a noble use, for it is a bearer vessel of the divine name, since it is said THAT HE BEAR MY NAME, because a certain name was necessary to be borne, since it was far from human beings, according to Isaiah 30:27: *Behold, the name of the Lord comes from afar.*

Of course Thomas cannot intend here to speak of the modern problems of relating dogmatics and apologetics. And rival modern conceptions of theology can or will in their rival ways have dealt with the very same texts that Thomas here comments upon and cites. Nevertheless Thomas's remarks in their own context do seem to exclude some of the modern options. It is Paul's office to bear the divine *name*. Paul is not therefore (according to Thomas) involved in teaching about God or divinity in general, or about human religiosity. Paul is according to Thomas about the business of telling his listeners about a specific, *nameable* character; and that name, furthermore, cannot be reduced to any description or function such as might be specified by structures of human reason, feelings of absolute dependence, or specifications of significance for salvation (*Heilsbedeutsamkeit*). The name it is Paul's office to bear is that of Jesus Christ. Thomas makes that explicit also in the gloss that the Isaiah commentary offers on the verse that the Romans commentary quotes: "[It says] 'Behold the name of the Lord' because the Son of God is the name of the Father, by which he is first made manifest,...second honored,...[and] third petitioned."[18] The name of God is here: Jesus Christ.[19] That is what Paul is here about.

And Paul carries that name "from afar." Thus he carries it precisely to those who are trapped in structures of injustice. It is thus precisely to those who are far from the name of Jesus Christ that Paul presents that name and not some other apparently more accessible to them. It would appear that here, just where the "from afar" suggests that Paul is practicing apologetics, the name specified subordinates it to or subsumes it into dogmatics.

Such a subordination or subsumption is necessary for two reasons, Thomas goes on to say:

> Now it is far from us on account of sin, according to Ps. 118 [119]:155: *Salvation is far from the wicked.*—It is also far from us on account of the obscurity of the intellect, whence to certain ones it is also said in Heb. 11:13, that they were ones having *seen it from afar,* and at Num. 24:17 it is said: *I will see him, but not now; I will behold him, but not nigh.*

Human religiosity is not to be trusted on account of human sin, and human reason is not to be trusted on account of the darkness of the intellect. Thus when Thomas concludes each of the Five Ways with a prime mover (etc.) "which everyone names God,"[20] we are not to think that the intellect has succeeded in delivering anything univocal with the name that Paul carries. For the name *he* carries comes from afar precisely to elevate the intellect; that is, to bring it closer to God, and in so doing to remedy its deficiencies—even the deficiencies of an intellect that functions more or less properly. I say "more or less" because Thomas says nothing to indicate that the distinction between the sinful will and the obscure intellect is so hard and fast as to divide the human person, or to make it impossible for the will to misdirect the intellect as the intellect misinforms the will: the distinction remains relative to an analysis that wants to locate sin in the will, not to one that wants to sequester the mind entirely from sin's effects. However that may be, revelation comes from afar, as to and not from us. The question will arise, of course, what Paul is up to when he comes, according to Thomas, to license and charge the theologian to pursue such other names of God. Will Paul be exercising some other office when he comes to do that, or the same one? Thomas gives no indication here of any other.

Rather he goes on to characterize Paul's office by comparison. The apostles have handed down the evangelical teaching of Christ just as the angels handed down divine illuminations, and the teaching of the apostles follows the preaching of the New Law in the New Testament just as the teaching of the prophets follows the reception of the Old Law in the Old Testament. The office of an apostle resembles that of an angel and a prophet.[21]

Such considerations lead Thomas to focus not on Paul's conversion but on his vocation. Election is first of all to serve God's purposes; Paul's bearing of Christ's name does not refer to his Christianity as such or his salvation as such; his Christianity and his salvation follow from his service of God's purposes, or, closer to Thomas's language, God's deputation of him for some particular use: Paul's service of God's purpose is not a goal that Paul chose independently on the basis of his conversion or for the sake of his salvation. Paul's apostleship is in Thomas's reading so tied up with his election that he can no more lay it aside for some other office than he could lay his election itself aside. Paul's apostleship is not an *option* for him as a Christian convert beside which he could, as a Christian, exercise some other office; it is his Christian constitution. It works similarly that the supernatural end of human beings generally is only secondarily for salvation: in the first place it is to fulfill God's original purpose for us in calling us into the trinitarian fellowship.

In the first comparison, furthermore, Thomas describes human beings "as standing apart from God" (*a Deo distantes*) while in the last he says "they delivered it to the faithful" (*fideles*). Thus Thomas characterizes those who receive Paul's word: They are in the first place distant from God, and in the second place faithful. The parallelism does not contrast but links the two characterizations. It is just *as* the ones standing apart from God that the angels—the prophets—the apostles—and Paul come to human beings; and just as they come to human beings they render them faithful in the Mosaic pattern to which Thomas implicitly adverts: "You shall be my people and I shall be your God." Paul speaks to his hearers, according to the comparison, with the sound of trumpets and the voice of a prophet: He does not allow the audience to determine the message, but he allows the message, as one reaching human beings *a Deo distantes* and leaving them *fideles*, to determine *them*.

Here follows a long section about what it means to bear the name of Christ. It turns out to mean what Luther might call preaching the gospel. For to bear the name of Christ means to bear Christ's grace and mercy. Yet the way that Thomas gets there looks convoluted.

> 5. Saint Paul bore furthermore the name of Christ. First of all even in his body, imitating Christ's manner of life and passion, according to Gal. 6:17: *For I bear on my body the marks of Jesus Christ.*
>
> 6. Second in his mouth, which appears in the fact that in his epistles he names Christ with great frequency: *for out of the abundance of the heart the mouth speaks,* as Mat. 12:34 says.

From that he can be signified by the dove, of which it is said, in Gen. 7:11, that it came to the ark bearing an olive branch in its mouth. Now since the olive signifies mercy, by the branch of the olive is fittingly understood the name of Jesus Christ, which also signifies mercy, according to Mat. 1:21: *You shall call his name Jesus, for he will save his people from their sins.*

Now the dove carried *this* branch, its leaves green, down to the ark, namely the Church, since the Church expresses the branch's excellence and significance in many ways, showing the grace and mercy of Christ. For that reason Paul says at I Tim. 1:16: *I received mercy for this reason, that in me, as the foremost, Jesus Christ might display his perfect patience.*

Why this business about the dove and the olive? Since it characterizes God to arrange not only words, as human beings can also do, but even things, events, or states of affairs to speak (I.1.10), images in Thomas's exegesis do not simply float free from their stories, but return us to them as to their source, context, and norm. So the comparison is not simply between doves and grace, olives and mercy, as random cultural references; it is between the *stories* of what the dove bore in its circumstances and what Paul bore in his. When that happens, and not when words simply resonate with each other, we have a genuine spiritual sense, intended (arranged) in the mind of God. So Thomas in turning here to images is not removing us to a level further from the ground than his earlier exegesis of words by reference to words. He is really simply moving to a level of comparing stories with stories, illuminating the way in which Paul serves God's purposes as a vessel of election by comparison to the way in which Noah's dove served God's purposes as a vessel of election. The association of stories with stories brings us *closer* to the ground than the association of words with words. It is in Thomas's hands a larger, not a more whimsical perspective, one that does not remove us from but returns us to the shape and circumstance of Paul's life.

Nor does a comparison so baroque to us distract Thomas from his christological exposition. "For since the olive signifies mercy, by the branch of the olive is fittingly [congrue] understood the Name of Jesus Christ, which also signifies mercy, according to Mt. 1:21: *You shall call his name Jesus, for he will save his people from their sins.*" Put another way, the olive branch, or the greenness of leaves having emerged from the flood, signified to the people of the ark the salvation from their sins. Again Thomas sufficiently motivates the explication; it does not so much juxtapose formally

similar messages as incorporate the Genesis story tightly into a christological framework so that the reader recognizes the olive branch as a type of
Christ or of his name, and the dove as a type of Paul. Those hearing Paul's
message may then place themselves as Christians in the ark, a sinful people
saved from God's wrath by a message of mercy and grace, *terra firma* and
the green leaves of the olive. The end of the comparison is that we readers
should find ourselves incorporated into the story.

The resemblance of the church to the ark on account of its carrying
sinners to their salvation is not the resemblance that Thomas adduces as a
reason for the comparison. They are no free-floating type and antitype that
he here associates: he associates them on the basis of their common relation
to *Christ*. It is in showing the grace and mercy of Christ that the church
multiply expresses *his* excellence and significance, and it is then for that reason ("*quando*") that the ark, in Thomas's exposition, resembles the church.
The ark and the church resemble each other, in short, on account of what
God, electing as instrument (*vas*, vessel), a dove or an apostle, *bestows* upon
them. The conclusion that Christians should recognize themselves as trav-
elers on the ark needs a qualification. Christians are to recognize themselves
as ark-travelers *in virtue of* their common experience (mediated by scripture
and church) of God's offer of mercy and grace. It is an offer that, as Thomas
elsewhere asserts (II–II.2.7) and here implies, involves for the elect of the Old
Testament too a faith that will reach fulfillment, unknown to them, in Jesus
Christ. Thus it follows that Paul should belong to the church as the dove to
the ark and for the same purpose.

The dove found its purpose on the ark in just such an errand, to be sure,
as that on which Noah sent it; Paul found his place in the church in just
such a mission as that for which God elected him. "For that reason Paul
says in I Tim. 1:16: *I received mercy for this reason, that in me, as foremost, Jesus Christ might display his perfect patience.*" The dove found itself on the ark for this reason, that in it, as foremost, God might display in
an olive branch God's perfect patience.

In an apparent *non sequitur*, Thomas's next paragraph goes on to characterize the Psalms of David in the Old Testament and the letters of Paul in
the New Testament as the writings in each Testament most prominent
in the church. How did we get from olives to psalms? Thomas concludes
the passage:

> [6. *continued*] And hence it is in the Church that as among the writings
> of the Old Testament the most frequently repeated are the Psalms of

David, who after his sin received forgiveness; so in the New Testament
the epistles of Paul are frequently repeated, who was followed by mercy;
in order that by this sinners might by excited to hope. It could, to be
sure, also have another reason, since in both writings is contained almost all theology's teaching.

The positive final clause, with its offer of hope, and the alternative
explanation, citing theology's teaching, both prevent us from taking the
sin-grace order as seriously as some Protestants later would. Rather the
comparison, as Thomas draws it, reinforces our identification with the passengers on the ark who stand, as we do, in some danger and navigate, as we
do, among the signs of God's apparent wrath. In that situation, our concrete
one, we cling to God's olive branches like seekers for land. Even so great a
sinner as David—even so great a sinner as Saul—even the remnant from
among such great sinners as those on whose account God apparently sought
to drown the whole world—even such great sinners as Christians are,
though "salvation is far from the wicked" may regard and cling to God's
mercy and even favor as evidenced in the advent from afar of a branch of the
olive or the name of Jesus Christ. It is just *because*—Thomas suggests—we
experience Paul as the dove returning to the passengers of the ark with an
olive branch in his mouth that the Church recurs in the New Testament to
his letters.

It is an interesting by-the-way that Thomas says that "in both writings
almost all theology's teaching is contained." Since he has just referred the
popularity of Paul and David to the remarkable sin-and-redemption character of their stories, the remark may reflect Thomas's openness to a law-
gospel dialectic that he rarely pursues.

> 8. Now in this office of bearing the name of God Paul's excellence is
> shown in three respects. First indeed with respect to election's grace,
> from which he is called a vessel of election. Eph. 1:4: *He elected us in*
> Christ *before the foundation of the world.*—Second with respect to fi-
> delity, since he wanted nothing of himself but Christ, according to II Cor.
> 4:5: *For we do not preach ourselves, but Christ Jesus.* Whence he says: HE
> IS A VESSEL OF ELECTION TO ME.—Third with respect to his individual ex-
> cellence, whence he says at I Cor. 15:10: *I worked harder than any of*
> *them.* Whence he says HE IS A VESSEL OF ELECTION FOR ME significantly, as
> if he were singled out before others.

Thomas's readers must now understand that preeminence as the result
and not the efficient cause or precondition of God's grace. Paul's more abun-

dant labor like his faithfulness is his own to be sure: but his own just as God-given and -driven and not otherwise. It works like merit, by which God involves us in God's plan to elevate precisely *us*.

Fruit: Election as usefulness, non-election apparent unusefulness

It befits those reflections that Thomas should finally come to the last part of the four-cause analysis that he announced at the Prologue's beginning. In this context readers will recognize the fruit of election too as God's doing, in such a way as not to exclude but to engage Paul as agent. Thus:

> 9. With respect to the fruit it is to be considered that some are apparently useless vessels [*quasi vasa inutilia*], either on account of sin or of error, according to Jeremiah 51:34: *Return to me as a useless vessel* [*vas inane*]. But St. Paul was purified from sin and error, whence he was a useful vessel of election [*vas electionis utile*], according to II Tim. 2:21: *If anyone purifies him or herself of those things,* namely errors and sins, *that one will be a vessel for a noble use, consecrated and useful to the Lord* [*utile Domino*].
>
> Thus the utility or the fruit of this vessel is expressed when it says BEFORE THE NATIONS, of whom he was the doctor according to I Tim. 2:7: *A teacher of the Gentiles in faith and truth;* AND TO MONARCHS, to whom he announced the faith of Christ, as to Agrippa, as Acts 16:38 has it, and even to Nero and his princes; whence it is said in Phil. 1:12–13: *What has happened to me has really served to advance the gospel, so that it has become known throughout the whole praetorian guard that my imprisonment is for Christ....*

What many theologians might call the rejected, Thomas here calls "*quasi inutiles*," the apparently useless. The worst that happens to them in this passage is that they return to the Lord, whence they may again go forth, if returning to the Lord indicates repentance, as useful vessels. Here Thomas seems to speak *only of vessels that are destined for God's use,* whether straightforwardly or by some reversal. The impression that Thomas here develops no doctrine of reprobation independent of the service of election is strengthened, and the notion that vessels of election become so either straightforwardly or through a reversal gets qualified. For *Thomas makes nothing of the possibility that someone may be a vessel of election straightforwardly.* He turns immediately to the *vasa inutiles* that become *utiles.* He has already characterized Paul and David as such vessels. Indeed it is their very transition from the one state to the other, from their apparent sinfulness to their actual calling, that he cited earlier as the reason (*felix culpa!*) for the preeminence of their writings in the Church. He gives the impression that concretely at least—under the conditions of the Fall, that is—there are only *vasa inutiles* become *utiles*. So a *vas inutile* gets explicated here at least as nothing more or less or other than a place-holder for a *vas utile*.[22]

Similarly, when we turn to the natural cognition of God we will discover that Thomas makes nothing of the possibility that anyone could come to an effective cognition of God straightforwardly. For the natural cognition of God without grace exists only to explicate the wrath of God for human *failure* to lean upon grace. There too, that is, the cognition of God will pass from a useless to a useful vessel, as it gets filled up, Thomas will insist, with the *"gratia evangelica Christi."* Nor will that be a case where a natural form determines the shape of the graced matter and thereby somehow ties God's hands. For as we have seen the election that has Christ as matter corresponds to a nature *trans*formed by God's bestowal of an integral supernatural end.

Just because the vessels are unuseful (Isaiah's *"quasi inane"*), God calls on them to return. But that call becomes the very means for their transformation, which renders their former state no longer the last but only the penultimate word, no longer their definitive but only their apparent determination (Thomas's *"quasi inutile"*). Thomas uses the Isaiah passage to make a remark similar to the one that concludes Barth's famous consideration of the reprobation of Judas (which also takes Paul as a central figure of election): we cannot say more than that God wills here a rejected one *elected*.[23]

The second paragraph again holds together Paul's election as a Christian with his vocation as an apostle. It treats as a piece what we tend to think of separately, namely his other-worldly fate and his this-worldly life: in a word, his predestination, and God's providence concerning him. As the *Summa* on predestination, merit, and hope makes clear, we cannot read off a fate from a life, but it does befit the two generally and for the most part to coincide (I–II.112.5 *in fin.*, II–II.18.4). Thus Thomas has no trouble moving from Paul's election before the foundation of the world in Christ (predestination) to his preaching Christ's name here and now before the Gentiles (providence). It would however be hard to see how to justify the reverse inference, from providence to predestination, since we neither have before us, nor could we discern it if we had it, the book in which God writes that full story. Indeed it is in the metaphor of the book of life where the relation of predestination and providence becomes explicit (I.24.1, esp. *ad* 1). And it returns us also, at the end of the paragraph, to the narrative of Paul's conversion and call, which forms the context, in the Prologue, for talk of vessels of election. In speaking of Saul rather than Paul it picks out the moment that Thomas has earlier considered in theory, election precisely as the *transformation* of a human being from an apparently useless to a useful vessel, from a place-holding to an active one.

We see that it is the story of Paul that governs this development of Thomas's exposition, the concrete analysis of God's action recorded in *sacra Scriptura*, rather than theoretical constraints. Thomas does not mention a case of place-holders failing to become active or of vessels always useful because that is not the story Acts gives him. It is one way in which Thomas allows the text to form him.[24]

Election and biblical inspiration

Thomas makes the transition between his four-cause analysis of the election of the author to a four-cause analysis, this time explicitly so called, of the author's work. The sequence in which an analysis of Paul precedes an analysis of his work serves a very interesting function. What would we expect of a modern prologue to a commentary on someone's work that began with something of a biography? We would expect a clue to the commentator's hermeneutical agenda. A certain sort of psychological portrait might attempt to locate an author's sub- or pre- or unconscious intentions. A certain sort of sociological portrait might attempt to trace the effect on the author of various economic forces. Even approaches that denied to the author's ascertainable intention any privileged view of the work would find in such determinations illuminating details to deploy *ad hoc*, perhaps in its deconstruction. Even those who would subordinate the author's intention to more powerful forces, psychological or economic, would co-opt the surface phenomenon as served their purposes. Thomas for his part identifies himself with the literal sense and an author's intention. But he pulls those apart and puts them together in ways that moderns would scarcely expect. As in Freudian and Marxist interpretations, the author's stated or apparent intentions do not control. Rather another authorial function supervenes, that of God arranging states of affairs to speak. So it is here that the story of Paul's call to apostleship controls the account of Paul's intentions. The *"sensus literalis vel historicus"* controls, but it is not identical with the text; the intention of God as divine author controls, but in the mind of God even figurative senses become literal precisely as divinely intended. So it is a fluid, flexible business in practice. Here the practice is very instructive: it subordinates the intentions of Paul to the story of Paul, the intentions of Paul to the intentions of God. Thomas does not here render God the author of scripture according to any theory of inspiration or dictation; in precise accord with the hermeneutics of *ST* I.1.10, he renders God the author first of Paul's election and vocation in Christ—of his life and fate, of his ministry and authorship—and only then of his letters.

God is the author of Paul's writings in the same way that God is the author of all good human acts. Those human acts—the ones that result in the canon of the Bible—do have a special place among human acts generally. They are not on the same level as good human acts that result in the composition of a *Summa* or of a novel. But that is not on account of some special theory of the words or of their inspiration. Rather it is on account of Paul's calling, a calling for which God had prepared him from before the founding of the world, but not different in that respect from the calling prepared for any other human creature. Formally, all human beings have a call to fulfill God's purposes for them. Materially, Paul's purpose was to hand down the name of Jesus Christ in letters that would receive a prominent, even canonical place in the church. So Paul possessed a high calling and a rare office, but beyond that the Prologue advances no special theory to explain the revelatory character of the Christian scriptures. Paul's office was not that of a plaything of the Holy Spirit such that he underwent a state qualitatively different from one another Christian could undergo; his rapture, although Thomas accepts it (II–II.175), plays nevertheless no role here; and his status in the Church does not arise from any works he produced under such influences.

Paul's office was that of an apostle and inseparable for him from his conversion to Christianity; the power of his writings arises like that of David's from the God-given depth of his repentance; and his status in the church arises likewise from the way in which others can also therefore find their own stories in his. Ephesians 1:4 does say as Thomas quotes it "[God] elected *us* in Christ before the creation of the world" (§8). And Thomas does say when he explains why Paul's letters recur in the church that Paul received mercy that we might—how else than by identifying ourselves with him?—have hope. Here too Thomas pursues the pattern of incorporating all human beings into the biblical story, rather than distinguishing them from its actors.

10. So therefore from the foregoing words we can find four causes of this work [*causa operis*], namely the epistles of Paul, which we have before our hands.

First, indeed, we have in the vessel [of election] the author [as agent]. Second we have in the name of Christ the matter, which is what fills the vessel, since this entire teaching is about the teaching of Christ.—Third we have in the use of the mails the means; for this teaching is carried by way of letters, which tend to be carried by messengers....—Fourth we have in the forementioned utility the distinctiveness of the work.

Note how Thomas uses the phrase *causa operis* to mean something like what we refer to as the meaning of a text. In a different way he also uses *sensus* to cover some of that ground. Cause-analysis gives him a structure for laying out some of the salient circumstances of the work without making immodest claims for any of those remarks. Note too the variety here opened up. In the first remark we have room to develop theological reflections such as the foregoing on God's election and providence. In the second we have an opportunity to make christocentric remarks about how it can be that Paul's whole teaching is of Christ. In the third, under the head of the mode of transmission we have room to ask historical-critical and sociological questions. And in the fourth the way lies open to consider how the letters were then and later received.

In the rest of the Prologue (sections 11–14 in the Marietti edition) Thomas goes on to propose a scheme for relating and ordering the different subject-matters of the letters, to ask why Romans comes first among them, where Paul was when he wrote it, and who preached first to Rome.

Thomas subordinates those matters too to the grace of Christ, which we are to consider in three ways (§11): first, as grace is in Christ as head of the church (Hebrews); second, as grace appears in Christ as in the individual congregations as the members of Christ's body (the letters to "prelates and princes"); and third as grace appears in Christ as in the mystical body, namely the church as such (the letters to Gentiles).

It has been a chief purpose of Thomas's Prologue to the Pauline epistles, as we have seen, to characterize Paul, to tell us who their author is. He is no philosopher or student of religion in the senses in which Barth disparages them. Thomas regards him rather as a figure of God's choosing and acting, a vessel of election. The plan in execution from the beginning of the world renders him not so much a pen in God's hand as an actor on God's stage. He is an actor whose part it is among other things to carry God's message as others, like Noah's dove and the David of the Psalms, have before him. In this case, as it happens, he plays his part by writing. His bearing of Christ's name as a follower and his bearing of Christ's name as an apostle arise from the same divine action; his election and his calling are one. That is who Paul is.

He is that as a vessel moving, according to a christological doctrine of election, from an unuseful to a useful state. The same pattern will appear in the following chapters with the human cognition of God; it too is empty until Christ fills it up, until, that is, it becomes faith.

4

Thomas's Commentary on Romans 1:1–16: The Gospel Grace of Christ, the Example of Paul, and the Structure of the Text

Thomas does disparate things in commenting upon Romans 1:1–16. That has to do, of course, with the genre of commentary. I will be picking out three features of the commentary upon these early verses that help to introduce the more concentrated consideration of the knowledge of God that we come to in Chapter 5. They are the grace of Christ, the example of Paul, and the way in which Thomas uses this section to structure or outline what is to follow.

It is evidence that nature-grace and law-gospel schemes have not yet come apart that the whole epistle, from 1:16b (§§97, 109) to 12:1, is about *"evangelica gratia,"* or "gospel grace," which Thomas ascribes, like the letter's entire matter, to Christ. As far as this chapter goes, *"gratia"* appears only to form or to abbreviate the compound, which we might coin as a technical term, *evangelic gratia Christi.* It is to bring out its bearing on the later polarization that I have translated the phrase "gospel grace" or "grace of the gospel." It does not look as if Thomas is distinguishing gospel grace from some other kind. Rather "gospel grace" provides a fuller characterization of the whole just because it straddles two conceptualities, not yet distinguished and each inadequate in itself. Here Paul is talking about the relation of the creature to the Creator (nature-grace scheme) *in order to* talk about the relation of redemption to sin (law-gospel scheme). Similarly, in the *Summa,* Thomas refuses to differentiate law-gospel and nature-grace schemes when he devotes a treatise, this time not to *gratia evangelica,* but to *"lex evangelica,* which is called the New Law." The treatise named after the New Law is in fact the treatise on grace (I–II.106–114). There too he seeks to follow the language of Paul (Rom. 3:27, 8:2). And there, since he is not commenting upon Paul verse by verse, he takes it upon himself to reflect upon and defend his language precisely *as Pauline.* The *Summa* can *insist* upon following Paul to the conflation of the later law-gospel and nature-grace schemes, whereas the commentary, closer to the authoritative text, need not. Thus in the response to the first article of the treatise, at I–II.106.1, Thomas comes to defend the juxtaposition, not of *"evangelica"* with *"gratia,"* but with *"lex,"* "a conception without equivalent in the Middle Ages."[1] The Pauline attempt to get beyond nature-grace and law-gospel schemes takes place in a few sentences (I–II.106.1):

> And therefore principally [*principaliter*] the new law *is grace itself* of the Holy Spirit, which is given by Christ to the faithful. And this clearly appears from the Apostle, who says at Rom. 3:27: *Then what becomes of your boasting? It is excluded. By what law? The law of works? No: but by the law of faith* for he calls grace faith's *law.* And more expressly at Rom. 8:2 it says: *The law of the Spirit of life in Christ Jesus has liberated me from the law of sin and death.*

Thus the *evangelica lex* is not a Lutheran law-that-accuses also in the New Testament, by making the commandment against adultery harder to fulfill: it is the Holy Spirit writing by grace upon the tablets of the heart; it is that which liberates, not that which accuses us. As a gift of structure in the Spirit, it is closer to the Torah of the Psalms. Thus if anyone should ask from *within* the law-gospel scheme whether the refusal to differentiate the schemes favors one or the other, we would have to answer: So far from rendering grace captive to law, Thomas insists upon the ability of grace to render even the law liberating.[2]

Thomas's insistence on reading the epistle to the Romans as a treatise on gospel grace appears unmistakably from the way in which he structures the commentary. Note that Thomas outlines the text in a nesting structure, like this: ([{|}]). Compare his outline of Romans[3] with Barth's (see table), since Barth follows the serial A, B, C outline with which we are perhaps more familiar:

Barth: *A Shorter Commentary on Romans* (table of contents)		Thomas: *Super epistolam ad Romanos lectura*	
1:1–17	Apostolic Office and the Gospel	1:1–7	Greeting
		1:8–16a	Disposition toward recipients
		1:16b–16:27	Teaching
		1:16b–11:36	Power of evangelical grace (*virtus evangelicae gratiae*)
1:18–3:20	The Gospel as God's Condemnation of the Human Being	1:16b–4:25	Necessity of grace

Barth:		Thomas:	
3:21–4:25	The Gospel as the Divine	1:16b–32	For Gentiles
	Justification of Those	2:1–4:25	For Jews
	Who Believe	ch. 2	Not justified by law
		ch. 3	Not by descent
		ch. 4	Not by circumcision

This chapter centers on the opening parenthesis, the verse that Thomas uses to set up Paul's entire teaching in the letter, 16b: "For the gospel is the power of God [*virtus Dei*] for the salvation of everyone believing, to the Jew first and also to the Greek." Thus we begin *in medias res*, with the verse that divides Paul's greeting and disposition from his teaching. First we will see how Thomas interprets the power of God "evangelically," that is, in terms of the gospel. Second we will see how he interprets *"virtus Dei"* christologically. Third we will look back to see how Thomas has used vv. 1–16a, Paul's greeting and disposition toward the recipients, to set up an *example* of that *virtus Dei*. Fourth we will look forward to how *virtus Dei* structures the rest of the verses that lead up to v. 1:20, which is where we are heading. Fifth we conclude with the second part of 16b, *For the Jew first and also for the Greek.* That phrase serves to set up the pericope "For the Gentiles" (1:16b–32). And "For the Gentiles" is finally the rubric that covers most closely all the verses (1:17–25) that comprise the immediate set-up and de-nouement of v. 1:20, and which form the topic of the chapter to follow.

"The power of gospel grace"

Recall the sweeping assertions of the Prologue. When Thomas had come to the "cause of this work" he specified four parameters for reading the letters of Paul. Among them was the name of Christ as material cause, "since all this teaching is about the teaching of Christ." In the section of the com-mentary leading up to what Thomas calls its teaching, beginning at 1:16b, Thomas takes numerous opportunities to remind the reader that the entire teaching belongs in the context of the grace of Christ.

At the same time Thomas carries out the procedure that he anticipated when at the beginning of the Prologue he said that God had elected Paul to be an example of virtue. Thus even Paul's greeting (1:1–7) and his disposi-tion toward its intended recipients (1:8–16a) become positively informative about its theological content for they specify precisely the disposition, or state of the will, of somebody who is an authority on the knowledge of God that Thomas will discuss. Paul exemplifies, the Prologue implies and the Commentary takes for granted, someone whose *cognitio Dei* is in good working order. It distinguishes Paul's constitution as a vessel of election to enjoy and exhibit all virtues. The moral virtues are necessary also for a good use of the intellect (I-II. 57.3 ad 2). In Aristotelian terms Paul is the wise person—in this case perhaps we should say the justified person—whom we should consult in cases we find doubtful or difficult (whether or not they are doubtful or difficult in themselves). That is not to say that only the wise person could act wisely or that only the justified person could act faithfully, but to say that we recognize the wisdom of wise and foolish actions, the justice of those who do and do not live by faith—we recognize what to us is partial and doubtful as justified and participating in the whole—by reference to the paradigm. Or so we saw Thomas interpreting the words of 1 Corinthians 2:15, "the spiritual person judges all things" in connection with the words of Aristotle about the virtuous one as the measure and rule of human action (I.1.6 *ad* 3). The Prologue has set Paul up as such a "spiritual person, the measure and rule of human acts," and the analysis of the greeting treats him as one.

In the commentary on 1:16b, which according to Thomas's plan sets up the entire theological exposition of the letter, he makes a threefold programmatic statement: "the power of evangelical grace is for the salvation of all human beings...is necessary for their salvation...is effective or sufficient."[4]

The intervening exposition has connected Christ as the letter's matter and Paul as wisdom's paradigm with that programmatic statement about the necessary and sufficient power of the grace of the gospel for the salvation of all human beings. The outline also gives a preliminary statement of Thomas's position, developing into a more direct account of *cognitio Dei* from v. 1:17 forward.

The power of gospel grace is Christ's

In his commentary on Romans 1:1 (§23), Thomas defines the gospel: it is "the same as good news." Then he specifies the good news as that of friendship with God as our good: "For in it [namely the gospel] is announced the joining [*coniunctio*, joining, especially in friendship or marriage] of the human being to God, which is the good of the human being."[5]

The gospel is announced by God, and the relationship is effected by grace (§24). "The material of the gospel... is Christ," as indeed of the whole scriptures, "for it is fittingly said that the Son of God is the material of Sacred Scripture" (§28).

That remark tends to confirm, in a different conceptual analysis, the centrality of Christ in sacred doctrine as argued in Chapter 1: this time the reference is not to Christ as the underlying rationale of the fourfold sense of scripture and the paradigm means of revelation, but to the content of the scriptures so read.

"One of those [goods], namely grace, is the first among the good things of God, since by it the impious are justified" (*In* 1:7, §72). Thomas adduces the christological reference of John 1:17: "Grace and truth have been brought about by Jesus Christ." Furthermore, "Paul also mentions the Lord Jesus Christ... on account of his human nature, by the mystery of which the gifts of grace reach us" (§72). That in the realm of knowledge the humanity of Christ counts as the paradigm form of demonstration is but the noetic elaboration of that mystery. And it is once again Paul's purpose "to teach the Romans about the truth of the grace of Christ" (§74).

So far the texts have reminded us that Thomas makes Christ inalienable from any part of the letter or even from any part of the scriptures, because Christ is its very matter. All exegesis therefore, all scriptural commentary, and, if the equation of *sacra doctrina seu scriptura* holds, all the theology of the *Summa* too is explicitly or implicitly Christ-filled. If Thomas's procedure allows Christ's material presence to go for longer or shorter stretches without saying, it cannot render it absent without ceasing to be Thomas's procedure.

Paul as implicit example of "the power of gospel grace"

From the opening of the commentary I want to pick out two affective attitudes that Thomas thinks characterize *cognitio Dei* in the context in which it is at home. In the presence of certain dispositions of the will, that is, *cognitio Dei* participates in the power of the grace of the gospel; and in their absence, I am arguing, true *cognitio Dei* fails. Thomas mentions these attitudes because he is commenting on the characteristics that Paul ascribes to himself. Thomas invests them with importance not just because they pertain to Paul's biography, or because Thomas's faculty-psychology attends to the way in which dispositions of the will, such as moral virtues, render effective or feckless the operations of the intellect. It may be hard for some moderns to take these attitudes with sufficient seriousness. We tend to think of attitudes as so separable from knowledge as to leave it unaffected. We dismiss them as mere emotion. Given Thomas's teaching on habits, however, we can see some dispositions as stable structures of character. It is important therefore to recall how differently Thomas regards them.

It is the passions that provide the energy of the soul both for mental and for physical acts, both for intention and for extension. Good mental acts need intellectual virtues and good physical acts need moral virtues, and in fact good mental acts need moral virtues too (I–II.57.3). Virtues perfect these embodied energies, the passions. Passions are energies *for* something. Because mind and will are so related in the soul, it matters therefore precisely for the isomorphism of the mind and the thing, that is, for the mental instantiation of the truth, which passion or embodied energy is being perfected in it and how. Thus when Thomas talks about non-epistemic concomitants of knowledge in the soul he is not talking about dispensable accompaniments, he is talking about necessary ingredients, however much they may lie in the background of syllogistic procedure. Thomas names syllogisms expressly when he answers an objection about the role of the moral virtues in speculative habits (I–II.57.3 *ad* 3). "So long as a geometrician demonstrates truth, it does not matter how he or she feels about it, whether joyful or angry;...But art gives only the ability to act well" (I–II.57.3). The good use and the very construction of a syllogism or of a passage of prose (*"constructio syllogismi aut orationis"*) require "a good will, which is perfected by moral virtue" (*ad* 3). For "it is through justice, which gives a right will, that an artisan is set on doing faithful work" (*ad* 2).[6] Now the construction of a syllogism applies to Aristotle's demonstrations of such propositions as "God exists," while the construction of a passage of prose applies to Paul's authorship of such writings as the Epistle to the Romans. Both appear in the *scientia* that is sacred doctrine.

In Romans 1:1–16a Thomas presents Paul as an artisan doing faithful work, one engaged in the construction both of syllogisms and passages of prose. Since the artisan who *uses* art well must also possess the *skills* of it (I–II.57.3 *ad* 1 *in fin.*), we have here, in Thomas's portrayal of Paul, an analysis of the paradigm case. With it Thomas will be able implicitly and explicitly to compare the case of the Gentiles depicted at the end of Romans chapter 1. As Thomas reads Paul, the Gentiles are among those who possess the skills of constructing signal syllogisms without the moral virtues to use them well.

The contrast is therefore between Paul as one who enjoys the moral virtues to use cosmological arguments well, and the Gentiles who lack those virtues. The contrast is not intellectual but moral. The Gentiles do not deploy the cosmological arguments with justice. Arguments leading to the conclusion "God exists" ought to change one's life. It is an understatement to observe that they tend not to. Thomas takes the observation as an indictment.

Since Thomas defines truth as "adequation of the mind to the thing," it does not subsist in extramental propositions except by abstraction from a knower. It is crucial therefore how the elements of the adequation, the words, dispose themselves in the mind of the knower. One of the best clues about how the words do in fact dispose themselves in the mind of the knower is the way in which he or she deploys them in connection with his or her human acts. Words or propositions about God deployed to justify unjust human acts, Thomas would reason, dispose themselves differently in the mind of the knower from the verbally identical propositions deployed to justify charitable human acts. Call such verbally identical propositions "homophones": they sound the same and function differently. Thus it is that Thomas writes at II–II.2.2 *ad* 2 that unbelievers who say "God exists" nevertheless do not do so "under the conditions that faith determines"[7] so that they do not truly believe that God, i.e., the "Abba" of Jesus Christ, exists.

Thomas would find it hard to describe intelligibly the mind of a human being acting unjustly as having been adequated to the state of affairs (*res*) about God in Jesus Christ. To preserve the intelligibility of the whole scheme of defining truth as adequation of mind to thing Thomas would prefer to say that such a deployment of the words or propositions detracts from the knowledge to be ascribed to the knower. I say "to be ascribed" because sometimes we will want to be able to talk about somebody involved in injustice as "knowing better." Sometimes, that is, the weight of the evidence will favor the ascription of knowledge in the face of injustice. But sometimes a person's acts will create such discord between what she says and what she does that we will want to say that she does not know "what she is talking about." In other words: The business of rendering human acts intelligible will sometimes be better served by the conclusion that someone "knows better," and other times by the conclusion that she "doesn't know what she is talking about." Thomas makes explicit room for both sorts of conclusion. They are ways of specifying the adequacy of the structural similarity or isomorphism between mind and thing. Since he thinks of Paul as someone whose words and deeds accord as well as those of anybody short of Jesus, he finds his dispositions worth noting.

Paul's knowledge is in good working order, Thomas implies, on account of his justice and gratitude; our knowledge is diminished by the absence of those qualities.

Paragraph 112, a passage to which we will return, tells us that human beings can hold truth captive in injustice, so that we prevent it from having its characteristic effect. "For true knowledge of God [vera Dei cognitio] in itself leads human beings to the good, but it is bound, as if held [detenta] in captivity, by the condition of injustice, by which, as Ps. 11(12):1 has it, *truths are diminished by the children of human beings.*"[8] *Cognitio Dei* under circumstances of injustice gets implicitly characterized as false, even, presumably, when it would seem to count as *scientia* by appearing at the end of a valid chain of deductive reasoning. Here we need only remember that full-fledged *cognitio Dei* cannot be a merely propositional matter. It must come embodied (to put it paradoxically) in a human soul.

The soul that embodies such knowledge, or comes to have built into its own structure an isomorphism with certain features of reality that come under *cognitio Dei*, is also characterized by gratitude. Early in the commentary (v. 8), and forming part of the background for what will follow, Thomas writes:

> It is truly necessary in all things that we put first our thanksgiving, according to I Thess. 5:18: *In all things give thanks. . . .*
>
> In all things, therefore, that we ask or do, we need the divine favor, and therefore, before all things, thanksgiving ought to come first.

The comment arises because Paul has given thanks. But Paul not only preaches the knowledge of God; he also exemplifies it. It was his office, we remember from the Prologue, not only to possess but also to exemplify the virtues that form the soul into beatitude. If the knowledge of God is ever effective in forming a human soul, it is so, Thomas thinks, in the case of Paul. Thus it is important that we learn in passing, on the way to the systematic exposition of the knowledge of God that comes after Romans 1:20, that Paul's knowledge of God is qualified by justice and gratitude. We will learn that those attitudes are not merely supererogatory virtues of his when Thomas comes to characterize the knowledge that comes without them.

It does not escape Thomas's notice that the *gratia* by which we return thanks (*eucharisto*) and the *gratia* of which Paul speaks (*charis*) throughout his letter bear some relation to each other. So he concludes: "Thanksgiving ought to return to God by the same token by which graces reach us from God, which is namely by Jesus Christ" (*In* 1:8). Here the grace of Jesus Christ and the example of Paul come together.

Now we are in a position to understand what Thomas does at the end of Romans 1 when Paul begins to talk about the knowledge of God in the context of the wrath of God (*ira Dei*). It is a paradox, an ineffectual knowledge, an apparent structure of the soul that manages not to structure the soul, or not to yield gratitude and justice. But we are getting ahead of the text.

The nesting structure of governing assertions in Romans 1

According to the nesting structure of Thomas's outline of the text, the verses of the *lectio* that covers *cognitio Dei*, namely 1:16b–20a, stand first in a number of much longer arguments that Paul will be making in the Epistle to the Romans. The verses lie within the innermost of a series of assertions that act like opening parentheses. An assertion, usually announced with the word *"primo,"* governs everything that comes between it and the "closing parenthesis," announced, if the intervening material is short, by the word *"secundo,"* or, if the intervening material is long, by a phrase like "after the Apostle shows that *x*, here he begins to (or shows that) *y*."[9] It is important to note that within an expository parenthesis the governing assertion need not be repeated, somewhat as in mathematics a negative sign governs the entire parenthesis that follows. One even gets the impression that Thomas tries not to repeat his governing assertions, as in mathematics the unnecessary repetition of signs violates canons of simplicity and elegance. One such characterization, "Here the apostle begins to instruct the Roman faithful about those things that pertain to the gospel teaching" (*In* 1:16b, §97), covers some fifteen chapters. So it is crucial not to lose sight of the rubrics even when they disappear from the immediate context. Because of the nesting structure of Thomas's organization, they provide a controlling context even at a distance. I stress the point because in the reading of the *Summa* it has been forgotten. Scholars have persisted in reading Question 2 as if it were independent of the governing assertions of question 1.

It is with a series of such nestled, hierarchically controlling assertions that *Lectio* VI (vv. 16b–20a, §§97–122) opens; they occupy paragraph §97. In what follows, the numbering spelled out in words is Thomas's; the paragraphing and bracketed section numbers are adapted from the Marietti edition; and the italicized outlining is mine. Those devices will help us see how earlier assertions govern the exegesis of Romans 1:20.

97. *Transition and introduction:* After the Apostle has rendered the Roman faithful well disposed toward himself, showing his affection for them [1:8, §74], here he begins to instruct them about those things that pertain to the gospel teaching for which he had proclaimed himself to be set apart. And

[*I.*] first he shows the power of gospel grace;

[*II.*] second they are exhorted to carry out the works of this grace, at 12[:1], where he says [§953], I APPEAL TO YOU THEREFORE.

Under the first heading [*I*] he makes two points:

[*I. A.*] First he asserts his thesis;

[*I. B.*] second he argues it, where he says [1:18, §109], FOR THE WRATH OF GOD IS REVEALED.

Under the first heading [*A*] he makes three points:

[*I. A. 1.*] First he asserts the power of gospel grace;

[*I. A. 2.*] second he explicates it, where he says [1:17, §102], FOR THE JUSTICE OF GOD,

[*I. A. 3.*] third he confirms the exposition where [1:17, §104] he says, AS IT IS WRITTEN.

The first statement that governs the exegesis of Romans 1:20 is the one that I have labeled "transition and introduction," i.e., that Paul seeks to instruct the Roman faithful about gospel teaching. It lacks anything to flag an ending for it. Domanyi takes it therefore to characterize the entire rest of the letter, including the greetings at the end.[10]

The next characterization, statement *I*, applies explicitly until the twelfth chapter. Paul is, according to Thomas, until then always concerned "to show the power of the gospel grace." That characterization does not cease to apply just because Thomas interpolates a set piece on arguments for the proposition "God exists" at Romans 1:19, §115. Rather any set piece that appears at Romans 1:19–20 must serve the intention of explicating the power of the grace of the gospel. To take it otherwise is to fly in the face of the text.

The next assertion that governs Romans 1:19–20 is the one I have labeled *I.B.* It says that Paul is engaged not in stating but in explicating his thesis that "the power of gospel grace is for the salvation of all human beings" (§109). Again Thomas insists that what follows is for the explication not only of just any grace, as if this grace could belong to one of those categories or divisions of grace of which Protestants like Barth are suspicious: it is for the explication unequivocally and insistently of the grace of the gospel. In this passage there is no talk of a grace of creation apart from the grace of the gospel, or of a grace (I) different from a grace (II), or of a grace preparatory to a grace effective, or anything like that. If such concepts prove useful for *ad hoc* purposes of analysis and clarification later, it is not because Thomas elevates them to any thematic or substantive importance. Here there is talk only and percussively of the grace of the gospel.

The current *lectio* is dense with the hierarchically ordered governing statements I have mentioned. Thomas is here setting out his outline of the entire letter. So it happens that also in the current paragraph we get a dense set of revealing parentheses. It is a side benefit of examining Romans 1:20 that by the time we get to it we will have passed through many of the opening parentheses that set up Thomas's exegesis, and we will get an idea of how the whole commentary goes. Paragraph 109:

> 109. Then when he says, FOR THE WRATH OF GOD IS REVEALED [*I. B.,* 1:18], he proves what he had said, namely that the power of gospel grace is for the salvation of all human beings [*virtutem evangelicae gratiae esse omnibus hominibus in salutem*]. And
>
> [*I. B. 1.*] first he shows that it is necessary for salvation;
>
> [*I. B. 2.*] second that it is efficacious or sufficient, at 5[:1], where he says [§381], THEREFORE, SINCE WE ARE JUSTIFIED BY FAITH.
>
> Under the first heading [*1*] he makes two points.
>
> [*I. B. 1. a.*] First he shows that the power of gospel grace is necessary to the Gentiles for salvation, precisely since the wisdom in which they were trusting has not been able to save them [*quia scilicet sapientia, de qua confidebant, salvare eos non potuit*];
>
> [*I. B. 1. b.*] second he shows that it has been necessary to the Jews, precisely since the circumcision and law and other things in which they were trusting have not attained salvation for them. Thus in 2[:1] he says [§169], THEREFORE YOU ARE INEXCUSABLE.
>
> Under the first heading [*a*] he makes two points.
>
> [*I. B. 1. a. i.*] First he asserts his thesis;
>
> [*I. B. 1. a. ii.*] second he defends it, where he says [§113], FOR WHAT IS KNOWN [*notum est*] ABOUT GOD.

Assertions *I.B.1* and *I.B.2* insist that grace is both necessary and sufficient. One of the theses of this chapter is that *I.B.1* and 2 also apply to the *cognitio Dei* by natural reason: grace is necessary and sufficient also for the functioning in good order of a human being's *concrete* natural powers.

Adam was created with nature *and*, out of God's superabundant mercies, in grace (*ST* I.95.1), or in a state of "original justice" (I.100.1). Grace was not constitutive of nature, any more than standing upright is constitutive of a human body; but being stood upright was both a good *of* the body and a gift *to* the body, the loss of which could not be restored by the body itself. As Pesch puts it: "Original righteousness is a good *of* nature, in that it neither altered nor added to its constituents; it is a 'supernatural,' 'gracious' *gift* to nature, because it cannot be made available by nature's own power."[11] Like life itself (strictly, in terms of God's gift of a soul), it could be passed on, but not recovered once lost.[12] Pesch comes to a careful conclusion. The "essence" of original sin "does not consist, like actual sins, in the loss of grace ..., but in the loss of the due harmony of nature [granted, a harmony worked by supernatural gift]. Fallen nature is sinful not because it *has* no grace, but because it is *unready*—'indisposed'—for grace."[13] Likewise bodies once dead decay and are shortly no longer disposed for life (or a soul). The result is that Thomas knows no cases of pure nature, neither ungraced nor unfallen, just as we know no cases of abstract bodies, in some state of suspended readiness for life, neither alive nor undecayed. Although both are logical possibilities, abstract nature and unsouled bodies, the real possibilities are nature graced or fallen, bodies living or decaying. If I am right about Thomas's contrast, then it makes sense for him to use Paul as an example of nature in good working order, nature under grace, and Paul's Gentiles as an example of nature *manqué.*[14]

It is interesting to note that *I.B.2* has faith explicate the sufficiency of *grace*. To talk about faith, that is, is not to talk about a human contribution to salvation: it is to unfold the sufficiency or total efficacy—*Allwirksamkeit*—of grace.[15] The problem in what we may call vulgar Protestantism according to which faith becomes, despite all attempts to the contrary, a rival to grace, so that paradoxically salvation by faith comes to say something different from salvation by grace, seems on Thomas's account to be effectively excluded. Indeed, for Thomas, concrete nature is no rival to grace, either. For grace could have no ultimate rivals (about which more in the comparison with Barth).

In Thomas's outline Romans 1:20 with its immediate context falls under the explication of grace's necessity. The natural knowledge of God, as Thomas understands and presents it, seeks to explicate not the independence of any realm of knowledge from the need for grace, but the need for grace precisely where natural human knowledge reaches its highest pretensions. The *closing* parenthesis (§381 at Rom. 5:1) that will, many pages later, end the presentation of grace's necessity confirms that impression:

"The apostle shows the necessity of the grace of Christ in that without it neither is cognition of the truth to the advantage of the Gentiles nor are circumcision and law to the advantage of the Jews." Thomas's conclusion leaves open what our reading of his intervening exposition will seek to determine: in what *sense* Thomas ascribes cognition of truth to the Gentiles. Already any reading which would fear the natural knowledge of God as a preparation for grace and thus a threat to its sole efficacy seems difficult to sustain. The natural knowledge of God seems to be either useless or already taken up into grace.

We can make more of the explicit structural parallels that Thomas makes at both the beginning and the end of the parenthesis between the Gentiles' knowledge of the truth and the Jews' knowledge of the law.[16] That seems to mean that both the natural knowledge of God and the law will prove good but self-consuming artifacts. It is for Thomas as if Paul had asked one of his notorious rhetorical questions, not, this time, about the law, but about the wisdom of the Gentiles, and Thomas has supplied the Pauline answer. Imagine Thomas as taking Paul's comparison between the knowledge of the Gentiles and the law of the Jews so seriously that he takes Paul's questions about the law as the best model for answering questions about Aristotle. Imagine Thomas asking: What shall we say then? Are we to continue in ignorance that revelation may abound? By no means! What then? Are we to proceed in ignorance because we are not under Aristotle but under revelation? By no means! What then shall we say? That philosophy is false? By no means! Yet, if it had not been for philosophy, I should not have known ignorance. Did that which is true, then, bring ignorance to me? By no means! It was sin, working ignorance in me through what is true, in order that sin might be shown to be sin (and not ignorance), and through the demonstration (of knowledge) sin might become sinful beyond measure.[17] Thomas would take both that adaptation and Paul's original as securing the location of sin in no other place than the human will.

The closing parenthesis of Romans 5 means furthermore that chapter one of Thomas's Romans commentary comprises at least one place, of several, where Thomas subordinates a nature-grace dialectic to a law-gospel one. That is, the *cognitio Dei* explicates *ira Dei*, and *ira Dei* serves *evangelica gratia Christi*. And that complication occurs in the very place where the nature-grace relation is at home. It confirms the observation that neither the law-gospel nor the nature-grace scheme is adequate alone, even in Thomas, to the complexities of the biblical stories.[18]

Consider now *I.B.1.a* together with *I.B.2*: "The power of gospel grace is necessary to the Gentiles for salvation, precisely since the wisdom in which they were trusting has not been able to save them." And grace "is efficacious or sufficient,... 'since we are justified by faith'." The two seem to imply the following alternative: *Either* the natural knowledge of God functions as part of the "wisdom, in which the Gentiles were trusting [and which] has not been able to save them"; or, if it counts as part of something by which they *are* saved, then it appears as part of the faith by which they are justified and unfolds the sufficiency alone of *grace.* The natural *cognitio Dei,* instantiated in a concrete human mind, belongs to one context or the other and participates in one constellation or the other, so that someone makes effective or ineffective *use* of it. Furthermore, the first alternative looks like knowledge used in "the theology that pertains to metaphysics," the second like knowledge used in "the theology that pertains to sacred doctrine" (I.1.1 *ad* 2). And ultimately (if not provisionally) knowledge used differently *means* differently. The point here is that Gentiles who rely upon the first are making an ineffective use of their cognition. Already Thomas anticipates the contention that that ineffective use is also a culpable use when he quotes Paul's conclusion, "Therefore you are inexcusable." For they are still relating to all things by understanding them with worldly wisdom or Aristotelian metaphysics, rather than relating to all things by trusting God, or in faith.[19] Since Thomas quotes Paul's conclusion, "Therefore you are inexcusable," we can anticipate that he will explicate the lack of the latter disposition as a culpable lack of the justice and gratitude he has found exemplary in Paul. Or so it appears from a preliminary examination of the assertions that govern Thomas's exposition.[20]

As we consider in order the intervening assertions that §109 anticipates and §381 concludes, we will see how they support, qualify, or undermine that alternative.

To conclude: *I.B.1.a.i* and *ii* make the natural knowledge of God not an assertion of Paul's or Thomas's in its own right. It is not a part of what Paul primarily "proposes or intends." Rather it is part of the *explication* of what Paul proposes and intends. It belongs to the part where Paul "shows what he proposes." It exists only for the sake of something else. According to the two-story system of the handbooks, grace appeared to top nature; nature was the foundation and substrate, grace the accidental, extrinsic icing above it; therein lay its empty graciousness. The model emerging here will leave that order reversed: nature functions conceptually to explicate grace, to help account for how it is *we human beings* that God takes hold of; ontologically, concrete nature depends—or *hangs*—from above; that is, from

God's gracious purpose. As the carrying out of God's plan, God's graciousness cannot be empty or content-free; God's purpose has something specific in store for the human creature. Grace and nature after it derive content from the fellowship that God wills for us.[21] That content lies implicit in the possessive Thomas deploys to qualify it: *evangelica gratia Christi.*

Let us return to the text at hand to consider *how* it is that the wisdom in which the Gentiles confided proved unable to save them. Thomas gives the reason that sets up the rest already in the last phrase of v. 16: "To the Jew first and [also] to the Greek." The phrase is one that already takes seriously the assertion that the power of the grace of the gospel is Christ's, for it follows what Thomas takes to be the logic of the biblical narrative composed of the history of Israel and the story of Jesus.

"Salvation is from the Jews"

In §101, Thomas takes up Paul's phrase "to the Jew first and [also] to the Greek." By "Greek" Paul means, according to Thomas, "all intelligent Gentiles," since it is from the Greeks that Gentile wisdom comes. Here Thomas is clearly using "Gentile" to mean non-Jew. By vv. 19–20, however, it will look as if he means those who rely upon their own wisdom instead of upon God. He thinks that for the most part the two designations cover the same people. The *"primo"* indicates that the Jews come first in the manner of the vine into which the Gentiles will be grafted; in the manner of the workers in the vineyard who received first and last the same wage there is however no longer a distinction between the groups. Thomas concludes the paragraph with a line that summarizes the whole of the biblical narrative, from the history of Israel to the story of Jesus: "Salvation is from the Jews" (John 4:22).

Consider a surprising suggestion. Imagine how differently we would have to read the Five Ways if we took them as really *of a piece* with an argument (*oratio*) including the assertion that salvation is from the Jews. In the context of a commentary on *Romans*, we are actually on a path that *relates* the history of Israel and the arguments of the philosophers. Thomas reads Paul so that the phrase *"Iudaeo primo et Graeco"* renders the history of Israel a controlling story, into which the arguments of the Gentiles must be grafted. The elements of the Gentiles can belong to the history of Israel just if sacred doctrine is the unitary science of I.1.3 that treats all things whatsoever as *revelabilia* and so renders them one with the biblical world. The two disparate data are of a piece, that is, if they *both* count as *revelabilia*. Namely, it is the Jews' story into which the *viae* of I.2.3 and of Romans 1:19–20, as so many paradigms of Gentile wisdom, have to be in-grafted. Only so may they become paradigms as well of Christian theologi-cal wisdom. For only so can they come to belong to the wisdom of sacred doctrine elevated by the more universal formal rationale of I.1.3, the ratio-nale of the *revelabilia*. The two disparate sorts of data—the apparently metaphysical *viae*, and the radically theological proposition that "salvation is from the Jews"—are of a piece under two conditions: if the Five Ways prove effective in calling forth justice, gratitude, and piety; and if the Jews form a correct part, at some greater or lesser remove, of the explanation for that unlikely occurrence. Just when the invisible things of God can be known from the things God has made, then *salvation* comes precisely *not* from that fact, but from those from whom, Thomas says, the savior was born. Here Thomas is open to one of Barth's most stringent formulations, which Barth takes to exclude natural theology: "[Paul] is speaking of the Gentiles as they are now confronted with the Gospel, whether they know it or not...,"[22] so that even the knowledge of God that they have or seem to have belongs to their confrontation with the Gospel. Thomas does the same thing when he makes the knowledge of God that the Gentiles have or seem to have belong to part of a demonstration that "salvation is from the Jews."

Those then are preliminary specifications of the "power of God" of v. 16b. It is necessary and sufficient for salvation; it is at home in the Gospel; it is specified by the grace of Christ; it governs the entire rest of the exposition of the letter; and it comes from the Jews.

That brings Thomas to verse 1:17 and the proximate context of verse 1:20. In the next chapter we will see how he causes such concepts as the faith by which the just live and the revelation of the wrath of God to deter-mine the ingrafted and uningrafted function of the Gentile wisdom there rendered as three *viae*.

5

Thomas's Commentary on Romans 1:17–25

So far we have finished the exposition of statement *I* in Thomas's outline. We need now to reach *I.B.1.a.ii,* where Paul defends his thesis. Paul's thesis (*I.B.1.a.i*), according to Thomas, is that the Gentiles "detain" the truth of God through their injustice (v. 18). That they "must" recognize the truth of God is, as Thomas explicates the passage, just an inference backwards from their having "detained" the truth, or from its effective *absence.* The positive assertion is a matter of backing and filling from our sinful state. It is not a matter of optimism about human potentialities.[1] Or so I shall argue.

In the text we had reached verse 17.

"The just shall live by faith"

Romans 1:17 is the verse that Luther made famous with his battle cry "by faith alone" and with his expositions of God's promise, the verse that occasioned so much controversy over whether the "justice of God" of which it speaks refers to the justice by which God justifies us or the justice by which God justifies God. None of those issues escapes Thomas's implicit notice or explicit comment.

Not only that, but, more important for our current purposes, Thomas also gets a chance to expound his doctrine of faith *before* his doctrine of a natural knowledge of God. The result is that we can see more of the theological context in which the natural knowledge of God is at home. In the *Summa,* by way of contrast, the teaching on faith comes over a *thousand articles* after the Five Ways. (A hasty count suggests some 1208). Thomas had already taken advantage of the very first question of the *Summa* to warn readers about the frailty of the human being set before long chains of reasoning. There he insists that such reasoning is followed "by a few and over a long time" (I.1.1). It can come as little surprise therefore that we find his own work no exception. It is all too easy in reading the *Summa* to miss the ramifications of the tractate on faith for the significance of the Five Ways. It is just too far away. Hence the advantage of the Romans commentary. There the ramifications of faith for the natural knowledge of God could hardly be clearer or appear in closer textual proximity.

That brings us to paragraph §102, which comments on v. 17: "For the justice of God is revealed in it [a pronoun Thomas takes in different ways] from faith to faith." Recall that Thomas regards the verse as part of Paul's exposition of the power of the grace of the gospel (proposition *I.A.2*). The logical relation in Thomas's exposition between this material and that of Romans 1:19–20 is indirect. For the *"A"* propositions precede but do not govern the *"B"* propositions. They provide context but not control.

Thomas announces first that the phrase *iustitia Dei* admits of two interpretations (anticipating Reformation controversies).

First, the justice by which God is just, namely in keeping God's promise; in that case the verse means that God's justness is revealed to the human being who believes the gospel, namely that God has fulfilled God's promise of sending the Messiah. The phrase *"ex fide"* emphasizes that the believer believes not just God as God, but, Thomas insists, the *promising* God, *"Deus promittens."*[2]

Thomas takes *"iustitia Dei"* to mean second the justice by which God justifies human beings. Thomas distinguishes therefore the justice of God (understood in this second way) from human justice. The justice of human beings is that by which human beings presume to justify themselves. The justice by which God justifies human beings, on the other hand, is according to Thomas (in both Old and New Testaments) the faithfulness of Christ, since by the same faith some believed in Christ as coming by which others believe in him as having come.[3] It is a matter of God's promise-keeping in the cases of both coming and having come. It is also a matter of God's promise-keeping in the cases of both the justness of God and the justification of human beings for it is crucial to Thomas that God persists in the original plan to elevate us, which comes to involve our justification. The natural knowledge of God will prove ineffectual unless by grace it is the knowledge of a God who keeps promises, a *justly* promising God, who therefore deserves in return justice, gratitude, and piety from us.

Thomas appends three other possible interpretations of *"ex fide in fidem"* that are of interest to us. It can mean "from the faith of the preacher to the faith of the hearers." It can mean from faith in one article to faith in all the articles of faith. And it can mean from the faith we now have to the faith that we will have in heaven. The last two possibilities indicate something about how Thomas expects reason to work within theology. Let us look at them in more detail.

"*Ex fide in fidem*" can mean from faith in one article to faith in another "because for justification faith in all articles is required" (§103). Does this mean that faith in one article counts for faith in all? It casts light on the way that a human being adheres to the first truth, which is whole and entire, by means of separable *enuntiabilia* or propositions accessible to reason working discursively under conditions of time and finitude. It marks human understanding to work by composing and dividing (I.85.5), and even when the object is simple in itself, like the first truth, human understanding divides it into linguistic units, *enuntiabilia*, or articles (II.1.2).[4] The propositions about the proposition "God exists" are such *enuntiabilia*, and as such they are, when they contribute to the justification of a sinner, propositions that belong in the series and context of *enuntiabilia* "*ex fide in fidem.*"

"*Ex fide in fidem*" can also mean from present faith to "the faith to come, that is, the full vision of God, which is indeed called faith by reason of a firm and certain cognition [*cognitio*], by reason, namely, of acquaintance with the *gospel* [*ratione evangelicae cognitionis*]." Nicholas Wolterstorff has suggested that it is a task of sacred doctrine according to Thomas to transmute faith as much as possible into knowledge (*scientia*), since the same person under the same circumstances cannot at the same time have faith and *scientia* of the same thing, and in the state of beatitude with God we have vision, which is *scientia*.[5] But in sacred doctrine, as I have said, we have *scientia* only as a borrowed discipline, not as a mental habit. We are not scientists in sacred doctrine but in glory alone. The firmness and certainty that belong both to faith and to the vision of God arise from the same source, the trustworthiness of God as first truth, and it is that *underlying* quality, different from *scientia*, in virtue of which the vision is called faith. Vision is not called faith in virtue of what *scientia* has in common with faith. Rather both grace and glory involve a nondiscursive (faithful or intuited) adherence by the human being to God as to the first truth. Even if the *scientia* enjoyed by God is an Aristotelian science in the sense of being the completed whole described by the *Posterior Analytics*, it is *not* an Aristotelian science in the sense of "proceeding from first principles": because nondiscursiveness means *no proceeding*, but intuition of the whole all at once, a sort of union of the knower and the known. In faith, however, we are already "united" (*coniugamur*) to God in this life, but precisely as unknown (*ignoto*, I.12.13 *ad* 1 and *In* Rom. 1:19, §114). In the beatific vision we are united to God, this time as seen, by the same union. For the union of faith is the union of glory working itself out in advance (the "something foreknown of the end" of I.1.1). The firmness and certainty that pertains both to faith and to vision belongs to our anticipatory and fulfilled union with God. Thus the vision of God is called faith on account of the union with God that the two states represent, one in glory, one in grace. Thomas's addition of the phrase *"evangelicae cognitionis"* tends to favor that reading. For it is the knowledge of the gospel that is the material basis of the union in this life and in the next. It is that union alone in which God's *scientia* contributes to the consummation of God's friendship with us, whether the union takes the finished form of the blessed's share in God's *scientia* in the next life, or the *scientia* of Aristotelian metaphysics that succeeds in referring to the unknowable God only as faith assumes it into sacred doctrine.

Thomas goes on to insert a set piece on faith in *quaestio* format. Such a procedure tends to confirm that the intention and content of the sacred doctrine of the *Summa* and the intention and content of the sacred doctrine of the commentaries are the same in execution as well as in intention. Sacred doctrine's two sub-genres, commentary and *Summa*, differ only in the order of presentation, and the order of presentation affects the way the context modulates the argument. If the reading of Question 1 of the *Summa* is right about Thomas's scripturalism, then it is in the commentary that the *quaestio* is at home. And given the history of Western Christian theology since Vatican I, a tendency to mistake the modulations of argument in the *Summa* will persist. Under those circumstances we ought to award interpretive priority to the commentaries. It makes a tremendous difference both in the way that beginning students in Thomas receive their first impression and in the way that Thomas's more serious modern proponents and opponents mount their arguments that despite the clear tendencies of Question 1 they read nothing of faith until hundreds of pages later. The ways in which the tractate on faith specifies and qualifies the remarks about the existence of sacred doctrine's subject get lost and misread because we read them where it is not faith that can be taken for granted but natural science. But Thomas occupies the entire space before the wrath-of-God passage under which Romans 1:20 stands with four *quaestiones* on faith: what faith is, whether faith is a virtue, whether faith persists as "continually the same" (*"idem numero"*) in the absence of charity, and how the soul lives by faith.

1. Thomas defines faith as "a certain assent with certitude, to that which is not seen, by the will, 'since no one believes [has faith] without

wanting to,' as Augustine says" (*In* 1:17, §105, *ca. init.*).[6] It differs from doubt, which assents to neutrality; from opinion, which assents to one part without certainty; and from *scientia*, which assents not by the will, but by reason's welcome or unwelcome coercion. Note that the certainty here is not the certainty of knowledge that would lead to pride, nor a reflexive certainty in the power of one's own belief; rather it is a certainty based on the God whose justness—whose promises—the believer trusts.[7] That was the first of the expositions of the verse Thomas is still commenting upon: "For the justice of God is revealed in it from faith to faith."

As in the *Summa*, so also here Thomas never speaks of the mental habit of the believer—even the believer who has an Aristotelian demonstration for something that pertains to faith—as *scientia*. The one use of *"sciendum est"* (*In* 1:19, §114) conforms to Preller's rule and that of II–II.9.2 confining the gift of *scientia* to second-order statements about which first-order statements are to be *believed* and which *disbelieved*. The same statement denies knowledge (*"notitia"*) of God's essence. Rather Thomas always confines himself, as in the passage under discussion, to the word *"cognitio."* Later in the Romans commentary (§327 at 4:3), Thomas will reflect on what he means by a "cognitive habit" (*habitus cognoscitivus*). A *cognitio* is an instance of that habit. But "cognitive habit" covers science and opinion as well as faith, so that the cognition of a piece of Aristotelian reasoning that may count as *scientia* according to one mode of adherence may count as faith by another.[8] *"Cognitio"* is not only the vaguest but also the weakest word for any sort of mental recognition. Preller's fuller conclusions are instructive here:

> "Cognitions of God," then, are not necessarily instances of intelligible knowledge of God. The ordinary word for "know" in Aquinas is *scire*, which is never used in connection with cognitions of God through natural reason. *Cognitio* and *cognoscere* are the broadest possible generic terms, referring to any state of mind connected with the apprehension of reality. To have a 'cognition' of God is to be in a state of mind that *in some way* takes account of God. To believe on the basis of external evidence that there is something inside of a closed box is to have a cognition of that which is in the box, even though one cannot say anything more about it than that 'it' is in the box. To believe on the basis of external evidence that the world is related in some fashion to an extrinsic and unknown principle is to have a cognition of that principle, even though one cannot say anything more about it than that it is not like anything else in existence.[9]

Because we in the modern world generally restrict the word "cognition" to empirically significant contexts, we tend to insist that Aquinas intend what we intend by the word; we thus insist that he fall into self-contradiction.[10]

It seems to be true that Thomas avoids the word *"scire"* in connections with cognitions of God through natural reason apart from revelation. Yet one might object that he does not hesitate to refer to some cognitions of natural reason, with reference to revelation, as "demonstrable" propositions. We are now in a position to give a preliminary answer to that objection. In sacred doctrine the word *"scientia"* and its kin are governed by the canons of Question 1, where *"scientia"* appears frequently, so that the term gets confined to the *scientia* that is a habit possessed only by God and the blessed, and the *scientia* or discipline of sacred doctrine subordinate to that habit. The remarkable absence of the word *"scientia"* in descriptions of propositions admittedly demonstrable in an Aristotelian sense seems to confirm the strong (literal) reading of I.1.8 *ad* 2, advocated by Preller, which calls them "extraneous and probable" in sacred doctrine, and therefore precisely *not* productive of *scientia* in the mode appropriate to *this* science. As even Cajetan notes (in the commentary reprinted in the *Leonina*), it is inappropriate for an Aristotelian science to prove the existence of its own subject. In an Aristotelian science, as we have seen, an existing reality founds a distinct science as its real first principle, and first principles are not susceptible of proof. Thomas has not forgotten in I.2.2 that in I.1.7 he made God *"subiectum principiorum,"* or the first principles' subject. Elsewhere Thomas confirms expressly that "demonstration does not proceed from extraneous first principles [*ex principiis extraneis*]."[11] That the Five Ways are called "demonstrable" is then a comment that sacred doctrine follows Romans 1:20 to make about *metaphysics* (I.2.2 *s.c.*), precisely in the office with which I.1.6 *ad* 2 charges it of judging other sciences. The warrant from which I.2.3 argues as a matter of sacred doctrine, on the other hand, *is* appropriate. It marks first principles as forms to manifest themselves. And so here we have the *self*-revelation of the existent's existence, when in Exodus 3:14 it is, as Thomas notes, none other than God who says, "I am" (I.2.3 *s.c.*).

For those reasons from now on I will use "cognition" for Thomas's *"cognitio,"* and leave his *"scientia"* untranslated. Those conventions will have the effect of banishing the natural "knowledge" of God, as almost always misleading, almost entirely from the discussion.

2. The second of the questions Thomas inserts here considers whether

faith is a virtue. Faith is not a virtue, to be sure, in the sense of that which is believed. In the sense of that by which one believes, however, it is sometimes a virtue and sometimes not. The virtue depends both upon the intellect and upon the will moving the intellect to assent (since if it were reason moving the intellect involuntarily we would have knowledge rather than faith). If the intellect alone should believe firmly and without coercion, without the adherence of the will, that particular instance of a conformity of *enuntiabilia* with reality would not count as faith formed by love. For faith is an adherence of a *human* mind to the truth, and in the absence of love the human being would show that he or she finally failed to understand what faith entails. Consider a crusader as an example of faith without love. "The crusader's battle cry *'Christus est Dominus'* is false when used to authorize cleaving the skull of the infidel (even though the same words in other contexts may be a true utterance)."[12] "By using *'Dominus'* in this context, the crusader shows that what he means by the term is a medieval knight errant, much like himself. But according to the normative patterns of Christian speech and action, Christ is not that kind of Lord; when the predicate *"Dominus'* has that meaning, it is not applicable to the subject *'Christus'*. . . . "[13]

Or consider two kinds of copied money. The usual kind of copied money is presented as legal tender in payment of a debt with an intent to defraud. The intent to defraud renders the copied money counterfeit. So far, so bad. Now when we seek to render intelligible what is going on in the transaction, we need ineliminable recourse to a human intention in order to do so. And the intentions of the producers and knowing distributors of counterfeit money are evil. The signal difference in rendering copies intelligible as counterfeits rather than postmodern art or Treasury engravers' models (quite different matters) is the intention of some human agent. Considered *entirely apart* from any intentions of human agents (admittedly a situation hard to imagine), copied bills become unintelligible (and just so hardly imaginable), purposeless paper.

In the first article of the *Prima Secunda* Thomas distinguishes intelligible actions from unintelligible when he contrasts a properly *human* action with the action of a human being. An action of a human being is just a movement (extension) abstracted from a reason (intention) and therefore not an "act" properly so called, but a surd jerk. Clifford Geertz distinguishes similarly between a twitch and a wink. A movement of an eyelid is unintelligible without an intention. We can also distinguish rehearsals of winks and parodies of winks from straightforward winks and mere twitches, given enough context to supply intention.[14] It is the intention, not the extension, the act, not the action, that makes the difference, or that makes the intelligibility. Thus Thomas tends to signal the distinction, at least implicitly, by speaking of a human act (*"actus"*) or action *proper* to an agent *as human*, which is marked by voluntariness, from the mere action (*"actio"*) of some human being.[15] An *actus*, literally the something-having-been-done of an agent, is defined in terms of exercising human freedom, and it is always related to *habitus*, or the character of a moral agent, either as leading toward the establishment of a stable disposition to act, or arising out of one. An action, on the other hand, does not attend to the character of a particular human being as agent, but prescinds from that character. An *actus* orders *actiones* intentionally, and an *actio* abstracts extension from an act. In a concrete case, the description may depend upon which feature of a complex situation one wishes to discuss. For faith, which is an *actus*, we need intention, since it is the properly human, voluntary character of faith that Thomas wants to identify in God's moving us to glory.

At the head of the *Secunda*, the distinction serves as a vehicle for the rendering intelligible of human acting as a whole, so that the specification of the final end of the human being specifies the intelligibility of humanness altogether. Since it is the revelation of Jesus Christ, as we saw in Part I, that defines the final human end, Thomas is actually using Aristotle to make all truly human acting, including, as a minor example, Aristotle's own, not finally intelligible kept apart from Jesus Christ. Faith is the human act whose inner or formal principle is Jesus Christ (another way of saying how Jesus Christ is our "way into God" precisely "as a human being," or how Jesus Christ, rather than Aristotle, finally defines *demonstratio* for Thomas).

And that, to come full circle, is why faith (by grace) must be a human act—so that human beings may be formed by Christ from the inside out. Propositions abstracted from the will would leave our desires unaffected, our subjective ends apart from the objective final end that God has granted us, our actions therefore finally unintelligible, our lives surd and unredeemed. The propositions of faith on a page are so many pieces of paper, not identifiable as God's tender until we see them in use.

3. What does it then mean to say that faith unformed by charity is no virtue? Does it mean that such "faith" does not count as faith? "Thirdly it is to be considered that the habit of faith is continuously the same [*idem*

numero], which without charity was unformed, becomes a virtue with the coming of charity, since, because charity is outside the essence of faith, by its coming and going the substance of faith is not changed" (§107). Faith, that is, does not cease to count as faith, at least as far as cognition goes, when charity is lacking.

Otto Pesch explains the matter this way. *Fides caritate formata* means

> that the assent to the first truth for its own sake is actually taken up into every existential, concrete act in which justification occurs as I–II.113.4 describes it.... The formula *fides caritate formata* does *not* mean that to a *complete* act, called "faith," still another act, called "love," must come forward, accidentally, in order that it possess justifying power; and it certainly does not mean that an external *work* of love (the love of neighbor) should have to step forward to faith, in order for it to justify. (If one asks about *fides formata* in the context of the question about 'faith and works,' then love belongs on the side of *faith*, not of works.)... With this interpretation it is also clear what *fides informis* is: an acceptance of the inevident first truth prompted under the pressure of a seeking after salvation *without* renunciation of sin, that is, *without* the renunciation of a final end in opposition to God....It is however for that reason a culpable form of faith's *failure*....That *fides informis* is nevertheless a "gift of God" can therefore have the meaning only that God, in withdrawing grace and love as punishment for sin, need not at the same time withdraw the assent of the understanding, and that the assent thus remains possessed by the sinner thereafter by God's mercy—but not that God first infuses *fides informis* into an innocent unbeliever and then love afterwards as form: for that would mean that God, through the infusion of a supernatural gift, moves a human being to a culpable, because defective, act of faith: *Fides informis* is a matter of the grave sinner, not of the personally innocent pagan.[16]

4. Thomas's fourth consideration insists that faith even formed by charity is not a human work but God's. That supports the contention that the love which forms it belongs on the side of what the Reformers would call faith. For Thomas describes it here not as a human act reaching out to God but as Christ's very inhabitation of the soul. Thus "just as the body lives by the soul in the life of nature, so the soul lives by God in the life of grace, first of all because God inhabits the soul by faith, according to Eph. 3:17: 'May Christ dwell in your hearts through faith'" (§108). It is not otherwise therefore than through faith, which is the indwelling of Jesus Christ in the heart, that we have the life of grace; the natural cognition of God cannot

therefore diminish the life of faith in the believer, since the life of faith has nothing to do with the quantity of propositions that get assigned to knowledge and to faith but with the indwelling of Christ. Nor can the natural cognition of God prepare a life of faith in the absence of grace. The indwelling of Christ could by grace establish a habit of justice that would dispose one to use the natural cognition of God well. But Paul requires Thomas to keep a different case in mind.

"Who detain the truth of God in injustice"

We come to the pericope where verse 1:20 will occur, "Ever since the creation of the world [God's] invisible nature, namely [God's] eternal power and deity, have been clearly perceived [*intellecta conspiciuntur*] in the things that have been made."[17] But Thomas governs that verse and the pericope by this one: "For the wrath of God is revealed from heaven against all ungodliness and wickedness of [human beings] who detain the truth of God in injustice [*qui veritatem Dei in iniustitia detinent*]" (v. 18).

The purpose of the revelation of the wrath of God was to prove that the power of the grace of the gospel is for salvation to all people, as necessary and sufficient for Jews and Gentiles. We are pursuing the necessity of grace for the Gentiles.

The natural cognition of God is not, after Adam's loss of original righteousness, a neutral thing. It is a feckless thing at once entrapping and culpable, like the loss of powers of someone drunk (*In* 1:20, §124). In its ineffectiveness it serves first of all to point to what we culpably cannot do (turn the cognition of God to the good), and thus to God's wrath. The postlapsarian indication of God's wrath in the natural cognition of God applies particularly for the demons, whom it characterizes to have more propositions count as natural cognition (perhaps even *scientia*) of God because their senses and their minds are more powerful than ours (II–II.5.2 *ad* 2). They suffer God's wrath more even as they recognize more. Similarly, when natural cognition of God occurs among believers it is not neutral either, but exercises charity, redounds to their credit, and yields them joy (II–II.2.10). Natural is not neutral but waits upon the will. God created the will and suffers it to persist in existing for friendship with God, that is, to lean upon grace.

God's wrath serves God's justice. We saw earlier that true cognition of God yields justice, gratitude, and obedience. So the wrath of God is directed against that recognition of God that Barth might call an impossible possibility, the recognition that does not yield justice but suppresses it. "God's wrath," Thomas writes, "is God's vindication [*vindicta*], which is called the wrath of God according to its similarity to human beings becoming angry, who seek vindication from without [*extra*]. But God brings vindication from within, from tranquility of character [*vindictam infert ex animi tranquilitate*]" (*In* 1:18, §110).

In the *Summa* (I–II.46.2) *"vindicta"* appears as a technical term to name one of two parts of anger. Anger seeks to avoid or stop some evil regarded as already present. In human beings it turns out to be a complex passion composed of two simpler ones. In one part it desires justice, that is, that a certain good be in someone; it counts therefore as love and requires hope. In another part it desires harm, that is, that a certain evil befall someone, and counts therefore as hatred. (If we remember that Thomas defines passions as embodied, and we think of the physical actions that accompany anger in a case where a great evil is encountered as already present but still able to be overcome, we are thinking of a case of fighting, where it is hard to separate the protection of one's just integrity from the harming of an aggressor. So it makes sense that the two objects should come together. And because it has within itself a double object, human anger has no opposite passion.) *"Vindicta"* or vindication is the name that Thomas gives to the restoration of a violated justice that anger rightly desires. God has additionally the resources to will good without harm; God's wrath consists therefore *only* of *vindicta*, of the will to restore justice without injury. The definition of *vindicta* as the part of anger that belongs to justice is here especially apt: We have just read about *iustitia Dei* as the justice by which God both preserves God's own justness—hence it involves God in no desire for harm—and restores justice to human beings—hence the desire for good in us. Thomas has here simply interpreted *ira Dei* in accord with *iustitia Dei*.

That brings us to another sense of *"vindicta,"* left tacit by the density of Thomas's exposition, one even more characteristic of the way *iustitia Dei* works to restore human creatures to life. We have in the glossing of *"ira"* by *"vindicta"* not only an explication of a more common by a more technical term, we have also a suggestive change of the semantic field that indicates a deep appreciation of characteristic Pauline themes. *"Vindico,"* unlike *"irascor,"* has as its root "to make a legal claim" (*vim dico*). The noun *"vindicta"* makes a specific sort of legal claim. It names the rod with which a praetor touched a slave who was to be manumitted; its literal sense is a manumission staff. Its first figurative sense is therefore not vengeance or punishment (although Thomas mentions that), but deliverance. And that too is apt, for

God's wrath seeks our freedom. Concretely: God's wrath is a staff of manumission by which God sets us free from the consequences of our detaining the truth. Consider how the passage works with that meaning:

> God's wrath is God's very delivering, which is called the wrath of God according to its similarity to human beings becoming angry, who seek deliverance from without [extra]. But God brings deliverance from within, from tranquility of character.

Unlike the human search for justice, which is "external" in the effects of anger, the imposition of penalties, and the manipulation of social conditions, all of which may leave the heart unjust, the person unjustified, the justice by which God makes us just and delivers us is also internal to us. God justifies and delivers us by involving us in God's work through the virtue of faith, by which, in leaning upon God, we live. God addresses and engages precisely our (restored) freedom when God makes us participants in the divine vindicta, the return to justice which is deliverance into life. It is the one confiding in the Son, Thomas reminds us with a quotation of John 3:36, who will see life. In the crucifixion and resurrection, the one confiding in the Son sees how God's justice becomes itself deliverance and life.

Thomas takes the wrath of God not only as God's seeking justice for both God and us; he takes it also as a penalty for sin. Paul asserts that the wrath of God has been revealed, Thomas says, "because certain philosophers used to say that the penalties for sin did not come from God, ... since they believed that God's providence was occupied with heavenly things, so that it did not extend itself to terrestrial matters" (§110 ca. med.). That changes the problem.

Now the problem is one about how we think the world relates to its intelligibility. Paul (thinks Thomas) will not let a secular view of the world go forward, one that leaves God in God's heaven and abandons human life to a terrestrial intelligibility internal to this world. Thomas sees Paul as advancing a claim about an entire realm of discourse, so that the world is not allowed to go without a theological explanation. That is of a piece with the passages we have seen from the John commentary where Thomas places secular sciences into a theologically governed hierarchy. A world-view worthy of the name must give an internal account of its rivals. It is one purpose of Thomas's exposition, both here and as it continues in the arguments for the proposition "God exists" that follow, to stake a claim, so that pretensions to the world's merely immanent intelligibility do not go unchallenged.

For Thomas it is already a nominal definition of God to govern the world

in providence (I.13.9c), and it already identifies God as a particular character to read in the sacred scriptures how God has arranged states of affairs to
speak (I.1.10c *in init.*); indeed, Thomas might have said that God has
arranged states of affairs, centered through the literal and figurative senses
on the events of Jesus, for self-disclosure. God as the author of providence,
God as the "Abba" of Jesus Christ, and God as the seeker of justice all three
require, as a condition for their possibility, that God prove active in human
affairs. Thomas supplies that presupposition here.

After Paul speaks of God's wrath as a consequence of sin, says Thomas,
he goes on to speak of the fault for which a discipline (*poena*) is inflicted.
The sins named in §111 turn out to be the very ones that we saw earlier in
this chapter as vitiating the effectiveness of the cognition of God: impiety
and injustice. Note that those are not sins of ignorance about bits of the
Christian story. Thomas is not here holding people blameworthy for doctrinal failings. He is advancing an explanation for sins on which he thinks one
might get a lot of trans-cultural agreement: injustice, and impiety in the
sense of ingratitude.

Those who have the true cognition of God—and lack it

Only now Thomas comes to speak of the cognition of God that the Gentiles
"had"—only now that he has explicated the faith from which alone effective cognition of God arises, the wrath of God that disciplines human beings by freeing them from the slavery they love, and the injustice and
ingratitude that would rob that cognition of any effectiveness.

> 112. Third he asserts the cognition that they possessed of God, when
> he adds [explaining whose impiety and injustice] OF THE HUMAN BEINGS
> OF THEM WHO DETAINED IN INJUSTICE, as held captive, THE TRUTH OF
> GOD, that is, true cognition of God. For true cognition of God [*vera Dei
> cognitio*], as far as it is in itself, leads human beings to the good; but it is
> bound, as if held hostage, by the disposition to injustice, by which, as Ps.
> 11(12):1 has it, *truths are diminished by the children of human beings.*
> [Nam vera Dei cognitio quantum est de se inducit homines ad bonum,
> sed ligatur, quasi captivitate detenta, per iniustitiae affectum, per quem,
> ut Ps. xi 1, *diminutae sunt veritates a filiis hominum.*]

So the cognition that Thomas goes on to describe is not the knowledge
that we possess, it is the knowledge that *effectively we lack.* "True cognition of God leads human beings to the good." But the cognition of Aris-

totelian demonstrations without faith does not lead to the good, "but is bound, as if held hostage." There is a cognition whose effectiveness we lack, and therefore it is knowledge we do not properly possess, since if we really possessed it, we would enjoy its effusiveness: but we bound and detained that effectiveness. We human beings saw a practical conclusion—do justice and in everything give thanks—and we doubled back to deny or domesticate the premises. In Part I we saw that the way in which knowledge (that time *scientia*) formed the soul in Aristotle but could be deprived of that forming power in Thomas. Thus the knowledge here in question is knowledge detained, captive, diminished, trapped: knowledge without its power, unable to form us, work in us, create effective conformity between ourselves and reality. Our cognition of God is unable to form us because somehow it has been deprived of its own form, and as thus actively *de*formed or denatured, it is lacking to us. It is a sort of virtual knowledge, would-be knowledge—or better: domesticated knowledge, *has-been* knowledge—knowledge as it were on paper but not in a mind: and that is a paradoxical situation for Thomas, if not for us, because cognition is defined as informing a mind. It is for Thomas a very odd sort of knowledge that proves as feckless as this does. If he were Barth, if he worked with Barth's categories, he would call it in virtue of its acknowledged ineffectiveness no knowledge at all. But since he is not, Thomas does call it *"cognitio,"* even *"vera cognitio."* For the offense is that it is precisely the true cognition of God that we hold captive. But we should not be misled. Thomas continues to call the cognition "true" by courtesy. It is the same courtesy by which he also continues to refer to unformed faith as "faith," even *"fides idem numero."*

And the captivity in which we hold off that true cognition is not a captivity in which we have placed it, previously having known it; it is the captivity in which we always already exist. It is precisely the wrath of God, as Paul says and Thomas recognizes, that first *reveals* the truth to us, first releases us from captivity and releases with us the recognition of the truth. Thus Thomas can say with Barth: "Paul is not speaking of the Gentiles as such and in general.... He is speaking of the Gentiles as they are now confronted with the Gospel, whether they know it or not [since they "detain the true knowledge of God with injustice"] and whether they like it or not [since it comes to them as *vindicta Dei*]. Paul...sees the Gentiles... in the reflected light of that fire of God's wrath which is the fire of [God's] love."[18]

The *vera cognitio Dei* of which Thomas speaks here (between Eden and the gospel) is always and everywhere a *vera cognitio Dei detenta*. It is a self-consuming artifact. It is a cognition Thomas affirms as deprived of its effectiveness—or affirms to deny.

The natural cognition of God in its immediate textual context

It is under those circumstances that we come at last to Thomas's exposition of the natural cognition of God.

113. [*I. B. 1. a. ii.*] Then when [Paul] says SINCE WHAT IS KNOWN [*notum est*], he shows what he asserted, although in reverse order.

[*I. B. 1. a. ii. aa.*] For first he agrees that the wise among the Gentiles recognized the truth about God [*sapientes gentilium de Deo cognoverunt veritatem*];

[*I. B. 1. a. ii. bb.*] second, he shows that in them were impiety and injustice, where he says [2:1, §123] SO THEY ARE WITHOUT EXCUSE;

[*I. B. 1. a. ii. cc.*] third, that they incur the wrath of God, where he says [1:32, §166], WHO, THOUGH [THEY HAD RECOGNIZED] THE JUSTICE OF GOD.

Under the first head [*aa*] he makes three points:

[*I. B. 1. a. ii. aa. aaa.*] First, he shows what they recognized about God [*quid de Deo cognoverunt*];

[*I. B. 1. a. ii. aa. bbb.*] second, he shows from whom they received such cognition [*huiusmodi cognitionem acceperunt*], where he says [1:19, §116], FOR GOD [HAS SHOWN IT] TO THEM;

[*I. B. 1. a. ii. aa. ccc.*] third, he shows by what means, where he says [1:20a, §117], FOR THE INVISIBLE THINGS [OF GOD].

Note 1) that the oddity of the self-consuming character of *vera cognitio Dei detenta* does not escape Thomas's notice. That is part of what Thomas signals when he remarks that Paul proceeds "in reverse order, however."

Note 2) how far down in the outline-hierarchy we are. A great many propositions govern "what they recognized about God," so that the natural cognition affirmed of God cannot be wrenched from that context and those constraints without a change in function and therefore in meaning. When Thomas addresses the issue in the *Summa* he does not, perhaps despite appearances, wrench it from that context and those constraints. For he directs the reader to Romans 1:20 as to a warrant and adverts therefore to the context and constraints governing it. The "little ones in Christ" for whom Thomas wrote the *Summa* were students attending lectures "in the sacred page." Yet because of the modern reversal of the *auctoritates* proper to natural science and natural theology—because after Locke we find ourselves in the position of an objector to I.1.8, rather than in the position of one accepting Thomas's response—we tend to imagine that a) the natural cognition of God, even in the presence of injustice and ingratitude, is surer than any knowledge based on revelation; b) that is because the human being is the ultimate source and measure of all cognition; c) such a human being is reliable only when her will is disengaged; and d) such cognition is not so called only by courtesy, but counts as the paradigm case. But Thomas denies, expressly or implicitly, all four of those propositions.

3) There is no mention at all in what follows here of triumphant human powers independent of grace. When there is mention earlier of apparent human powers, or of what is "in them," it turns out to be *impietas* and *iniustitia*. When we get to the question "from what source" (*a quo auctore*) the knowledge comes, the mention is of "God." Thomas will, to be sure, come to define natural cognition of God as "what is recognizable about God by the human being through reason [*quod cognoscibile est de Deo ab homine per rationem*]" (*In* 1:19, §114). But *"per rationem"* forms no hard contrast with the category *"a Deo,"* even if Thomas allows the compatibility to go without saying. All things that are "recognizable by the human being" are, for Thomas, "recognizable through reason" in *some* way, just as all things that are recognizable by the human being are also in some way recognizable through the senses. Nothing is "cognizable by the human being" through some faculty *other* than reason; that would be absurd. Until we know more the characterization need look no more than analytic.

Thomas, speaking in the voice of Paul, begins his exposition with a protest: "I *properly* [*recte*] say that they detained the truth of God, for it was in them." The first person verb is unusual, and the "properly" indicates that the whole assertion of a positive possession of a cognition of God serves the coherence of asserting its absence. He asserts the positive as a matter of backing and filling. It is not a theologoumenon in its *own* right. It is not a proposition to which Thomas owes *primary* allegiance. It is part of a second-order theory. It is part of an attempt to make *sense* not of knowledge but of ignorance. It answers an objection. Therefore Thomas protests: "I say properly." And it is also only therefore that Thomas continues "for it was in them."

The positive assertion of a natural cognition of God serves to make the Gentiles guiltier, not prouder. Thomas does not miss the "so they are without excuse!" with which Paul closes his trap. By §128 it turns out that Thomas is talking about cognition that, as he describes it, nobody concretely possesses, and demonstrations that no one concretely can follow to the identification of that with which they conclude—until, perhaps, the advent of the gospel. In a moment we will finally come to Thomas's set piece on the natural cognition of God, where three *viae* to the proposition "God exists" serve to explicate Romans 1:19. It is worth pointing out the relative isolation of that set piece from what precedes and follows it. That is, the set piece is not a climax to which the foregoing exposition builds; it is nothing that Thomas has been working towards; it is a matter of filling in a gap in the argument about the Gentiles' *fault.* Nor is it a stepping stone on the way to something else. In context, it is a digression. It is a digression, furthermore, of a particular type. It is not a random digression that relates to what comes before and after it merely by free association in the author's mind or because of a passing relevance to contemporary circumstances, which might, for those reasons, also go somewhere else. It is a digression ordered, as I have said, to the argument, an elaboration that arises organically from its context, one that belongs here and not elsewhere, a well-governed investigation of a point emerging in the course of exposition. Thomas had a word for such digressions; we have seen one already upon the topic of faith. We have a *quaestio.* The *quaestio* arose, after all, in commentaries on scripture. And commentaries on scripture are where the *quaestio* is at home. But first a peek is in order at the way Thomas's argument will resume after the digression has passed.

The argument resumes, after the digression with the conclusion, as we have seen, "So they are without excuse" (*In* Rom. 1:20b, §123). After discussing at some length the possible logical relations of ignorance and culpability, Thomas comes to this conclusion (§129): The Gentiles caused their cognition of God to become empty or vain (*"evanuerunt"*) because they did not have faith. True cognition of God was unstable in faith's absence. It could not stand upright without leaning upon God. Despite all Thomas's emphasis elsewhere upon the location of sin in the will and the relative reliability of the mind, here he is willing to talk about the fallenness also of the intellect just in its dependence upon the will. They did not, he says, trust God; therefore their cognition too must fail. And the word he uses for "faith" is the Reformers' own *"fiducia."*

We can characterize Thomas's remarks so far as falling into three strains, the compatibility or incompatibility of which is to be established.

1) The natural cognition of God is a cognition that no one in the text actually has, because all spoken of have already "become empty in their own thoughts [*evanuerunt in cogitationibus suis*]" (*In* 1:21 §129 *in fin.*). Everyone is concretely in a state of culpable ignorance for not leaning upon God. So the natural cognition of God is a self-consuming artifact. It exists only in

order to show what is being denied. It does not show what people possess, but what they lack. Their cognition amounts, in Preller's words, to "a felt ignorance," and it is in that sense alone a cognition rather than a failure of cognition.[19]

2) The natural cognition of God is still available to everyone. But the propositions included receive the designation "cognition" by courtesy, in the same way that *"fides informata"* continues to be called faith, for, lacking a form, it is unable to impose a form upon the soul. Such cognition is empty, feckless, lying. Barth would call it no knowledge at all. When he does so he is speaking of the same truth as Thomas. Thomas would go further, however. Thomas would defend the retention of the term *"cognitio,"* so that *in the presence* of faith—not as a mere addition, but as a filling-up (the opposite of *evanuerunt*), as a bringing to life—the same propositions could count as knowledge again (*cognitio* able to participate in sacred doctrine.) Unless those propositions live and move and have their being in God, they are like fish out of water. So as mere cognitions of the Unknown called "God" that stand at the end of the ways—the three of the Romans commentary as well as the five of the *Summa*—they are merely detained cognitions, or cognition so called by courtesy, until and unless they are held in the right medium, that is, a mind indwellt by God. Both a page and a godless mind are inappropriate, indeed impossible media.

3) The natural cognition of God is neither cognition that nobody concretely has, nor virtual cognition of God that is waiting for the right medium. It is a rhetorical trope. The "natural cognition of God" that the Gentiles had was either mistaken or so called by another of Paul's rhetorical traps. It is "really" one of three sorts of "theology of the Gentiles" that Thomas mentions at the end: "civil theology," which is idolatry; "fabular theology," which is lying; and "natural theology" (*"theologia naturalis"*), which serves the creature rather than the Creator.

Can those three strains be reconciled? Yes, if we elevate the second, the notion that the natural cognition of God is virtual cognition of God: cognition of that of which we know not what it is or how to identify it. In the mind that God causes to lean by faith upon God, it is real, effective knowledge in that it can reproduce its form within the knower or impress itself upon her. It can in short *change* her. If such effective cognition of God should become self-conscious as a discipline, Thomas would explain its effectiveness by saying that it does come to participate in *scientia*, yet not the *scientia* that arises from demonstrations such as Aristotle offered, but the *scientia* that arises from the demonstration Christ offered—a demon-

stration of the image of God working love and justice and causing the
scientia of the blessed.

In the first situation, that of Gentiles without the gospel, none of them
actually possesses cognition of the relevant sort—salvific cognition, knowledge properly so called, cognition that could find a place in the science into
which sacred doctrine is formulable rather than the science into which
metaphysics is formulable. Natural cognition therefore in the sense of
knowledge effective in conforming the mind to itself, and therefore *properly so called*, and natural in the sense of *in the absence of faith* does not in
fact exist, now or ever, because the two qualifications "properly so called"
and "in the absence of faith" cancel each other out.

In the second case, that of virtual cognition of God, which is cognition
of "God," we see that natural cognition of "God" can become by grace
the natural cognition of God, of the One, that is, of whom Jesus Christ is
the *via demonstrationis in veritatem*. Contrary to some usages, the cognition can be "natural by grace," since "grace does not take away nature"
(I.1.8 *ad* 2, I.2.2 *ad* 1). That happens in the mind that, by grace, relies faithfully upon God's self-revelation in him, that is, upon that other demonstration. *Then* it becomes the *cognitio evangelica gratiae Christi* of which the
Romans commentary repeatedly speaks.

We can see a real continuity between the cognition of "God" that preceded faith and the cognition of God that exists after faith in the same way
that we can see a real continuity in life between the one coming to believe
and the one actually believing: in both cases we can see (or construct) the
continuity from belief's side backwards. To us the continuity describes a
genealogy rather than a development. According to Thomas, someone like
Paul, who has experienced the gospel, knows how to go back and take up
the statue of the Athenians into the Unknown God as something to which
he can make a retrospective connection. Since the connection is retrospective, not prospective, Paul can make sense both of the claim to represent
God and the admission that God remains unknown ("*ignotum*," to which
Thomas characteristically adds the intensifier "*omnino*," "entirely"). In
other words, faith can, by analogy, relate a word for a concept to the name
for a person, or "'God'" to "God."

In the third case, finally, "the natural cognition of God" is presented as a
misnomer. The true name for the thing is "the service of the creature rather
than the Creator," as explicated by the parallels of idolatry and mendacity.
That is a description of the natural cognition of God not virtual or neutral
on a page but in a mind engaged in impiety, injustice, and ingratitude. So

too revealed statements, like "Jesus is Lord" can be falsified when they are mouthed by someone capable of holding them in a mind that can also direct the cleaving of a Muslim skull. That too is mendacity, idolatry, and service of the creature at the expense of the Creator, of the sort that Thomas describes. "For by infidelity a human being is maximally separated from God, since neither does she have true cognition of God; for by false cognition of God one does not approach God, but is rather further separated from God...since that which that one opines is not God" (II–II.10.3).[20]

So in the concrete situation of human beings the natural cognition of God is explicitly and logically dependent upon the revealed cognition of God—that is upon the revealed cognitions of God properly and effectively so called or the *revelabilia* as God's form in the world, engaged in informing human beings toward their end of friendship with God. That will become clearer when, later, we will come to the end of *Lectio* VII—the end of the "without excuse" pericope—and Thomas begins to characterize three ways to do natural theology wrong. In fact, Thomas uses the term *"theologia naturalis"* only in that negative sense. Thomas never uses the phrase "natural theology" to describe what he is up to in the Romans commentary or the *Summa*. He thinks of both as biblical, dogmatic theology, of the sort described in Part I's characterization of sacred doctrine. After Deism, however, one thought that the whole point of natural theology was to be *the same thing* when believers and non-believers practiced it (and after Deism it *was* the same thing): one of Thomas's genres had been lost, and Barth rightly rejected it in theology as a category mistake. But Thomas did not make that mistake. Thomas made a distinction.

Preliminary conditions on the natural cognition of God

Soon the text will come to the "natural theology" that Thomas actually does. He describes an effect of God's self-vindication in the gospel grace of Christ, a resulting cognition of God that depends for its laudability or culpability upon the context, usually contained within a human mind, of the other propositions and behaviors that constitute, Wittgenstein might say, its use. It belongs to the Gentiles as a reconstruction of something they concretely lack, a zero to hold that place in the argument. It belongs to Christians only by courtesy until it is formed by faith, as faith belongs to them only by courtesy until it is formed by love. Within the theology that pertains to sacred doctrine it belongs to sacred doctrine's genus and genre; it stands, that is, under scripture, and gets taken up, finally, into the story of Jesus

Christ that Thomas calls its demonstration. Outside the theology that pertains to sacred doctrine it belongs to a genus that Thomas sometimes calls (neutrally) "the theology that pertains to metaphysics" and sometimes (disparagingly) "natural theology," which worships and serves the creature rather than the Creator. It adds to the merit of believing when the believer has a positive disposition of the will toward it, that is, desires and embraces the knowledge as a source of joy (II–II.2.10 *ad* 2); it takes away from the merit of believing if the believer has a negative *or neutral* disposition toward it, as when a rational creature "has no will to believe except on the basis of proof" (II–II.2.10 *ad* 1): for that is but one step from the reason for which the demons, according to Thomas, "believe and tremble" (II–II.5.2 *ad* 3). The problem is, at root, not that they have a neutral attitude toward the knowledge in the abstract, but that the knowledge should not be abstract; it should lead to justice—and to have a neutral attitude toward something leading to justice is a sin. Furthermore the *enuntiabilia* that are concretely subject to proof also depend upon the power of the intellects available to understand them, so that the case of the demons, who can see more with their stronger senses and intellects (II–II.5.2 *ad* 2) renders the domain of preambles (the place where the theology that pertains to metaphysics overlaps with the theology that pertains to sacred doctrine) somewhat relative. Since human reasoning is subject to error, not only about demonstrations but also about demonstrability,[21] and since human beings can also sometimes recognize their error, the line between what is provable and what is not may move. But cognition without justice and piety is not only ineffective; it is, in this passage and in the test case of the demons, dangerous: so that the more human beings claim to know about God by the power of their unaided reason without justice and gratitude, the more demonic (in terms of stronger intellects and less willingness to believe) they become.

But Thomas cannot simply give up talk of a *natural* cognition of God, properly so called with faith, justice and piety—a cognition that is possible as grace disposes or redisposes nature for it. For to do so would be to deliver up the *enuntiabilia* to dwell only in contexts or minds where an *inade-quate* context or mental isomorphism obtained; to give them up, that is, to a context that "detained their truth." In a few pages we will see more of how Thomas uses cosmological arguments to claim the *effective* natural knowledge of God for the realm of *revelabilia* and the sacred doctrine that studies them.

Those are collected together some of the explicit and implicit conditions of the natural cognition of God that Thomas tends to take for granted and we tend to forget.

From notum *to* cognoscibile

The next passage is remarkable for the way in which Thomas distances himself from a balder assertion of a natural knowledge of God. The most obvious surprise is that he glosses Paul's *"quod notum est"* with his own *"quod cognoscibile est."*

> 114. Therefore [Paul] states the first thing. I say correctly that they detained the truth of God, for the true cognition of God [*vera Dei cognitio*], in some sort of way, was within their power, since [Paul says] WHAT IS KNOWN OF GOD [*quod notum est Dei*], that is, what is recognizable about God [*quod cognoscibile est de Deo*] by a human being through reason, HAS BEEN MANIFESTED IN THEM, that is, has been manifested to them by that which is in them, that is by an intrinsic light.

First of all, Thomas stays away from a possible gloss of *"notum est"* with *"scire,"* and confines himself to *"cognoscere."* That tends to confirm Preller's rule. Paul's *"quod notum est"* deploys a verb that Thomas prefers to reserve for the expression of our ignorance: When he denies knowledge of God's essence in this life, he uses the phrase *"omnino ignotum."*

Second, what is or has been noted (past participle) becomes what is recognizable (another *-ibile* suffix). After we have seen the sharp distinction Thomas draws between *revelatum* and *revelabile* this move must seem fairly bold. Without making it explicit, Thomas observes an ambiguity in the passive statement of *quod notum est*: it can refer either to the subjective fact of *somebody's* actually having noted something, or to the objective fact of the notedness of a thing, with the possibility that, as it happens, the notedness does not now inhere in anybody's mind. The latter interpretation is difficult, because Paul adds the clause "has been manifested in them." Fortunately for Thomas's exploitation of the ambiguity, Paul's gloss comes only in the next phrase, after Thomas has already gotten a distinct interpretation under way. Thomas chooses the second, objective meaning: Something may have been recognized about God without anybody's actually recognizing it now; or better, its having-been-recognized-ness does not depend upon the presence in a particular time and circumstances of a mind containing that truth. In that case the clearer way of putting the matter is of course as Thomas does: it is recogniz*able, cognosc*ibile.

The point here is that Thomas chooses a possible interpretation, a *lectio dificilior*, according to which he prescinds from describing God as known with any sort of past participle—even though Paul does—in favor of an adjective of potentiality. Thomas steps back from describing God as *cognitum* just where he has most reason to, in favor of describing God as *cognoscibile*. That is remarkable, it bears repeating, when Thomas is used both to making sharp distinctions among such words and to conforming his usage to that of the scriptures.

Perhaps Thomas is treating the world in the same way as he treats scripture. The move works differently, however, with regard to scripture and the world. With regard to scripture, the move from *revelatum* to *revelabile* serves to *expand* the scriptural realm to include the world. All things whatsoever are *revelabilia*. One expects to move from *notum* to *cognoscibile*: what is known to us may be small, but what is cognoscible to us is great. This time, however, the emphasis falls differently. This time the move serves to *contract* the realm of knowledge actually claimed (*nota*) to that of knowledge merely possible. The move from *revelata* to *revelabilia* is a move from actuality to possibility that expands the possible: the move from *nota* to *cognoscibilia* is a move from actuality to possibility that contracts the actual. Worse: it gets contracted to that of merely possible *cognition*. It is hard to see how Thomas could further attenuate the connection of the mind with the extrascriptural world. The fact that *nota* become *cognoscibilia* leaves room open that *cognoscibilia* may turn out in fact, on account of injustice and impiety, to be mere ig*nota*. As *ignota*, however, those things may be revealed; the way is open to take them, as the Thomas of the Romans commentary would have it, as a matter of the grace of the gospel revealing to us what our sin had obscured, or, as the Thomas of the *Summa* would have it, as *revelabilia*. So Thomas contracts the realm of *notae* to make room (*quoad nos*) for *revelabilia*.

So Thomas silences what might look to us moderns like epistemology in Paul's *quod notum est* and treats it under a field in which he has much greater interest, that of moral psychology. He does that the better to make heard what he takes to be Paul's purpose, the demonstration of the necessity of the grace of the gospel. In making that move Thomas would not regard himself as departing from Paul, but rather as cleaning up a bit of terminology remaining from a time when the words like *"notum"* and *"cognoscibile"* had yet to acquire the technical senses in which he uses them. And also in making that move, Thomas anticipates a move of Karl Barth at just this point. Barth glosses the verse in his *Shorter Commentary* by saying "the Gentiles have always *had the opportunity* of knowing God."[22] Barth too says this because he sees Paul's purpose as explicating the necessity of the grace of the gospel.

We are now in a position to venture a reading of what Thomas means when he says "the true cognition of God, in some sort of way, was within their power [*fuit enim in illis, quantum ad aliquid, vera Dei cognitio*]." We have seen that the true cognition of God is only in them, so Thomas glosses the verse, as *cognoscibile*, and as *notum* only in respect of God's own intelligibility (the distinction Thomas usually makes with the phrases *"quoad nos"* and *"in se"*). If it is in them as *cognoscibile* rather than as *notum*, then it is in them not as actuality but as potentiality. That is, we ought to read *"fuit enim in eis"* as "it lay within them" or "within their power"—i.e., not actually, but potentially. It is a potentiality actualized only, in the world that Thomas depicts, with grace, whether Adam's or Christ's. Should that interpretation seem strained, we have only to return to the text again, where we find Thomas insisting that the knowledge is "in them" only in a modified sense. The qualifier *"quantum ad aliquid"* distances the knowledge as possessed only "in some kind of way," or possibly, with an archness unusual in Thomas, "to some purpose," i.e., to render them without excuse. The gloss *"cognoscibile"* leaves no doubt as to what qualification Thomas intends: potentiality without actuality.

It is that determined move from *notum* to *cognoscibile* that controls what Thomas does with what comes next, when Paul says *"manifestum est in illis."* Now the way lies open for Thomas to interpret these passages too so that, paradoxically, something can be "manifest in them" without their realizing it. That should come as little surprise, if the cognition under discussion here is the ineffectual, therefore paradoxical sort I have been suggesting.

The positive claim of the natural cognition of God

The denial of any sort of cognition in this life of God's essence contains the germ of the positive claim that the natural cognition of God makes in Thomas: it is a claim not on behalf of human powers but upon the world.[23]

> [114 continued.] It is therefore to be known [*sciendum est!*] that one thing about God is entirely unknown [*omnino ignotum*] to a human being in this life, namely what God is. Hence Paul too found the altar at Athens inscribed: *To the unknown God* [Acts 17:23]. And that was be-

cause the cognition of a human being begins from those things that are connatural to a human being, namely from created sensible things, which are not capable even of analogizing[24] the divine essence.

Thomas begins with yet another qualification: that about God's uncognizable essence. God's essence is uncognizable in a way different from the way in which truths are unrecognizable in injustice and ingratitude. The uncognizability of God's essence has to do with human finitude; the uncognizability of the invisible things of God that can, under certain conditions, be recognized from the things God has made has to do with human sinfulness.

The questions Thomas asks of the natural cognition of God are three: what is it? (*quid*); from what source does it come? (*a quo auctore*); and through what faculty (*per quem*). He has answered the *quid* by exclusion: we do not know God's essence in this life. That is, we do not, on account of our finitude, participate in it by a mental isomorphism with it. That does not mean we do not participate in God in this life by any means. Rather it is by faith that we are joined to God. Such conformity as we have with God is given to us so as to engage and involve us. Thomas even specifies that it is *without* knowledge that we participate in this way in God: faith joins us to God as to One unknown: *"quasi ignoto coniugamur"* (I.12.13 *ad* 1). For the "place" where God infuses faith—its locus—is not the intellect but the will. So cognition (of whatever sort) proves no rival to faith as it would become after Locke.[25] Rather a cognition when it acquires a structure or becomes articulated is a working out of faith's desire and delight. After faith has joined us to God as to One unknown, it may be a result of the joining that we construct deductive arguments to connect creation to Creator. The sort of *via* represented by deductive argument may be a *via* into the enunciable proposition *"Deum esse,"* but it is not, since finite human beings remain incapable of comprehending the infinite, our *via in Deum*. That title, as we have seen, Thomas reserves for Jesus Christ, who is finite and infinite in one. And since God has graciously chosen to become our end it is necessary, as we recall from I.1.1, that God give us a revelation, which *is* our *via in Deum*. The *quid* of the natural knowledge of God is defined, therefore, in such a way as to point to the necessity of a cognition of God (faith) *elevating* to nature (thus supernatural but not anti-natural) by means of a non-cognitive union (grace). That is not an accident of the logic of the *Summa* here imported as part of a set piece into a commentary on a text with a different logic. Rather it reflects the purpose of Paul, as

Thomas reads him, to throw all human beings upon the mercy of *evangelica gratia*. Paul's purpose would be thwarted, given Thomas's Aristotelian scheme, were God's essence included.

Since Anselm's ontological argument does appear to reach God's essence, and Thomas's cosmological arguments do not, it will be useful here to turn to the ramifications of the different sorts of argument for the programmatic and textual purposes that Thomas has here in view. Thomas rejected Anselm's ontological argument for the existence of God on the ground that it requires *scientia* of God's essence (I.2.1c *in fin.*). The purely philosophical reasons for that rejection, warranted or not, are well known. We are pursuing the theological ones.

Those who *advocate* Anselm's approach, such as Karl Barth,[26] prefer it for this reason: Abstracting from the world of natural science, it offers an *intratextual* or *intrasystemic* account of the necessity of God's existence, one that explicates God's necessity in the light of other theological propositions. It seems to confirm therefore even in the case where "the demonstrative office of a theologian comes most clearly to expression"[27] the rule that it is scripture that defines the world. It preserves the proposition "God exists" as *revelatum* by explicating it in terms of *revelata*. It preserves integrity of sacred doctrine by confirming that no way lies open (*"non remanet amplius via"*) to meet the unbeliever on her own terms if she concedes nothing—except deconstruction of her arguments from within (*"solvare rationes contra fidem,"* I.1.8c). Thus Anselm's ontological way fits Barth's program of defining theology as *faith* seeking understanding.

It may look as if Thomas's cosmological way does not. For cosmological *viae* seem to run afoul of the principle on which Thomas, Anselm, and Barth all agree; they look like an attempt to find precisely an *amplius via*, an attempt to do more than *solvare rationes contra fidem*. But to read cosmological *viae* as *ampliae viae*—as the sort of ways that Thomas is committed to excluding—involves him in a contradiction as blatant as it is quick. So it is only fair to see whether we cannot find some other way to read them.

Since it is the task and intention of sacred doctrine as *scientia* to *incorporate* the whole physical world into the intratextual world of the scriptures (I.1.3 with I.1.10), and since Thomas's announcement and fulfillment of that charge comes in part in his turn to the category of *revelabilia* (I.1.1, I.1.3 *ad* 2, I.1.7, 8, and 10) for things considered under the aspect of their revealability, he will take advantage of the next two paragraphs (§§114–15) to work out some of the consequences of those decisions. Things in the world really possess the form, thanks to God, of *revelabilia*; that form is therefore notable in principle, since it is precisely forms that we note, or forms that locate intelligibility. Things are on Thomas's account God's to reveal, and because that determines their form, it is also ours to understand, if we can.

Recall that *revelabilia* are not simply things that we regard in a certain way, as we regard a thing as edible; rather we recognize a feature of a thing that renders it *revelabile*—we recognize a form—as we recognize something in an apple. Even if we were different (say we were Martians), apples would still be edible (to human beings even if there were none). That is a statement about the form of apples. *Revelabilia* need not appear among *revelata* just as edibles need not get eaten. When in sacred doctrine as *scientia* we recognize things under the formality of *revelabilia*, we take account of that feature of *theirs*.

The intelligibility of things is a part of their truth that human beings have detained through injustice. That means for Thomas that the intelligibility of things as *revelabilia* is notable in itself (*manifestum est*) as having that God–given form, and in human beings (*in illis*) as ordered by God toward that intelligibility—had we not disordered ourselves with injustice and impiety.

The intelligibility of things as God-revealable has a subjective and an objective moment. God reveals *them* (reveals them, that is, *as* something: as *ordered to God*), and therefore they in turn reveal God. In them, that is, God also makes a self-disclosure. Thus Thomas moves on to the next words of Paul: "For God has manifested [or revealed] it to them." That restates and carries forward the move to take things in the world under the formal rationale of revelation. And this formal rationale is not something additional to the things themselves, as if form could be simply added to matter; the formal rationale is constitutive of the reality itself. The object of what God reveals is reality-under-a-description. It is reality-under-a-description *not* as if *res* were simples and *res* under a description were complexes. Rather, under the description of the world *in sacris paginis* we get a new apperception of *quod quid est*, or what *is*. We get a new apperception of what *simples* are, by revealed contact with "what is known about God." The *revelabile* is not a complex; it is a simple.

And it is precisely things in the world that Thomas presents to us as such simples. When we play that language game, it is the *revelabilia* that are the primitive concepts. That is the beauty of a cosmological demonstration—or, as suits this context better, a cosmological *claim*. It is not a claim of human reason upon God: it is a claim of God upon human reason, a claim that charges them: Think about the world under God. If we suppose that a demonstration of that sort attempts to move from one conceptual realm (that of modern or even Aristotelian natural science, where the intelligibility of things rests in themselves, and the end of inquiry comes therefore with that-which-is) to another conceptual realm (that of natural theology, where the intelligibility of God derives from things, and the end of inquiry comes again with that-which-is, this time God existing), then we have entirely missed the point. The point is to take up, assume, co-opt all things into the Christian language game, so that Thomas can trace the connections within it between the created (intelligible as such only in terms of its Creator) and the Creator (partially and imperfectly intelligible in terms of the created effects while remaining entirely unknown in terms of essence). The cosmological demonstration renders the world homogeneous under God, *not* so as to place God and things into a single genus, but so as to *deny* to any created thing a pretension to God-forsakenness or its own God-forsaken realm. The primitive of Aristotelian *scientia* was "that-which-is," which stood for "that-which-is-intelligible." But in sacred doctrine "that-which-is" abbreviates something different. Here it stands for "that-which-is-revealable." The things that *are* in the world, *are* precisely as God-related. The cosmological *via* does not lead from the world up to God, but from God down to the world; it does not render the world Babel-building, it renders God world-enveloping. It elaborates the claim that in God we live and move and have our being. If Thomas had wanted to present the cosmological *viae* as Babel-building, he could not have preceded them in the *Summa* with a definition of its subject-matter as *revelabilia*, he could not have characterized them in the Romans commentary as God-revealed, and he could not have arranged natural science under theology in the commentary on John.

Meanwhile, such reflections on the cosmological *via* restate the problem with the ontological *via*. The ontological *via* abstracts from things in the world. In so doing it leaves them undescribed. It neglects them as they truly are, as *revelabilia*. Thus it delivers them up to human control, and in so doing it delivers up God to human control, a symptom of which abdication is that it claims to have God's definition.

One way to avoid trying to control God and losing the whole world is to answer the question *a quo* as Thomas does, by seeing the knowledge and thereby the world as from *God*. *Were* the knowledge entirely our own, the world would become in turn our creature, and we, willy-nilly, Kant's world-makers, curved in upon and trapped inside our own minds, the thing-in-itself escaped from our grasp. We would be angels both cut off from sense-impressions and deprived of God's infusing them.

Thomas wants to throw a much wider net than the *revelatum*. He wants not only to "confine" himself to the scriptural realm and remain in that sense intratextual; he wants to open the *whole world*, the entire cosmos to the scriptural realm, and render *it too* intratextual. That is what it means for Thomas, as I have said, to have a doctrine of creation; that is what it means for Thomas to bring every understanding, including cosmological ones, into captivity to Christ; that is what it means for Thomas to speak of the object of theology not as *revelata* but as *revelabilia*. In cosmological proofs within sacred doctrine Thomas upholds the world of *revelabilia*. He does not abandon the non-*revelata* to an extra-scriptural realm when he defines reality in terms of that text, with the result that part of the world would get left outside the text and suffer in ontological status.

Since it is characteristic of the intratextually defined realm—the realm defined by Question 1, articles 1 and 10—that it is revealable to us, it is also therefore somehow *giveable* to us. One whose essence we understood would *not* be revealable to us, because there would be nothing opaque about that one to us, no veil to lift, no wrapping to remove, no gift to receive, no friendship freely granted. Something within our power, transparent to us, cannot be revealable to us, cannot come to us as mystery. Knowledge of essences eliminates mystery. The ontological argument, Thomas suggests, impugns the gratuity of revelation, and worse, for the present purpose, runs counter to the conclusion that Paul is about to reach, namely that every human being stands in need of it. Above we saw that Barth thought he had to *defend* Anselm's ontological argument in order to remain intrascriptural and protect revelation: here we see that Thomas thinks he has to *reject* Anselm's ontological argument in order to remain intrascriptural and protect revelation.

That is so because for Thomas to "remain intrascriptural" means *to absorb the world within the scriptural realm*, in short to keep the world inside. And that means that Thomas not only thinks he has to reject Anselm's argument to *protect* the account of God's revealability; he also thinks that cosmological arguments *contribute* to the account of God's revealability. As used in sacred doctrine—as elements of a Pauline rather than an Aristotelian "construction of a syllogism or a passage of prose"— the cosmological arguments claim created things as *revelabilia*. *Without* them the claim of I.1.3 to pass from Scripture (*revelata*) to the world ("everything whatsoever" as revealables) would remain empty. Without them, the unity of sacred doctrine arising from the integrity of its formal rationale and justifying its claim to call itself a distinct Aristotelian science would fall into heterogeneity. And without them, the charge of I.1.8 to "take every understanding captive into obedience to Christ" would go unfulfilled. Therefore Thomas must demonstrate sacred doctrine's cosmological claim. We will see in detail how that works in the paragraphs that follow. For that is the burden of Thomas's next question, the question *a quo*.

The demonstration of God's cosmological claim

What follows in that context might well seem to be Thomas's most optimistic estimation of the capacities of human reason in the Romans commentary.

115. The human being can, however, from created things of that sort, recognize [*cognoscere*] God in three ways, as Dionysius says in his book *On the Divine Names* [ch. 7, *lect.* 4].

One way, to be sure, is by causality [*per causalitatem*]. For since such creatures are defectible and changeable, it is necessary to reduce them to some principle immovable and perfect. And according to this it is recognized about God whether God exists.

Second, by the way of preeminence [*per viam excellentiae*]. For not everything is reduced into a first principle, as into its first and univocal cause, as a human being generates a human being, but into a common and transcendent cause [*in causam communem et excedentem*]. And from this it is recognized what is over all.

The third way is that of negation [*per viam negationis*]. For if there is a transcendent cause, nothing of those things that are among created things can compare with it, as also no heavenly body is properly said to be heavy or light or hot or cold. And according to that we call God immovable and infinite and whatever else is said of that sort.

Such then is the cognition that [the Gentiles] had by the light of reason having been set into place [*cognitionem habuerunt per lumine rationis inditum*].—Ps. 4:6: *Many say, "Who has shown good things to us?" The light of your countenance, Lord, has set a seal upon us.*

Two qualifications bear repeating here so that we will not take *Thomas's* optimism as of the same sort as the *Enlightenment* optimism with which we are more familiar.

First, if we isolate the source of the account's optimism, we find it prompted by no praise of human powers *apart from God*, but rather praise of the light of the countenance of the Lord. Both before, as we have seen, and after, as we shall see shortly, Thomas qualifies the concrete extent of human powers in use. It is consistent with the whole passage we have been examining in this chapter that Thomas treat the light-of-the-divine-countenance-become-intrinsic-to-us-as-human-reason under two aspects: under the aspect of the goodness of God's gift, and under the aspect of the human being's culpable *in*ability to use it.

The second qualification is just that Thomas has not, in the current passage, forgotten, even temporarily, his previous exposition of the second aspect. Thomas is still talking about a mode of manifestation that human beings have *detained*, about the mode of manifestation to them that is, through their impiety and injustice, precisely *not* manifest to them.

The entire section §§114-115, for all its claims about what about God is "in them" and "cognizable by the human being through reason" and "by the light of reason having been set into place" insists on those characterizations *not* to locate the intelligibility of the created world or of God's connection to it in those places; rather it continues to locate in those places precisely the paradox, the problem, the fault, the lack: it continues to locate in those places precisely what Thomas said his purpose would be to locate: the necessity of the grace of the gospel of Jesus Christ. Only under that influence does the paradox, problem, fault, and lack disappear. That is not to uphold a sort of Christian philosophy according to which Christian faith can show natural reason truths that it would not have discovered without the faith but accessible to it unaided thereafter. For under faith the whole matter proceeds under different presuppositions that radically change the context, and therefore the use and sense, of the truths to be demonstrated. It proceeds, that is, under the presupposition of explicit theological premises, articles of faith, with far-reaching ramifications, like those of creation, christology, and Trinity.

That said, we may pass rather quickly over the three *viae* offered, since it is our purpose to ascertain their function rather than to evaluate their content. A few remarks therefore:

1. The three *viae* here name *categories* of ways rather than specific ones. Thomas bills all of the Five Ways of the *Summa* as reasonings from effect to cause (I.2.1), that is, as examples of what he here calls the first way, the way of causality.

2. Nevertheless he must use the categories of ways with some fluidity, because the example that he here gives for the second category, the *via ex-*

cellentiae or way of preeminence, happens to match the *Summa's* third way, at least as the reply to the second objection (I.2.3 *ad* 2) refers to it.

3. The difference in labels (as well as in content) between these ways and those of the *Summa* may indicate a penultimate difference in purpose. Later in the commentary, Thomas will make explicit some theological ramifications of these ways that, in the *Summa*, the tight articular structure and the desire to maintain a simple order of instruction leave implicit. But the version of the ways in the *Summa* left other theological ramifications implicit because Thomas can expect a reader who has just finished Question 1 not to have forgotten them.

4. Perhaps it is significant which examples Thomas chose. The example of the way from causality anticipates Paul's conclusion "therefore they are without excuse" when it characterizes creatures as "defectible." The example of the way from preeminence recalls the necessity of regarding the locus of the world's intelligibility as outside of it when it denies the reducibility of the world to a proper and univocal (i.e., this-worldly) first cause, in favor of a first cause "common to and transcending" all others. And we can take the example of the way of negation to complement that reading when it characterizes God as a transcendent cause that suffers no comparison with anything created.

In his next comments Thomas confirms what we have concluded before, that it is to praise God rather than human beings that we find here an apparent epistemic optimism also for that reason so different from that of the Enlightenment.

> 116. Then when he says, GOD HAS MANIFESTED IT TO THEM, he shows from what source [*a quo auctore*] such cognition had been made manifest to them, and he says that God manifested it to them, according to Job 35:11: *He teaches us more than lowly beasts of burden.*

That is, if we should recognize more than beasts of burden do, then it is *God's* doing. For it is our nature to lean upon *God*, even if God permits us to do it in the way (or place) proper to us, namely through reason and will. Thomas continues:

> At that it is to be considered that one human being manifests something to another by explicating her conception by certain exterior signs, as by voice or in writing. God, however, can manifest something to a human being in two ways. In one way, by infusing an interior light, by which the human being recognizes something, as in Ps. 42:3: *Send forth your light and your truth.*—In the other way, by proposing God's wisdom

by exterior signs, namely sensible created things. As in Eccl. 1:10: [God] *pours it out*, namely wisdom, *over all God's works.*

In that way therefore God manifested it to them either interiorly infusing light, or exteriorly tendering visible created things, in which, as in some book, the cognition of God might be read.

The natural recognition of God without the (implicit or explicit) grace of the Mediator is therefore not a present possibility for anyone of whom the text speaks.[28]

Thomas has also already told us, in any case, that neither of the two ways is infallible. We are not therefore to think of the infusion of light as *ipso facto* the infusion of cognition. The parallelism of the interior infusion of light with the exterior production of signs confirms that conclusion, since it has been the deliberate, explicit, and repeated assertion of the commentary that the exterior signs of God's creation have failed to work. Even miracles ensure credence only from demons, their intellects too powerful to resist them.[29] Little reason, therefore, to expect more from the interior light. The passive-voice, subjunctive conclusion that "the cognition of God might be read" leaves open the possibility that the signs, legible in themselves, proved illegible to the Gentiles, and that the light, illuminating in itself, got blocked by human ingratitude and injustice. It does not take greater optimism about the human mind to move beyond that impasse as the Enlightenment version of natural theology so confidently would; it takes greater optimism about the human will, which can mislead the mind; or better, it takes a greater *separation* between mind and will than Thomas, despite his faculty psychology, would ever countenance. Rather Thomas might well assimilate to demons those unwillingly coerced by the evidence of signs such as the Enlightenment appeared to pride itself upon.[30]

Thomas implies more, however, when he adduces the simile of reading the creation as God's book. Such a reading requires certain unspecified theological premises. In the case of the sacred scriptures all of the spiritual senses depend on being able to read the states of affairs as significant, and the project of interpreting the Hebrew scriptures christologically, reading them as the Old Testament, and uniting them as such with the New, depends on the spiritual senses. Therefore being able to read the states of affairs as significant depends logically, for Thomas, upon doctrines of christology and providence as conditions *sine quibus non*. In the case of reading creation as God's book we are also engaged in taking states of affairs as significant. We will not be able to do that, either, without certain theological presuppositions, like that of providence. For we can imagine Thomas putting this argument into almost parallel form: The author of all creation is God, in whose power it is to accommodate not only sacred scriptures for signifying meanings, but also states of affairs themselves. The proposal that the world speaks of God raises the problem of theodicy (as Thomas recognizes, for example, at I.22.2 obj. 2), and the answer to the problem of theodicy, even for Thomas, is finally christological. For it is in christology that Christians answer the question of how God freely chooses to assume even our suffering and death.[31] Just as reading the scriptures as God's book also depends, for Thomas, on premises as theological as those about the divinity of Christ, so too the reading of creation as God's book ultimately depends, for Thomas, upon premises as theological as those about the divinity of Christ. Here too Thomas's construal of the world admits of reconstruction as one in which rationality is penultimately Aristotelian and ultimately christological, so that reason is generally and for the most part deficient christology. Such ramifications will seem more plausible when we come shortly to see what trinitarian conclusions Thomas is willing to draw from the construal of nature as God's book.

It is instructive to push the parallelism a step further. In I.1.10 we learn that God can arrange states of affairs to speak. In context the remark explains how the spiritual senses of scripture depend upon the providentially arranged events narrated in the literal sense. But nothing limits it to the states of affairs narrated in scripture (the *revelata*). We may not be able to read other states of affairs. But some of them, at least, were manifested to us. And all of them are revealable to us (*revelabilia*). That is the burden of the article about the unity of sacred doctrine as a science: "sacred doctrine treats [*determinat*]...of creatures according as they are referred to God as to their beginning or end, for which reason the unity of the science is not impeded" (I.1.3 *ad* 1). The current passage treats of created things as they are referred to God as to their beginning. It does so not merely in order to contribute to the unity and comprehensiveness of sacred doctrine as a science, although it does. Rather it does so primarily to elaborate upon Paul's argument, to adduce three ways (*viae*) in which Thomas sees Paul to be right. It is therefore no mere set piece, nor does it, for the extent of an excursus, smuggle in metaphysical norms. It is an integral part of a commentary that seeks to explicate theological matters that ramify deeply and wide. The extent of any overlap between metaphysics and sacred doctrine depends upon the changing state of metaphysics. When therefore we see similar matter in place in the *Summa*, we may know that it contributes to the unity and comprehensiveness of the theology that pertains to sacred doctrine neither to ornament a *fideist* scripturalism that could also do without it, nor to prove the existence of God as the nineteenth century would understand that at the beginning of a foundationalist exercise. Rather it contributes to the unity and comprehensiveness of the theology that pertains to sacred doctrine in a concretely specifiable way, namely that of recalling it to the whole context of the proof of the necessity of the grace of the gospel of Jesus Christ. Similarly, when we read this bit of the Romans commentary we may see it as exemplifying in its whole context and elaboration the *Summa's* move to take all created things as *revelabilia.* For here too, since knowledge unformed by the gospel proves incapable of informing human beings toward that justice and gratitude that anticipate life with God, the ultimate result is that demonstration itself, at some distance to be sure, must follow the master demonstration that Thomas ascribes to "Our Savior the Lord Jesus Christ" (III prol.). Thomas's use of the scriptures is not fideist, because he does not seal them off from cosmology, and his use of cosmology is not foundationalist, because he interprets it in light of the scriptures. Rather his use of both scriptures and cosmology is deeply if often tacitly christological.

Transition to a trinitarian cognition of God

"Next," Thomas writes, "when Paul says 'for the invisible things of God from the beginning of the world,'" etc., he shows by what way [*per quem modum*] they received such cognition" (§117), or "what those things are, which they recognized [*cognoverunt*] about God." Romans 1:20 itself lists three things: the invisible things of God, God's eternal power, and God's divinity ("*invisibilia Dei*," "*sempiterna quoque virtus*," and "*eius divinitas*").

What is invisible about God is what we human beings cannot see in this life, namely God's essence. But Paul says that "the invisible things of God are perceived as intellectual things [*invisibilia Dei intellecta conspiciuntur*]." It is the plural number of "*invisibilia*" that saves the truth of the assertion for Thomas. He takes the *invisibilia* as those participants in God's essence that, when we do see the essence we will see as one, like God's goodness, wisdom, power, and so on.

God's *virtus* becomes the specific power of creation, which Thomas interprets as perpetually keeping things in being. Even philosophers interpret it that way, he remarks. So it is that Paul calls it *sempiterna.* It is an attempt to *co-opt* into sacred doctrine a "homophonous" statement that functions quite differently in each realm. The metaphysical correlate of the statement about God's power would not cohere with the purpose of showing the necessity of the grace of the gospel of Jesus Christ, or of rendering the metaphysicians culpably ignorant.

Thomas interprets *divinitas* as the good to which all creatures tend as their final end. But the final end of human beings in friendship with God is just what Question 1 of the *Summa* declares that we need a *revelation* to know with any content. The revelation just is something pre-cognized about the human *end*. That too Thomas renders content-free apart from sacred doctrine.

With some elegance Thomas advances a preliminary, antepenultimate summing up of much of the argument, as he relates each of the three things that can be known of God to one of the three *viae*. The invisible things of God, which participate in God's unknowable essence, belong for that reason to the *via negativa*. The power of God, which corresponds to God as beginning or Creator, belongs for that reason to the *via causalitatis*. And the divinity of God, which corresponds to God as the good toward which things tend as end, belongs for that reason to the *via eminentiae*. An even more elegant penultimate conclusion will build on that false cadence.

Recall the conclusion of Otto Pesch above on the matter of formed and unformed faith: "*Fides informis* is a matter of the great sinner, not of the personally innocent pagan." If we want here to speak of the unformed natural cognition of God in a similar way, we must, however, have a somewhat different situation. Here it *is* a matter not of a sinful Christian but of an innocent Gentile. Or is it?

In the earlier *quaestio* on faith we saw Thomas considering faith's paradigmatic act, complete with all its complements, to which its formation by love is no supplement. Rather form is no more alienable from it than its matter is. And love is no accident to faith properly so called, but its very form. Faith unformed by love retains that name by virtue of God's grace in leaving a defective, residual "faith" behind.

A similar analysis makes sense of Thomas's use of *cognitio Dei*. *Cognitio Dei*, if it is effective, properly so called, salvific—the "*vera Dei cognitio*" that "as far as it is in itself, leads human beings to the good" (§112)—occurs also in the context of certain named attitudes of the will, like gratitude, justice, and piety; all of those, Thomas's analysis of a human act tells us (II–II.23.7), require love for their perfection. Such love is possible with two sorts of divine grace: that that held Adam and Eve upright in Eden, and that

that remedies sin. For both are ordered to justice, whether Eden's original righteousness, or the sinner's justification. The integral act of *cognitio Dei* is possible to innocent human beings relying upon grace in Eden, and to sinful human beings being healed by the grace of Christ. For the present purpose we do not need to worry about how far for Thomas the grace of Christ proleptically or unreflexively extends. We do need to specify that in relying upon grace both the innocent and the redeemed do something not merely but thoroughly natural in Thomas's understanding of the word. For it marks the creature precisely by *nature* to lean upon *grace.* Thus the integral act of *cognitio Dei* as here described, and still excluding things that are cognizable of God only by revelation, can, to put it starkly, be called the true or justice-inducing "natural knowledge of God" just insofar as it leans upon grace, and not otherwise.

For it is the role of the *defective* knowledge of God, unmarked by justice, gratitude, and piety and unformed by love, to specify the "otherwise"; it is the role of *that* knowledge to be characterized as unnatural precisely as it relies upon itself (the "wisdom in which they were confiding [that] was not able to save them" of §109) and not upon God; to be the wisdom characterized therefore as uncreaturely: and it is thus, Thomas supposes, that Paul concludes "they worshipped and served the creature rather than the Creator" (1:25). It is a paradoxical knowledge of God—ineffective to form us, feckless to save us, even culpable—because it is unformed, which is to say denatured, or unnatural; it is unnatural because it fails to lean upon grace, and because it is unnatural and because it is impotent to exhibit its form it proves scarcely intelligible, almost unaccountable.

The passage is difficult because Thomas is bending and straining an Aristotelian scheme that depends upon well-formed natures as principles of intelligibility. And he bends it in at least three interrelated ways. First, he locates the principle of intelligibility outside creation. Second, he defines well-formed nature not as independent but in the context of grace. Third, he undertakes to use a scheme based on form to describe form's distortion.

Which *cognitio Dei* is Thomas describing when he speaks of the three *viae?* He seems insensibly to shift from the defective or residual to the complete version. For he began to specify that "the wise of the Gentiles recognized truth about God [*de Deo cognoverunt veritatem*]" (§113). He ends—and here we come to the last paragraph of the *lectio*—with reflections explicitly trinitarian. The movement is *insensible* because "natural theology" has not yet acquired the baggage that would accrue to it during the Enlightenment. The movement *occurs* because, from the point of view of the

Christian theologian commenting upon Paul, Thomas has two purposes. One is to follow Paul's argument so as to explicate the defective, unformed cognition of God that Paul will find "inexcusable." The other is however to illustrate how real, fully formed cognition of God actually works in the context where it is at home, namely within Christian theology.

A trinitarian natural cognition of God perfected by faith

And *there* the cognition of the Creator will have ramifications for the account of the Trinity, ramifications that Thomas does not overlook.

> 122. The Glossa even says that by *the invisible things of God* is understood the person of the Father....—By *eternal power*, the person of the Son....[And] by *divinity*, the person of the Holy Spirit, to whom is appropriated goodness. Not that the philosophers, led by reason, were able to reach, by those things that have been made, as far as the cognition of the persons with respect to things proper [*propria*] to them, but according to the things *ap*propriated [*appropriata*] to them. They are said however to be lacking in the third sign, that is in the Holy Spirit, since they held something corresponding to the Father, namely the first principle itself, and something corresponding to the Son, namely the first created mind, which they called the fatherly intellect....

The identification of the three named features of the Godhead with the persons of the Trinity proceeds here on two levels. The Gentiles sometimes know that there is something without knowing how to identify it (the distinction between "someone is coming" and "Peter is coming" of I.2.1 *ad* 1, and the distinction that enforces the use of the word *"cognitio"* when we do not know *quid est*). Thus they have concepts that Christians will want to appropriate to the persons of the Trinity. They do not have concepts proper to the Trinity in itself (generation, filiation, spiration), nor do they know that the concepts they do have correspond to the Trinity in Christian discourse, or as Thomas and Christians generally would say, they do not know that the concepts they have really belong to particular members of the Trinity in the mode of appropriation.

It is hard to understand why Thomas would even bring the matter up of trinitarian correspondences to the three *viae* if he has only the Gentiles in mind. Rather he has already moved from cosmological arguments to the center of dogmatics. Indeed, it is not a shift of genre at all, if cosmological arguments and trinitarian appropriations have become, at least in the last stage of Thomas's authorship, of a piece. Given that such and such concepts are available in the Gentile world, which can Christians co-opt for explications of the Trinity? Which prove most easily assimilable into Christian discourse?

More: Thomas makes an implicit connection between the three *viae* here discussed and the persons of the Trinity. The *via negationis*, as it elaborates upon the *invisibilia Dei*, turns out to apply to God the Father. The *via causalitatis*, by elaborating upon God's *sempiterna virtus*, gets applied here to God the Son. And the *via eminentiae*, by elaborating upon God's *divinitas*, gets applied to God the Holy Spirit. Those insights are irreducibly Christian theological ones; they belong to the articles of faith (II–II.2.8). They belong therefore to the *cognitio Dei* "under the rationale by which the act of faith is established" or "under the conditions that faith requires" (II–II.2.2 *ad* 3), not under the conditions of ineffective Gentile cognition. But it is the overlap in the unformed material—the overlap in underdetermined talk of first cause and created mind—that causes the word *"cognitio"* still to apply here. These are matters that the theology pertaining to metaphysics also mentions. I say overlap in unformed matter or underdetermined talk because it is metaphysics and sacred doctrine that respectively impose the formal rationale under which the things are considered, as the earth gets considered differently by the geometer and the astronomer. We do not know enough about the use of a homophone like "first cause" until we know in what context it stands and what sort of semantic range it has and what sort of form of life it conditions.

That is not to say that there will be nothing in common between graced and ungraced uses of the word. Only for Thomas it is Christian theology rather than metaphysics that specifies the commonality. It is the commonality that creation shares with redemption. Since redemption proceeds under the sign of the Holy Spirit, which blows where it will, we cannot specify in advance what the commonality will be, but perhaps we can see it from the other side, retrospectively. To say that the Gentiles are lacking in the third sign, that of the Holy Spirit, is precisely to say that the logic of redemption is not predictable from the logic of creation, or that the logic of coming to believe follows the logic of belief, and not otherwise.[32] Just as the convert can make subjective sense of the continuities of her life from the after side of the conversion—under the sign, that is, of the Holy Spirit—but could not have foreseen it beforehand, so too even the Gentile cognition of God looks trinitarian to the believer, without, of course, the metaphysician's having any notion of it.

Cognitio detenta *and* scientia subtracta

Now we turn to the denouement of this development, *lectio* VII, which begins with Paul's conclusion "therefore they are without excuse" (1:20b) and ends with his explanation that "they converted the truth of God into a lie and worshiped and served the creature rather than the Creator" (1:25).

Thomas characterizes what has gone before as Paul's showing that the truth of God was recognized by the Gentiles in such a way as to leave them culpable (§123). Thomas elaborates on the paradox in two ways. First he distinguishes between exculpatory and culpable ignorance in Aristotelian fashion (§124). Then he confirms expressly the implication that the cognition in question is to be characterized as deficient:

> Therefore those are called inexcusable SINCE, ALTHOUGH THEY HAD RECOGNIZED [*cognovissent*] GOD [i.e., in some way], THEY DID NOT GLORIFY GOD AS GOD, either because they did not pay the cult due to God, or because they imposed an end to [or a limit on] God's power and knowledge, subtracting somewhat from God's power and knowledge [*quia virtuti eius et scientiae terminum imposuerunt, aliqua eius potentiae et scientiae subtrahentes*], against what is said in Ecclesiasticus 43:30: *Be glorifiers of God as much as you are able* §127 ca. med.

Here we have culpable ignorance, that is, ignorance that takes on the will's pattern of sin and guilt—a pattern that is both trap and fault, a pattern from which we cannot rescue ourselves but from which God rescues us in no other way than by restoring our selves to us. I want to call attention to the two phrases in which the word *scientia* appears. First, they conform to Preller's rule about *"cognitio"* and *"scientia."* *Cognitio* can belong to human beings; *scientia,* in divine things, only to God. Second, they tend to confirm the conjecture that Thomas sometimes implicitly, sometimes explicitly distinguishes knowledge (of either sort) according to whether or not it is formed. Here we have explicit reference to a "subtracted" version of God's *scientia.* Thomas says that the Gentiles "impose a limit on God's *scientia,*" and, more tellingly, he characterizes them as themselves "subtracters somewhat from God's *scientia*"—thereby detaining or disarming any cognition they may have enjoyed of their own. They subtract from God's *scientia* precisely as they subtract grace from nature and leave it deficient. For that also goes, Thomas says, for God's powers: "they imposed a limit on God's power...subtracting somewhat from [it]." The power that we Gentiles, in turn, have by nature is denatured when it imposes a limit on God's, or when it leans no more upon grace, and the cognition that we have by nature is evacuated when it leans no more upon faith, or leans no more by faith upon the *scientia* of God that faith adheres to uncomprehended. Adam and Eve, similarly, had (infused not investigated) *scientia* of natural things, like the names of animals and they put an end to it, Thomas implies, comparing their knowledge to sight lost by the blind (I.94.3 *ad* 1).

It might be possible even at this point in the commentary to entertain the supposition that if some Gentiles are "subtracters from God's *scientia*," others might be "integrators of God's *scientia*," that is, if some culpably take away from God's *scientia*, detaining their own cognition of God, others concretely existing in this life may be able to build up toward it, freeing their own cognition of God. But we have already seen a number of considerations sufficient to defeat that supposition.

1) To suppose that that possibility exists for anyone now flies in the face of the commentary's logic, which is to assert the necessity and sufficiency alone of the "gospel grace of Christ."

2) It exempts some Gentiles from the conclusion that Thomas is here explicating, that *all* are without excuse.

3) It ignores the strictures against use of the word *"scientia"* to describe human knowledge of divine things: even the Holy Spirit's "gift of *scientia*" tells us only which humanly formed propositions to *believe*, while we lack the comprehension of them that would count as *scientia* of our own (II–II.9.3). And even the *donum scientiae* testifies to the need for grace, since it is a gift of the Holy Spirit.

4) The supposition misses the way in which the entire movement of the passage recapitulates the theology of the Fall. Thomas preserves rational powers in the human being not to assert a human power of coming to know God,[33] but to *locate* the Fall in the will. In this passage the point is not to assert a human ability: it is to castigate a human *aversion*. It is a turning away from God that is *willful* and *desired* (in an odd sense of desire) that the present passage seeks to assert. Thomas distinguishes will and intellect in the one soul as parts of just such an analysis as this.

Finally, 5), the supposition of a knowledge from us up forgets the implication of the preterite verbs "God did manifest...it might be read" that a possibility once open (like the possibility of upholding righteousness) has *passed*. For those reasons the supposition is excluded. And for those reasons too it is attractive to gloss the divine *scientia* from which we Gentiles have subtracted as a divine *scientia* from which Adam and Eve fell. Certainly the "subtraction from" God's *scientia* and "detention of" human cognition that Thomas explicates here *participate* in the logic and the effects of the

Fall. Culpable ignorance began *with* Adam and Eve and continues *in* them. But whether we may *identify,* as it were temporally, the *scientia* from which the rest have subtracted, with the *scientia* from which the first fell, is a question for a chapter unwritten.[34]

The next move is to elaborate upon the evacuation of cognition in the absence of faith. Thomas takes up Paul's words "they became empty [*evanuerunt;* RSV has "futile"] in their own thoughts" with the gloss: "In their own thoughts they became empty, insofar as they had trust [*fiduciam*] in themselves, and not in God, ascribing their good to themselves, and not to God, according to the Psalm 11(12):5, [*May the Lord cut off*] our [*flattering*] *lips*" (§129 *in fin.*). Ascribing their good to themselves and not to God is precisely (in the context of the knowledge of God) to claim knowledge of God by nature abstracted from grace; and not to have *fiducia* in God in the context of knowledge is to want to know all things otherwise than by trusting God, or, in a word, as *intelligibilia* rather than *revelabilia.* The passage is in effect another recommendation of the *analogia fidei* for *cognitio vera.* Beside *cognitio vera* we now have *scientia subtracta:* "an insult delivered to God, a skimping of God's glory, that consists...in a refusal of due worship."[35]

It would be a mistake to suppose that since *cognitio* is sometimes less than *scientia, cognitio vera* is on the way to *scientia subtracta,* which is on the way to *scientia integra.* We have already eliminated the possibility of the second move. For *cognitio vera* "induces human beings to the good," whereas *scientia subtracta* is a result and cause of sin. So far from being on a continuum, they point away from each other. *Cognitio vera* participates in the cognition of *faith,* and *scientia subtracta* falls away from trusting God. Within the narrative structure of sin and redemption implicit and explicit in the whole text, *scientia subtracta* participates in the Fall, and *cognitio vera* in the redemptive "gospel grace of Christ." The one points to Adam, the other to Christ.

Meanwhile, few will miss the Lutheran-sounding use of the word *fiducia* to characterize how it is that the Gentiles subtract from God's *scientia.* Thomas makes here unmistakable that any natural cognition of God deserving that name belongs *with fiducia.* Thus: the full natural cognition of God belongs not on the side of Protestant nature but on the side of Protestant grace. On behalf of the natural cognition of God that in Thomas is so called by courtesy when it unnaturally and denaturedly *lacks* grace, no disturbing claims are made.

What follows twice confirms that conclusion. In paragraph §130

Thomas describes the subsequently, culpably ignorant as "lacking the light of wisdom." That is the situation of concrete human beings not joined to God by faith. In paragraph §131 he characterizes them as "ascribing wisdom to themselves by themselves" and as "acting *against* the divine wisdom." He concludes by applying Jeremiah 10:14: "'Every human being is rendered foolish by his or her own wisdom [*scientia*—the Vulgate's word, not Thomas's]'—when, that is, they presume upon it." For *scientia*, according to Preller's rule, is just what human beings cannot presume upon *in divinis*.

At last he sums up the argument we have been tracing throughout these two chapters synoptically rather than playing it out as the order of the text demands. This then is what he and his readers have learned from Paul:

> 139....God is not said to abandon human beings into uncleanness directly, inclining the disposition of a human being toward evil, because God ordains everything to God, as in Prov. 16:4: *The Lord has made everything for the Lord;* but sin is something by aversion from God. Yet indirectly God does lead human beings into sin, in that God justly subtracts the grace by which human beings were being kept from sinning, as someone taking away someone else's prop might be said to cause her fall. And in this way the first sin is the cause of following sins; indeed a following sin is a penalty for the first.
>
> In order for that to be evident it is necessary to know that one sin can be the cause of another indirectly and directly....
>
> Indirectly, to be sure, as the first sin merits the exclusion of grace, which being subtracted, a human being falls into another sin. And thus the first sin is the cause of the second indirectly or by accident, as removing something that prevents it.

I will elaborate on the logic and consequences of that passage in the following chapter, which collects together the conclusions of the Romans Commentary for the natural cognition of God.

What Thomas means by "theologia naturalis"

At the end of the *lectio* Thomas mentions "natural theology" (*In Rom.* 1:25, §145; cf. II–II.94.1) for the first and only time in the passage that we have read. He takes the reference from Augustine (*De civitate Dei* 7.5–7, 12), who has specific ancient philosophers in mind. "Natural theology" also appears in the company of two other Augustinian labels, "civil theology" and "fabular theology," which seem to lack easily identifiable modern

counterparts. The first refers to explicit idol worship such as Thomas interprets Roman civil religion to have involved. The second refers to the theology "that the poets carried on in the theaters." In that company and from
that source, therefore, there is no evidence that Thomas had a general tendency of human religiosity in mind, at which Barth's polemic sometimes
seems to be directed. Neither however is the description offered of natural
theology entirely like the description given of the others. Thomas says
nothing explicit to limit "natural theology" to the specific philosophers
that Augustine had in mind, although certainly they must have counted for
him as paradigm cases. He leaves the description open. As he deploys it in
the text, where it stands last in the *lectio*, he says nothing to exclude the
application of the description where it logically as well as historically fits.
Thus: "The Apostle seems furthermore to touch upon the theology of the
Gentiles in three ways....He touches third upon natural theology, which
the philosophers in the world have practiced, worshiping parts of the world;
and with regard to that he says: *They have worshiped and served the creature more than the Creator.*"

To *explicate* that verse as implicating the natural theologians of the nineteenth and early twentieth centuries as if Thomas had or could have had
them in mind would be to bestow Thomas with prescience. But we may
credit him with the identification of a logical category that we may attempt
to apply as an extension not of his foresight but of his reasoning. Even such
an extension would have to proceed with caution. For most of the natural
theologians of the nineteenth and twentieth centuries thought of themselves as Christian apologists rather than philosophers in the style of the an-
cients. The categories have shifted enough to make application difficult and
arguable. Many of them, if asked to align themselves with some category of
Thomas Aquinas, would probably identify themselves more nearly with the
perceived project of the *Summa* contra *gentiles* than with the Gentiles coun-
tered in the Romans commentary. Indeed that identification happened
enough, at least in the imagination of both Thomists and anti-Thomists,
that Thomas got identified, in reverse, with the natural theology after Kant.

It is enough here to point out what neither Thomists nor anti-Thomists
seemed to realize who made that identification: that Thomas did in fact
possess the resources for developing an entirely different, even *opposed*
category for the evaluation of the post-Kantian apologetic project; he did in
fact possess the resources for developing a dogmatic counter-project like
that of Karl Barth. Had Thomas encountered Barth's opponents, he might
have identified them with the culpably ignorant Gentiles of the Romans

commentary. Whether he would in fact have done so, and whether he would have regarded it as charitable to do so, we cannot know; but he would have had the resources to do so and to have made common cause with Barth. Barth did not see that opening in Thomas. If he had, he may well have considered it his duty, as one who sought always to interpret others *in optimam partem,* to exploit it, and to read Thomas as an ally, as he read Anslem. Whether we must do so is another question. Here it is enough to pose the question of Thomas and Barth where both sides thought the matter closed.

6

Conclusions about the Natural Cognition of God from Thomas's Romans Commentary

How are we then finally to evaluate the natural "knowledge" of God? I take the theologian's license to sum up *thesenhaft*. Some ten conclusions follow. An excursus on the Romans commentary's threefold analysis of faith and its relation to *scientia*, or at least to Aristotelianly demonstrated cognitions, comes at the end of the chapter.

1. There is a paradigmatic use of the natural cognition of God which occurs with fiducial faith (*In* Rom. 1:21, §129) in the context of justice, piety, gratitude, and finally the infused grace of charity (§§1, 106–108, 11, 127). This is the cognition of God that sacred doctrine uses and turns into wine.

2. There is a defective use of the natural cognition of God which occurs without faith in the context of injustice, impiety, ingratitude, and finally the direction of the will away from God. This is the cognition of God that every concrete, existing Gentile[1] seems to have according to the Romans commentary, the cognition of God that cries out for the grace of the gospel of Jesus Christ. Otherwise it is wine into vinegar.

But did we not earlier mention a third, neutral use?

3. The Enlightenment imagines neutral human beings, neither delivered up to injustice, impiety, and ingratitude, nor religious enthusiasts; it imagines human beings who *disengage* their wills from their knowing. Thomas does mention human beings "with no will to believe except on the basis of proof" (II–II.2.10 *ad* 1). Even the love of truth, however, is a movement of the will toward the good. Having no will to believe can, for Thomas, only reflect a flight from the good, an aversion of desire from it. Those rational creatures with no will to believe except on the basis of proof whom Thomas accords more than a mention are already those with no *will* to believe even in the *face* of proof, which becomes a case of intellectual coercion; they are "in some way driven [*coacta*] by the evidence"; they are the demons who believe and tremble (II.II.5.2 *ad* 1). Furthermore, those who debate with *infideles* "not supposing the truth of the faith as

certain," or even *"as if* doubting" commit a sin, although to do so for refut-
ing errors (to the opponent's good) or as practice (to the good of the debating believer who lets herself be corrected) is laudable (II–II.10.7c and *ad* 3).

4. But does Thomas not in fact mount just such a neutral project in the
Summa contra gentiles? Yes and no. He mounts the project, but he does not
complete it. He changes course mid-work. Either he cannot carry it through,
or he intended merely to adopt the *pose* of neutrality, switching later to a
conceptuality incompatible with neutrality, one that anticipates that of the
Summa, which exemplifies the first, paradigmatic use of the natural
knowledge of God. It is not irrational to pursue the latter course, nor is it
cynical. Thomas does not take up the pose of the sincere doubter, so as to
deceive readers about his commitments, but takes up a temporary position,
as a teacher, which he will pull up from behind him like a used ladder.
Thomas begins in the *Summa contra gentiles* with a strategic and temporary, self-consuming division of the truth into two modes. When he moves
them toward coherence, however, he moves the use of the natural cognition of God away from neutrality toward the use that obtains under the
conditions of faith. In so doing he mimics in the academic presentation of
theology what happens in the life of a convert. The coherence of a life is
able to be constructed only in retrospect. Similarly the penultimate coherence possible in this life of arguments, say, for asserting the proposition
"God exists," comes only within sacred doctrine. Thomas merely begins
with a fragment that looks quite different in its final context. Either we
must say that the *Summa contra gentiles* executes its transition to another
genre as an intentional rhetorical trope, one that seeks not to trick but to
sublate, and deliberately turns water into wine; or we must say that
Thomas allows the project of the *Contra gentiles* to fall into a category mistake. If we allow Thomas the charity of the first interpretation, we will see
that the awkwardness of the transition comes from its prospective arrange-
ment: retrospectively it makes sense. The miracle of water into wine
makes sense, after all, only after the fact, when it forms part of a gospel narrative that seeks to tell the story of Jesus. From the standpoint of the water,
if you like, the transition to wine is entirely opaque.[2]

The Enlightenment and its neo-Thomist critics could only imagine a
neutral use of what they took to be straightforward proofs for the existence
of a God univocally understood because they had put themselves into the
position of coming to believe and the logic thereof—rather than the position of belief and its logic—imagining that they had the example of the
Contra gentiles to recommend the first procedure. In so doing they mistook

two things. First, they mistook the project of the beginning of the *Summa contra gentiles* for something that controlled the interpretation of Thomas's entire corpus, including the *Summa theologiae*, because it seemed to accord well with their own project. Perhaps it was all but inevitable that they should do so. But that *Summa* belongs to a manifestly different genre from that of the beginning (at least) of the *Contra gentiles*. Second, they mistook the beginning of the *Contra gentiles* for the whole. But the project was never carried through as it was begun. Either it *mis*carried, or it carried out a project that proved coherent only in the *end*. And it was from that end, and not from that beginning, that the *Summa theologiae* began.

5. The discussion of the natural knowledge of God in its integral form—as objectively trinitarian (*In* Rom. 1:20a, §122, read with §§115 and 117) and as issuing effectively in justice, piety, and gratitude—represents nature as completed and perfected by *grace*. Under conditions of sin, the completion and perfection of nature by grace involve the redemption that comes to the *faithful*.

6. *Cognitio naturalis* is always and everywhere *cognitio naturalis gratia evangelica Christi*: namely an acquaintance of nature by the grace of the gospel of Christ: for *without* the grace of Christ working in advance we would have died outside Eden. But it comes in two forms: "detained" (*In* Rom. 1:18, §§111–112 and 1:21, §§ 127–130) and redeemed.

At I–II.109.1 Thomas affirms that a human being can have a cognition of something true without grace: This does not deny that a human being still lives and knows by the grace of creation, but it affirms that some knowledge is possible without the grace of elevation.[3] We have seen that the two are one grace, one plan of God, broken in its execution by human sin. Thus Thomas's affirmation of cognition "without grace" praises the persistence of God's intention even before its execution. It does not set human knowing apart from God. It affirms what we may call *cognitio naturalis detenta*. Thomas's affirmation does a knowledge that denies the glory of God, and fails to issue in gratitude, the courtesy of calling it by what it has been and might be. In calling it in virtue of what it has been, the affirmation accuses it of failure, and recalls it to its vocation. In so doing, the affirmation refuses to deny the cognition to the *intellect*, just so that it can assign the subtraction to the *will*.

We Gentiles have "subtracted from God's knowledge" (*In* Rom. 1:21, §127) as we have rejected God's aid, so that our knowledge fails to form us as our nature fails to hold us upright. Through injustice and ingratitude we confine ourselves to *cognitio Dei subtracta*, that is, a cognition of God without the ramifications or the full coherence that faith requires, without *fiducia* (§129). That is *because* we have been *a scientia Dei subtrahentes* (§127), i.e., holders of a cognoscitive habit without the deeds and attitudes of charity (*In* Rom. 1:17, §§105–108), like the justice, gratitude, and piety here mentioned. Without the Godward and God-given attitudes like those Thomas finds in Paul (Prologue, §§1–3), of justice, gratitude, and piety, we lose too the cognition's objective trinitarian coherence.

For convenience we can invent technical terms that imitate or keep close to Thomas's language. Call the defective form *"cognitio detenta,"* after the Pauline phrase "they detained the truth in unrighteousness" of Romans 1:18; or *"cognitio subtracta,"* since it results from subtracting from or insulting the power and *scientia* that God possesses, on which it should depend. Call the full form *"cognitio iustitia formata,"* to reflect Thomas's constant preoccupation with justice in this passage (occasioned by Paul's), and to show the parallel to "faith formed by love." Or call it more briefly *"cognitio integra,"* in contrast to *"detenta"* or *"subtracta"*; or *"cognitio evangelica,"* a phrase that appears at paragraph §103 in explication of the *"ex fide in fidem"* passage, since it is the cognition of the *gratia evangelica* that Thomas makes the theme of the entire letter (*In* Rom. 1:16b, §94); or *"cognitio salutifera,"* after the phrase at *In* I Cor. 1:21, §55. Or borrow Thomas's description of what it is supposed to accomplish and call it *"cognitio vera,* which leads human beings to the good" (*In* Rom. 1:18, §112).

7. Thomas says in the Romans commentary that we have the faith of which he speaks only under the condition of trusting God, but note that he does not exclude the possibility of *also* in appropriate cases trusting human reasons and natural signs; only they are *"not yet"* faith if they are all we trust (*In* Rom. 4:3, §327, *ST* II–II.2.2). They are precisely in that sense of "not yet" *preambles.* Contrary to popular belief, preambles are "pre-" not because they are foundational (in the sense of logically prior or more generally accessible), but because they are serviceable (in the sense of standing at sacred doctrine's disposal).[4] They are things that may *become* faith; in that sense, as possible manuductions for the faithful, they precede it; but they need not. And *should* they be taken up into faith, they contribute nothing to it, for faith *properly* so called depends upon nothing else than trusting God. Still, we can distinguish preambles from things that could not be taken up into faith, such as "God is a creature."

The contrast between preambles and articles, within limits, is relative. Some things will never be susceptible of proof. Other things must be susceptible of proof, because the scriptures tell us so reliably. Still other things do not have that status specified. Both preambles and articles come into sacred doctrine under the conditions specified by their lying *sub ratione Dei* or by their status as *revelabilia*. That is, a verbally identical demonstration will function otherwise in the theology that pertains to metaphysics than in the theology that pertains to sacred doctrine, because the context that specifies the use and therefore the meaning of the words will differ. The context proper to sacred doctrine is specified by the formal rationale of trusting God (I.1.3, etc.).

The contrast between preambles and apparently demonstrated articles, or between serviceably and unserviceably demonstrated truths, however, is sharper. At I.46.2 Thomas lists no fewer than *eight* apparently demonstrative arguments for the proposition that the world had a beginning instead of having always existed. Were the presence of a demonstrative argument enough, Thomas would have to consider it a preamble that the world had a beginning. But Thomas knows, as I.1.1 has it, that even demonstrations sometimes turn out to have an "admixture of error." Therefore he does not rely upon them, but upon the Creed. What counts as preamble does not depend upon what science demonstrates: "And this is useful to consider, lest perchance anyone, presuming to demonstrate what is of faith, should adduce insufficient reasons, which would provide material for ridicule among the infidels, finding us believing for such reasons the things that are of faith" (*ST* I.46.2). Since it is the Creed rather than the state of metaphysics that tells Thomas what is demonstrable and what not, he goes on to find errors in each of the demonstrations. He would have had to look for errors in the Five Ways, too—and would also have found them[5]—had revelation not guaranteed that some such ways would work. And the fact that most people today would not consider them to work would bother Thomas, would "provide material for ridicule" among the cultured despisers, only if Thomas's argument in I.2.3 actually depended upon the cogency of the demonstrations.

But it does not. Like the argument in I.46.2, it depends formally on trusting what God says (I.1.8), for I.2.3 in Romans, for I.46.2 in the creed. In both places we have apparently valid demonstrations. In both cases Thomas is prepared in principle and in advance to find the demonstrations mistaken. In both cases we nowadays tend to find them mistaken. The fact that Thomas tends to find one set mistaken and another set not has to do not with the contingent state of human learning, but with the authority of scripture, when well interpreted, to judge it (I.1.6 *ad* 2). Only if he judges human learning capable—yes in the case of whether God exists, no in the case of whether the world had a beginning—does he then use it "as an architect uses builders, a citizen a soldier" for the "easier leading by the hand" (*manuductio*) of our defective intellects (I.1.6 *ad* 2). That then is the difference between demonstrations that serve as preambles and those that do not: sacred doctrine's formal rationale tells Thomas which secular arguments overlapping with sacred doctrine's matter will prove serviceable and which not. Preambles do not prove their own serviceability; that depends on how sacred doctrine presses them into service.

The interpretation of preambles in terms of serviceability, or in Thomas's terms, as manuductions, gives us no reason to deny that if a preamble is Aristotelianly demonstrated *cognitio*, then it must count in some non-equivocal sense as *scientia*. It counts as *scientia* in metaphysics, for example. And just if our use of the word "*scientia*" is not to equivocate, then there must be some continuity between the scientific character of preambles in metaphysics and some scientific character in sacred doctrine, even if they are strictly extraneous to it (*ST* I.1.8). Otherwise scientific character fades in and out according to discipline, one sealed hermetically off from another. Then not only theology, but all sciences would be fideistic.

The difference between the current interpretation of the status of preambles in the *Summa* and other possible interpretations is that rival interpretations tend to articulate the continuity of scientific character from the bottom up. For many of them, preambles are the paradigms of demonstration which sacred doctrine must match. According to the interpretation defended here, however, the order is reversed. The paradigm of demonstration is the "demonstration of the Father" (*ST* I.42.6 *ad* 2), Jesus Christ, "who, as a human being, is the 'demonstration' [*via*] stretched out for us into God" (*ST* I, proem. to q. 2). According to the philosophy of science implicit in the *Summa*, it is other scientific disciplines that mimic *that*. The scientific character of other, Aristotelian demonstrations comes from the top down; to call Aristotelian and christoform arguments both "demonstrations" and both "scientific" is not equivocal, according to sacred doctrine, just because Aristotelian demonstrations too participate in the Logos by analogy.

The "other" *viae*—the *quinque viae*—do not represent the *paradigm* of demonstration. Rather Thomas's theological appropriation of the Five Ways saves our penultimate and provisional demonstrations from equivocity, from not counting as demonstrations after all. The appropriation saves our *cognitio subtracta*, the cognition we have generally and for the most part, which was enough for Aristotle, but which Thomas relegates to the theology that belongs to metaphysics. The appropriation saves the Five Ways by taking them up into the realm of *revelabilia*, in which, through God-bestowed faith, they are joined with the first truth they cannot otherwise reach.

The Five Ways are caused to assert the unGod-forsakenness of nature under conditions short of the will's assent to God. They are caused to assert the unGod-forsakenness of nature even in conditions of a will's dissent from God. In so doing they save Paul's usage; they save *cognitio subtracta*. And in so doing they claim the world for the realm of *revelabilia*. The point is not that Aristotle is outside the realm of the *revelata:* he led by the hand into the world of *revelabilia*.

The second form of *cognitio naturalis gratia evangelica Christi* is what we have been calling *cognitio integra*. This is what Thomas has in mind when he abbreviates the long form as *"cognitio evangelica."* This paradigm form of human cognition of God comes in several forms, among them *fides.*[6]

8. Since we have seen that the *cognitio Dei* functions only in the presence of grace, we know something about the conditions under which we can have an Aristotelian science whose subject is God. For an Aristotelian science requires that propositions be put in order so as to deliver *effective* knowledge—"true cognition, which leads human beings to the good" (*In* Rom. 1:18, §122). For Aristotle, a science *just is* that structuring of propositions—as in demonstrations—to render the mind formed or structured in accord with the form or structure of reality. For sacred doctrine, Aristotelian science requires some wrenching.

For it has been the further point of Thomas's entire exposition of Romans 1—and indeed of the eleven following chapters that will carry him to chapter 12—to explicate the necessity and sufficiency, for the integral and effective knowledge of God, the *evangelica gratia Christi*. "Evangelica gratia Christi" specifies the conditions under which Thomas thinks human beings can, through restoration and elevation of their natures, enjoy effective *cognitio Dei*. Thus he has defined the discipline, moral and intellectual, of what Aristotle calls *scientia*, even the virtues, moral and intellectual, of that ordered series of mental acts. So Thomas has defined sacred doctrine as *scientia* according to the conditions under which alone sacred doctrine could count as a science by the lights of Aristotle: he causes sacred doctrine to follow from Revelation, a form from outside the world, as he causes other Aristotelian sciences to follow from revelations or forms in the world. He has gotten the *scientia* and the knowers (recognizers, never called *scientes*) back together again as well as he might, that the doctrine of creation had put asunder. He has done so under the power, the *virtus*, or the revelation of the *evangelica gratia Christi*, since only thus could it be effective. At the same time Thomas has defined sacred doctrine as *scientia* according to the conditions under which alone it could retain its integrity as sacred doctrine. Once again Thomas causes Aristotle's notion of a science to serve sacred doctrine and not the other way around. For Thomas has once again set things up so that the more scientific it is, the more sacred doctrine looks to the gospel of Christ. Taking the Aristotelian concept of science captive to Christ, as Summa 1.1.8 deploys 2 Corinthians 10:5, requires the following further distinction.

9. Since Aristotle's language of *scientia* as of things seen and the Bible's language of faith as of things not seen (II–II.4.1) makes a division, then when the natural cognition of God becomes effective by grace, its effectiveness belongs on the side of faith, not on the side of *scientia*. For it is by faith that we are united to God, and faith that motivates and structures (infuses and habituates) change in the human soul. That is the logic of Thomas's Romans Commentary.

In Part I, I read the first question of the *Summa* to give the following *account* of that logic. It is not *because* of the account in the *Summa* that things go that way in the Romans commentary; it is *because* of the account in Paul. *Like* Aristotle Thomas maintains a secondary and penultimate distinction between the structured discipline (like German *Wissenschaft*) and the structured habit (like German *Erkenntnis*) of effective cognition, and *unlike* Aristotle Thomas introduces, in sacred doctrine, a terminological distinction for two reasons. 1) The disciplined or scientific character of sacred doctrine is *borrowed* by revelation from the *scientia* enjoyed by God and the blessed: it does not inhere in the human intellect in this life. The work of the theory of subalternation is to claim the title *"scientia"* for a discipline that cannot, of its *own* habit, so change the soul as to save it, that cannot, in short, reach its purpose. Meanwhile (2) the habitual or soul-structuring character of the believer is not gained from studying the science of sacred doctrine, since its subject lies outside the realm of the humanly comprehensible; the habit is *infused*. Because sacred doctrine seeks a source of intelligibility for the world that lies outside the world, and a source of intelligibility for the mind that lies beyond its powers, its real and mental instantiations remain apart, its discipline borrowed, its habit infused. Thus Thomas must retain *"scientia"* for the structuring of the discipline, in virtue of the reliability of the reality of revelation, and *"fides"* for the structuring of the soul, in virtue of the gratuity of salvation. The discipline deserves the title of "science" by leaning upon the science of God and the blessed (I.1.2), but the habit is denied the title of science because sacred doctrine is a science unable to operate *by itself* to structure the soul; its operating comes *by faith*, and even so operation is denied (by the invention of the word "cooperation") to faith, since faith is a movement of the soul by God (I–II.111.2).

So too demonstration differs in this structuring of cognition. Jesus Christ structures the discipline by being himself the real light, the new feature of reality, that demands a new real science; Jesus Christ (as a human being) is himself the primary demonstration in the proemium to Question 2, and he is himself the primary state of affairs to which other states of affairs point forward and backward according to the theory of scripture as sacred doctrine's authority at the end of Question 1. At the same time Jesus Christ structures the soul by dwelling within it. The intellectual counterpart of that indwelling, by which God unites us to God precisely as One unknown, is not *scientia* but faith. Thus even as we study the *scientia* of sacred doctrine we become not its scientists but its believers. Thus the necessity and sole effectiveness of the *gratia evangelica Christi* in the Romans commentary. The Aristotelian structure of the soul does accompany faith, and the Aristotelian structure of the discipline does belong to sacred doctrine: both arise from the same structure of reality understood as the real first principle of an Aristotelian science. And the connection therefore between the real first principle and the structures of discipline and habit that follow from it is rightly called a demonstration. But that first principle and its demonstration, both in the extramental discipline and in the intramental habit, are both Jesus Christ. Sacred doctrine assumes metaphysics into christology.

Thomas is not kidding when he distinguishes the formality of the theology that belongs to metaphysics from the theology that belongs to sacred doctrine. And yet here again the appellation of Aristotelian science is justified for sacred doctrine just by reference to Jesus Christ. For only by reference to Jesus Christ does sacred doctrine keep together the structures that come together in Aristotelian *epistêmê*: the structure of reality, the structure of the academic discipline, and the structure of the soul to be formed in accord with the end of inquiry and its full possession, the *scientia beatorum*, or the vision of God.

Thus it is no accident, and no expression of mere pious sentiment that Thomas calls the humanity of Christ *via* and *demonstratio*. Those words most fittingly portray the figure of science put at sacred doctrine's disposal. They represent the language appropriate when sacred doctrine trains philosophy seriously as *ancilla theologiae*. They do not merely turn water into wine, they make argument flesh.

That is the logic of Questions 1 and 2, as partially confirmed by the commentary on Romans, of the *Summa's Prima Pars* in sequence.

Excursus: The Romans Commentary
and the threefold division of faith

We can also be more systematic about those conclusions. In the Romans commentary the account of integral, formed natural cognition of God as objectively trinitarian and issuing in justice, piety, and gratitude seems to involve three elements: 1) a proposition that has the *possibility* of conforming to reality—i.e., it is assimilable to *cognitio integra* or *vera*—if the mind that holds it does so under these additional conditions: 2) conditions of coherence, as with other propositions about, say, the Trinity; and 3) conditions of the will, as attitudes of gratitude, piety, and justice.

Bruce Marshall has elegantly worked out Thomas's threefold analysis of faith in his article, "Aquinas as Postliberal Theologian."[7] My arguments reach similar conclusions somewhat differently. Besides interpreting the Romans commentary, their purpose is to contribute in two ways to the support of the view he espouses: 1) to show that Thomas implies and deploys the view ascribed to him also in a *sustained* section of biblical commentary where he may be read (as a matter of textual if not intellectual-historical argument) as implicitly developing it from *Paul*, and 2) to adduce an argument from Thomas's analysis of a human act in clarification of the matter of faith versus *scientia*, or the cognition of God demonstrated in Aristotelian manner.

That threefold division, by which we sum up Thomas's actual interpretive practice in following Paul over an extended argument, actually emerges later in the Romans commentary in programmatic remarks about the way that cognitive habits work in general among the faithful, and reappears in the *Summa*'s tractate on faith (II–II.2.2 *ad* 3). Here we will look at the distinction that Thomas presents at *In* Romans 4:3 (§327) as rising to thematic status out of his reflection upon Paul. There he says that the cognition of faith has three elements (which correspond to the three we have observed actually at work in the exposition of Romans 1), which Thomas calls *credere Deum*, *credere Deo*, and *credere in Deum*. Corresponding aspects qualify the ascription of *cognitio Dei* to all human minds, faithful and unfaithful.

At Romans 4:3, the Vulgate has Paul say, "For what does the scripture say? 'Abraham believed God, and it was reckoned to him as righteousness [Gen. 15:6].'" Paul's use of the verse gives Thomas an opportunity to consider the cognitive conditions accompanying salvation, the question he considered at the end of Romans 1. He comments:

> 327. . . . Now it must be considered that the justice that God counts as paid [*scriptam*] [Paul] has represented not as some exterior work, but as the interior faith of the heart, which God alone sees. For since the act of faith is said to be threefold, namely, *to believe that God exists, to believe God,* and *to believe into God* [*credere Deum, Deo, et in Deum*] he has put down the act which of trusting God [*credere Deo*], which is more properly the act of faith, showing its species. For to believe in God [*in Deum,* literally "into God"] shows how faith is ordered to its end, which is by charity; for to believe in God is, believing, to go into God [*credendo in Deum ire*], which charity causes. And from that follows faith's species.
>
> Now to believe that God exists shows the matter of faith, according to which it is a theological virtue, having God for its object. And therefore this act does not yet attain to the species of faith, since if anyone should believe that God exists by any human reasons and natural signs, that one is not yet said to have faith, but only when he or she believes for this reason, that it is said by God, which is designated by what is called *credere Deo,* trusting God; and from this is faith specified, as also whatever cognoscitive habit by reason according to which it assents to anything. For someone having the habit of *scientia* is inclined by a different reason to assent, namely by a demonstration, and someone having the habit of opinion is inclined by another reason, namely by a dialectical syllogism [inductive argument].[8]

Thomas actually has two distinct sets of threefold distinctions in play. Among cognitive habits he distinguishes faith, *scientia,* and opinion. For the cognitive habit under discussion he goes on to distinguish three aspects, *credere Deum, credere Deo,* and *credere in Deum.* A similar analysis also applies, the exposition of Romans 1 suggests, to the other cognitive habits. First let us turn to the analysis of faith. Later we will turn to the possibility or impossibility of overlap between faith and *scientia.* Or, more precisely: between faith and Aristotelianly demonstrated propositions that may or may not count as *scientia* under the canons specific to the *scientia* of sacred doctrine.

    A. In the phrase *"credere Deum,"* the accusative abbreviates an accusative-plus-infinitive clause. The context usually suggests *credere Deum esse,* "to believe that God exists." The grammar also permits *credere Deum esse x, y, z,* "to believe that God is something or other," or even *credere Deum facere x, y, z,* "to believe that God does something or other."

For the context of the natural cognition of God that Paul defends the phrase would seem to take the most obvious completion, "that God exists." Yet since in its integral form the natural cognition of God also by grace 1) coheres with trinitarian statements and 2) issues in justice, piety, and gratitude, it makes sense to hold open the other possibilities. Furthermore, the analysis purports to be general about the act of faith. For that reason too, other completions of accusative-plus-infinitive construction will be possible and necessary. The grammatical form of the accusative serves therefore as a placeholder for an infinite series of propositions p about the subject of the abbreviated clause, God.

We may regard *credere Deum* as a function that picks out the propositional element from the Creed. Since it uses the form "*Credo in unum Deum,...,*" the Creed verbally combines two elements (*credere Deum* and *credere in Deum*) that Thomas wants here, for purposes of analysis, to distinguish; but it goes on to add a long series of appositional accusatives that identify the God "into whom," as Thomas has put it, the believer "goes," and the accusatives in apposition have propositional force. So we may imagine an integral "*credere Deum*," or "belief that God..." as abbreviating completions like this: Belief that God is one, that God is Creator of heaven and earth, that God has for us human beings and for our salvation descended from heaven, that God has become incarnate and has been made human, and so on, mimicking the Creed—all of which clauses are statable in Latin in accusative-with-infinitive constructions of the form "*credere Deum esse....*"[9] Thus Thomas calls *credere Deum* the whole *materia fidei*, as the passage goes on to say.[10]

B. Thomas calls *credere Deo* faith's "proper act." By that he means two things. Most broadly he means the existential attitude of trusting God. We have seen that at Romans 1:21 (§129) Thomas used the word "*fiducia*" to describe that attitude. In that he seems to agree with the position the Reformers would take up in following Paul to see faith as primarily the name for the way in which by grace God leans the will upon none other than God. It is by this God-given leaning upon God that human beings come to desire God as their good and seek God as their end; it is thus, that is, that the promise of the *praecognitum finis*, the revelation of the gospel, comes to take effect in us, and God sets us on the way to becoming God's friends. The relation of this trust to the revelation of God's designs for us brings us to the second, narrower meaning of *credere Deo*. Trusting God also involves trusting what God says, namely in the scriptures. Thus it is that the *quaestio* that begins with the *praecognitum finis* (I.1.1) must end with articles on the interpretation of the scriptures (I.1.9 and 10). Both senses come into play in the passage we have been considering. Abraham trusts God (broader sense), and Paul invites us to trust the scriptures where Abraham's trust is written (narrower sense).

We find confirmation in Thomas's comments on 1 Corinthians 1:21 (§55 *in fin.*), where Romans 1:20 gets mentioned again. The verse runs, "For since, in the wisdom of God, the world did not know God through wisdom, it pleased God through the folly of what we preach to save those who believe." There Romans 1:20 is taken to represent the instruction of the human being by God as teacher—so that *credere Deo* (broader sense) is in order—by means of created things not trusted alone. The human being in such a case is said to hear God's words (*credere Deo*, narrower sense). But those who trusted in created things alone were accounted ignorant. The commentary continues with a summary of the argument appearing in Romans, and ending with a reference to a salvation-bearing cognition, "*cognitio salutifera*," comparable to what I have been calling "*cognitio integra*" or "*vera*."[11]

Thus too we saw Thomas say that Paul's condemnation applied to the "*philosophi in mundo*," because they "worshiped and served the creature rather than the Creator": because, that is, *fiducia* or *credere Deo* was lacking.

Credere Deo in the sense of trusting God as teacher is necessary also in another way. It requires above all trusting God in the description of the object of faith, as *revelabilia*, in the description, that is, of the human mental function *credere Deum*. Therefore Thomas follows Hebrews in characterizing the object of faith as "argument of things not appearing" (II–II.1.4 *s.c.*, citing Heb. 11:1). And precisely because faith is thus of things not seen, it must always return to trusting God. That has the result not of diminishing but of protecting the integrity of sacred doctrine as "single science" (I.1.3), its dignity as having its certainty "from the light of the divine *scientia*, which is not able to deceive" (I.1.5), its wisdom as considering only the highest cause (I.1.6), its focus upon all things "*sub ratione Dei*" (I.1.7), its argumentative character as relying on God's authority (I.1.8), its characteristic use of scripture (I.1.9 and 10), and its reliance upon revelation as upon the first principles of a science, that is, as Corbin would put it, for its very *scientificité* (I.1.1 and 2).

We saw Thomas say that *credere Deum* is effective "only when one believes for this reason, that it [or what] has been said by God, because by this is designated what is said by believing God." Thus in the Five Ways the reason for God's existence given in the *sed contra* (I.2.2) is God's own "I am" of Exodus 3:14. For sacred doctrine's cognitive habit of God "believes God," namely "what has been said by God," and that is the clue that establishes the status of the *credere Deum* that follows.

c. In the 1 Corinthians as in the Romans commentary Thomas has an account of how human beings passed from *credere Deum* under the conditions of *credere Deo* to *credere Deum* under the conditions of "to worship and serve the creature rather than the Creator," from the integral to the defective cognition of God. That account comes under the head of *credere in Deum. Credere in Deum*, we saw, means "to go into God," or to undergo the process of elevation toward friendship with God, to be sanctified. It means, in a word, love, as Thomas said: "To believe into God demonstrates the order of [any] faith to the faith that is [formed] through charity." Without love of God by the will, trust of God by the intellect will fail. It lacks a structure, a form, to motivate it and keep it in order, to keep it upright. Structureless it collapses. Nature cannot even lean upon grace by its own power; grace must *attract* it, since "none comes to the Father except whom the Father shall draw";[12] and the being-attracted is love. The attraction once withdrawn, the trust fails upon which the integrity, the salvation-bearing capacity, of the cognition of God depends. That unformed faith is still called faith and unformed cognitions of God still cognitions happens by the sort of courtesy that is grace, by which Thomas marks the persistence of God's will to elevate even the fallen. Like unformed faith, unformed cognition in general does not refer to a cognition that of its own power built up well-formed propositions about God (*credere Deum*) in the right linguistic context of others supported by God's authority (*credere Deo*). Since the right linguistic context gets established by trusting God existentially, which depends upon love, such an upbuilding could not happen in love's absence. Rather in both cases the unformed version represents, if Pesch is right,[13] a *falling away* from the integral version.

That falling away corresponds to the movement of Thomas in his commentary upon Romans 1, who insists that the Gentiles subtracted from and detained the cognition of God. *Credere Deo* exists in the mind only as a result of *credere in Deum* in the will, even if the *credere Deo* is only left behind by a *credere in Deum* that has since departed. That is why formed and unformed faith must be "continuously the same" habit (*"idem numero"*): the unformed faith *persists*, habitual in the bad sense of the word—lingering and unmotivated—after the God-given initiative has departed. Unformed faith could not be discontinuous, for then it could reappear without the explanation of previously existing love in the heart and trust in the mind that alone make sense of its continued if empty existence. Its continuous identity asserts its left-over-ness.

Now for a preliminary summing up: Since cognitive habits come in three forms, faith, *scientia*, and opinion, the *cognitio* of the Gentiles could belong to any of those three species. For it to be effective *cognitio*, the *cognitio salutifera* of the commentary on 1 Corinthians 1:21 (§55) and the *cognitio evangelica* of the commentary on Romans, it must belong in the use- and meaning-defining context of other, often surprising propositions specified by *credere Deo*, such as the one we saw early on in Romans, "salvation is from the Jews." That follows from a whole series of remarks in the Romans commentary: the necessity that *cognitio Dei* be describable as *evangelica gratia Christi*, that it involve *fiducia*, and that its integral form be describable as trinitarian. In order for the mind to trust God in that way, *credere in Deum*, God's drawing the human being by love to the good in God, must exist or have existed in the heart, as follows from Thomas's repeated assertions that effective *cognitio Dei* involves justice, gratitude, and piety. The happenstance that a proposition held in a mind moved by such a heart also has an Aristotelian demonstration for its assertibility does nothing to change those conditions. Indeed, if the believer should love and embrace such a demonstration, it would add to the merit of believing (II–II.2.10c and *ad* 2). But that the demonstrable proposition makes salvific sense—or begins to succeed in conforming the soul to reality— only in the *presence* of faith (*credere Deo*); and that it can have arisen with that sense only as a *result* of faith (*credere in Deum*) does not *quite* mean that it belongs to the *species* of faith (*credere Deo* again).

That inconclusive result brings us to the relation of faith and *scientia*. In different places, Thomas presents three ways of describing the matter, two of which appear, at least, to oppose one another. a) The *species* of the act depends upon the reason (*ratio*) for believing. That is the position that the Romans commentary asserts (§327). b) The *terminus* of the act depends upon the *terminus* of the action, that is, the way in which the object puts a temporary or permanent stop to the activity of the mind regarding it. After *scientia*, that is, the mind has no further place to go (an interpretation of II–II.1.5). So *scientia* diminishes the reason (*ratio*) for but not the merit of believing (II–II.2.10 *ad* 2). c) The *habit* exercised *"diversifies"* the act into two species (I–II.54.2, II–II.1.4). Two further considerations will try to reconcile those possibilities: a short exposition of Thomas's analysis of a human act, and the example of doubting Thomas, who "saw and believed."

A human act involves that which is peculiarly human, namely the ability to order actions toward an end. A human act instantiates human freedom, always incipiently or deeply habitual. A human act is the intelligible behavior of a free *agent*, it is, literally, something-having-been-(intelligibly)-done, and we explicate intelligibility of acts by supplying them with intentions (*fines*).[14] An action, on the other hand, is an exterior or interior movement considered as the product of an act; it is a making. The same action (running) may participate in any number of different human acts, and a human act of the same species may involve different actions (I–II.18.7 *ad* 1, quoted below). Acts are always susceptible of moral evaluation (whether an instance of running was to save a life); actions are susceptible of technical analysis (whether the running was fast). The opposite of "action" is "something undergone" (*passio*); the opposite of "act" is "something involuntary."

In the evaluation of human acts, therefore, Thomas first considers what renders human acts involuntary, in which case agency is itself vitiated (I–II.6). For acts properly so called, he considers the circumstances (I–II.7). There we learn that the most important consideration in the analysis of an act is its *end* (*finis*), and not, as in civil law, the thing which is done: "The principal one of all the circumstances is the one that connects the act with the end, namely *for what purpose*; the second, on the other hand, is the one that touches the very substance of the act, that is *what one did*." The analysis applies even when the end and the thing done seem not to cohere: "The end, even if it does not have to do with the substance of the act, is nevertheless the principal (*principalissima*) cause of the act, insofar as it moves [the agent] to thing to be done. Hence too a moral act has its species most of all from the end" (I–II.74 *ad* 2).

Just in case that should remain unclear, Thomas asks whether the species which is from the end is contained under the species which is from the object, or vice versa. That is directly relevant to the question at issue. For we may put the question like this: In the case of an Aristotelian demonstration of something that is of faith, we seem to have an object (*credere Deum*), which according to II–II.1.5 is clearly an instance of Aristotelian *scientia* in an Aristotelian context, that differs from its end, which in the relevant case is clearly love and trust toward God (*credere in Deum* and *credere Deo*). In the Aristotelian context the end would be different, namely the investigation of things as such, not of their relation to God. The analysis of an act considers a more mundane case in which the object and the end do not cohere in the ordinary way, one in which the agent steals in order to commit adultery (I–II.18.7). Does the act count as adultery or theft?[15]

"According to its substance, nothing can be in two species, of which one is not ordered under another." Thus it is that the same person cannot have both *fides* and *scientia* of the same thing—according to the substance, the *quid fecit* of the act. "But according to those things which are added (*adveniunt*) to the thing, something can be contained under diverse species." The example that follows specifies different formal rationales—color and odor—that differentiate the considerations of things in somewhat the same way as Thomas's differentiation of the theology that pertains to metaphysics from the theology that pertains to sacred doctrine. "And similarly an act which according to its substance is in one natural species [say an act of knowing], can belong to two species according to supervening *moral* conditions" (I–II.18.7 *ad* 2). So the supervening moral conditions (*credere Deo* and *in Deum*) do specify the *act*, even when other conditions (those of the theology that pertains to metaphysics) might cohere with the object of the act so as *not* to differentiate its species. Thus the species of an act that comes from the end does govern the species of an act that comes from its object, and not the reverse. In that respect, metaphysics in sacred doctrine counts as faith, not *scientia*, since faith specifies the end of the act even when *scientia* specifies the terminus.

The person who steals in order to commit adultery perpetrates "two counts of malice in one act." The two results—*"duas malitias,"* two deeds done or *quid fecit*, two *termini*—are adultery and theft. But the one *act* of the agent is adultery. Or, put another way, the agent counts as an adulterer rather than a thief. To call the person a thief would be misleading in terms of getting the moral species wrong, even though he or she had committed a theft. Similarly, the one who demonstrates a preamble gets two results, does two *quid fecit*, reaches two *termini*, in a singular act. The two results or *quid fecit* are delight and *scientia*. But the one *act* of the agent is faith, which takes delight in its exercise. It would be misleading in terms of moral species to characterize the demonstrator as a knower, even though she has *scientia*. The demonstrator is better characterized as a believer.

An objection might proceed as follows. A human act is not only a voluntary but also a rational act, for reason has to tell the will enough to choose what to do, "whence even the free will is said to be 'a faculty of will *and* of reason'."[16] Now to demonstrate something is a human act of the intellect alone, quite apart from reference to the will, and comprises an exception to the notion that the *will's* end specifies the species of an act. The intellect

has its own end, namely the truth, that gives its acts a relative independence from those of the will. The reading offered of Thomas on acts makes
acts of reason merely instrumental to the will and becomes therefore too
voluntarist.

Answer: the activity of reason does supply its own end to reasoning in
the realm of metaphysics; there the will too reaches its end in demonstration. But the end, even love of truth, remains in the will, for there is a sense
in which the intellect acting in abstraction from the will operates involuntarily. With regard to the exercise of the act (*"exercitum actus"*), the act of
the intellect can always be commanded (*"imperari"*), "as when it is indicated to someone that she pay attention, and use her reason." In another
way the act of reason may be beyond our power because we simply are not
able to understand the thing considered. And in still another way the act of
reason lies beyond our power "when it assents to what it apprehends." The
first sense, that of commanding the exercise of reason, is that in which
Thomas finds merit in the student of sacred doctrine, as seeking a demonstration to elaborate what she adheres to with certainty on faith. But that
command is the command of grace moving the heart to love and the mind
to trust God, rather than the evidence of signs for its own sake. As for the
evidence of signs itself, the third way of considering the act of reason applies: "Assent to or dissent from such things is not in our power, but in the
order of nature. And therefore, properly speaking, neither does it lie under
our command" (I–II.17.6). For "the intellect is moved to its object *out of
necessity*" (I–II.10.2 obj. 2, emphasis added). That is the sense in which
Thomas must say that *scientia* diminishes the *ratio fidei*. It does not
change the reason *for* adherence, the motive or end (*finis*), only the reason
by which adherence takes place, which is accidental to whether the intellect apprehends something that causes its assent.

Even though Thomas wants to recognize the peculiarly human function
of reasoning and continues to call the operation of reason an act, in the third
case its motion is reduced to the category of action, a making abstracted
from the will. (He needs to call it human because it gives the will enough to
act *on*.)

The conclusion of the demonstration marks a stopping place for the
human agent in at least four distinct senses.

First, if the reason has been able to apprehend the demonstration in its
cogency, it reaches a stopping place in the sense of something to which it
must assent by necessity as apprehended. That sort of stopping by necessity
is the terminus of an action, not the *finis* of an act. It is as if I am eager to

press on *past* a certain milepost and find the milepost closer than expected. I have not desired the milepost moved, but I embrace it when I meet it, and my focus (*ratio*) remains chiefly beyond it, although the milepost passed passes out of it. The thing demonstrated drops behind me and therefore out of my horizon (*ratio* again).[17] It is in that sense that the *ratio* of faith diminishes. We do not intend to terminate our action (running to this milepost, demonstrating this proposition); we intend to perfect our acts. In *this* case, *scientia* terminates an operation, *fides* perfects an act—and the termination of an action is accidental to the perfection of an act.

Second, division of action and act is more relative than the metaphor implies, since acts are composed of actions, and actions take their intelligibility from acts. In metaphysics the action of demonstrating would have been commanded by the will as a separate act that would also reach its *finis* coterminously there—the mile- and goalpost would be one. To be sure, Thomas does supply, if not Aristotelian demonstrations, at least spaces where they might appear. He does so in the office of the "teacher of Catholic truth" of the Prologue to the *Summa*, as testimony to that persistence of God's intention that we call nature. It is precisely such a witness that "adds to the merit of believing," because it treats human powers not as taken for granted but as a gift in the movement from grace to grace. That is why they appear as provoking God's wrath and inviting God's compassion—because they are places in which God's sustaining will has already invested itself.

Third, in sacred doctrine the action of demonstrating as commanded by the will reaches a penultimate resting place, a temporary *finis* that is *instrumental* to the love and trust of God exhibited in the whole articulation of sacred doctrine as *scientia* as the discipline of interpreting the scriptures. But the will's real *finis* is *credere in Deum*, which definitively places the act—the act of an integral human agent rather than as an operation of the faculty of reason alone—under the species of faith. "For a movement does not receive its species from that which is its terminus by accident, but only from that which is its terminus in itself"—which for the will is a moral end. "For moral ends (*fines*) are accidental to natural things, and conversely the account of the natural end is accidental to the moral. And therefore nothing prevents acts that are the same according to their natural species to be diverse according to their moral species" (I–II.1.3 *ad* 3 *in fin.*).

Hence when Thomas says that the same person may not have faith and *scientia* of the same thing, he distinguishes *actiones* of the intellect according to their natural species, not *actus* of the will according to their moral species. He distinguishes *termini* not *fines*. And when he says that demonstration may add to the merit of believing and that the theology that pertains to metaphysics differs from the theology that pertains to sacred doctrine, he distinguishes *actus* of the will according to their moral species. *Scientia* names the terminus of an action, *fides* the motive of an act.

Fourth, the act of reason terminates in the conclusion of a demonstration also in the sense of reaching a dead end. It reaches only what people call "God." Since it cannot say (and even faith cannot say) what God is (*In* Rom. 1:19, §114 *in med.*; I.2.1), it warrants the assertion of the existence of something (or non-thing) of which it knows not what it is. It ends in a certain *je ne sais quoi*. In this sense the metaphor of milepost and goalpost completely breaks down. For neither does faith reach a cognition of God's essence. And, as we saw before, "faith is not merely a further extension of or addition to conceptual knowledge. For this reason, Aquinas can say that faith *perfects* [not "terminates"] reason. Faith is a perfection precisely because it is *not* merely an extension (and an incomplete extension at that) of the natural powers of the intellect. Faith perfects the language of natural reason by enabling it to do what it cannot do on its own—point toward the God of faith. . . . And that 'pointing toward' is not even in the light of faith an intelligible 'terminating in'—God is not rendered intelligible even by faith."[18]

An example will complete the account.

The human being is in the position of the doubting Thomas of II–II.1.4 obj. 1 and *ad* 1. Doubting Thomas, says Aquinas (quoting Gregory), "saw one thing and believed another. He saw the human being and, believing, confessed God, as he said, my Lord and my God." The *argumentum* was diminished with regard to whether the human being before him was Jesus, and increased with regard to whether the human being before him was God. He gained vision of the one and faith of the other. Similarly when a believer demonstrates (say) the existence of God, the act, habit, and merit of faith remain or are increased. The *ratio* or content of faith diminishes only in one respect. For the god that stands at the end of one of the Five Ways is *not yet* (the "*nondum*" of *In* Rom. 4:1) the God of Christian faith just because a demonstration works: it is as if the demonstrator should say, in a poor imitation of Thomas: "my prime mover and my God." Or, since the Five Ways all end as linguistic remarks like "and this everyone calls God," it is as if the believing demonstrator said "my 'God' and my God." Here too we see one thing and believe another. It is just so that the objects of faith and *scientia* are different: so that we should never mistake *scientia* for faith. They remain distinct, even when propositions previously taken on faith get

proved, by a sort of cognitive division. Under those circumstances it is misleading to say that *scientia* replaces faith or that faith is transmuted into
scientia. The act of faith, it bears repeating, remains; only the division has
focused it a little more intently upon God.

To say with Wolterstorff that the believer transmutes faith into sight[19]
makes it sound as if the believer has a rival intention to believe on the basis
of natural signs and human reasons even when she believes God with all
the good will in the world. What is disturbing about that formulation is
that it contemplates precisely a change in the intention of the act, so that
not even the same habit is instantiated. And it flies in the face of the demand that demonstration add to the merit of believing precisely when "believing" specifies the act. Rather it is the object, or perhaps better, the *focus*
of the act, the same, uni-intentional act, that changes.

Earlier in the Romans commentary we saw Thomas talk about one
transformation from faith into sight, namely into the sight of the beatific
vision, which Wolterstorff, following some strains in Thomas, does want to
assimilate to *scientia*.[20] But the Romans commentary, cognizant of the
sameness of the act's intention, characterized the movement as "from present faith to future faith" (§103 *in fin.*): faith on both sides, faith into faith,
because the intention making for adherence, and therefore the act's species,
remains invariably the same. The characterization "from faith into *scientia*" is correct only as regards the *argumentum*. As a characterization of the
believer it is strictly false. For as a characterization of the *believer* it is a
characterization of the *agent*, and therefore of faith as act and not as *enun-
tiabilium* or proposition. It is no part of the *believer's* project as an *agent* to
turn her *act* of faith into an *act* of *scientia*, by changing the *reasons* for belief. That would be to *withdraw* confidence in the first truth and *repose* it
in the evidence of signs, and *such* a project Thomas could only regard as
morally dangerous (II–II.10.7) and even demonizing (II–II.2.2 *ad* 2). Precisely
however if the act remains the *same*, Thomas can allow some of the *ratio* of
faith to "diminish" into *scientia*, in order, like doubting Thomas, that love
of God and the act of faith may be strengthened and the *ratio* of faith be focused, its mystery picked out, and the God to whom we are joined in this
life by faith specified as precisely *outside* the control of our minds, that is,
as One *Unknown* (I.12.13).

One way of describing what happens when doubting Thomas says "my
Lord and my God" in Aquinas's explication is that the doubter has diversified his cognitive habits. The objection imagines that the doubter sees and
believes the same thing in the same way, but the answer distinguishes two

habits according as he considers the body of Jesus (one physical object) in two ways (as human and as also divine). We may say that the one preceding cognitive habit, *fides*, got *diversified* at that point into *two* habits, one for each of the *rationes formales* under which the doubter took the matter. The twin twins the habits. And he is a good example for it, since as a twin doubting Thomas may have been sensitive to being himself considered under the wrong formal rationale, that of his brother. Here we can see quite clearly the way in which the material object of faith is and is not diminished. Doubting Thomas is no longer in faith, doubt, or opinion as to whether the human being before him is Jesus. Of that he is persuaded, without action of the will, by the evidence of signs. Faith does not leave sensible perception behind; perception too is addressed and engaged in the believer. To describe what happens *merely* as a diminishment of faith, however, implies that faith has nothing left to do. Faith has rather something more focused to do. That is why Thomas Aquinas chooses to describe the matter well in advance of the faith-*scientia* passage as a diversification of habits.

At I.II.54.2 Thomas considers explicitly the way in which habits are diversified according to the aspect under which something is considered. The reply to objection 1 insists that the material object itself—the *actio* or *quid fecit*—when abstracted from the formality under which a habit considers it, does *not* diversify habits. So both the doubter's faith and his sight have still to consider the body of Jesus. The reply to objection two repeats an example from I.1.1 *ad* 2. When a person has two sorts of demonstrations, say of the shape of the earth, one from astronomy and one from geometry, she *does* have two habits, one for each of the ways of thinking about the earth. And that makes sense: studying eclipses makes her a better astronomer, and studying the movements of heavy objects makes her more knowledgeable about gravity. By the diversification of habits, doubting Thomas's *habit* of faith is not diminished sight, since it continues to regard Jesus as God, and it is even strengthened because its joy in seeing the human being as Jesus increases the habit of love. It is by the diversification of habits that Aquinas articulates the way in which faith involves and engages the doubter's habit of perception. Demonstration by the believer diversifies, focuses, and strengthens both the habits that it distinctly and separately exercises, metaphysical and faithful.

When Aquinas writes that the same person cannot have *scientia* and *fides* of the same thing, he leaves open the possibility just deployed in the preceding article, that the same material object may be considered under two formal rationales and therefore count as *not* "the same thing" (*"idem"*). It is necessary to *deny* faith of the things of which one has *scientia* precisely in order to keep the two formal rationales of metaphysics and sacred doctrine *distinct*. Otherwise one might think that one had done with the proposition *Deus est* after one had a demonstrative argument for it. A demonstrative argument, Aquinas insists here, would leave even the believer in the lurch, if she thought that in exercising the habit of *scientia* with regard to this proposition she was exercising also the habit of faith with regard to it. But to exercise the habit of faith with regard to the proposition *"Deus est"* is precisely *not* to have *scientia* about it, just because the *ratio* of faith is "diminished," as Aquinas says: its focus is narrowed. Not that the *scita* cease to be *revelabilia* or *credibilia*: but with focus narrowed, light intensified, faith is free to zoom in on what is more proper to it: "My Lord," the doubter says, "and my God."

If that analysis is correct, why not say then that the unbelieving philosopher who has a demonstrative argument for the existence of God has the same intention when she believes first on that basis and then on the basis of faith, since both the demonstration and the faith have the same intention, God, but a changing object, now the God of the philosophers, now the God of the Bible? The Thomistic analysis of that situation is clear: the intentions can be the same only if we know enough about the object for both intentions to succeed. In this case, however, the first intention fails.

So Thomas says that unbelievers with a demonstrative argument "do not truly believe that God exists [*nec vere Deum credunt*]" (II–II.2.2 *ad* 3). The proposition *credere Deum* fails for lack of the appropriate use- and meaning-specifying context or *credere Deo*, which arises only from present or left over *credere in Deum*. Thomas makes the same contrast immediately before the Five Ways, in fact, when at I.2.1 he distinguishes between knowing that someone is coming and knowing that it is Peter coming; he characterizes the cognition of God that we have by demonstrative argument as like knowing that someone is coming.[21]

To take its proper part in God's gracious ordering of the human being toward divine friendship, the will needs enough in the mind to act upon, but no Aristotelian demonstration under conditions of *cognitio subtracta* can supply it. For *cognitio subtracta* arises from the insult the human will delivers to God's *scientia*. Enough for the will to act upon comes rather from the "something foreknown of the end" of I.1.1 that is God's self-revelation in Jesus Christ. The *praecognitum finis* arises from revelation just because it exceeds the *cognitiones* of Aristotelian *scientia* and requires another light. So it is that in evaluating the matters of faith that prove susceptible of Aristotelian demonstration we have to consider not the object but the act of faith. For only the act of *faith* is in touch with the *relevant scientia*, that "of God and the blessed." And only in faith's *act* can grace engage what is human about God's human creature, the ability "to order actions and intentions to an *end*," that is, to *act*. To take hold of some part of the human creature other than the act of the will would be to leave unassumed and unredeemed the very image of God (I–II prol.). It would be to leave the *demonstratio* of that image in Jesus Christ ineffective in saving us (III prol.). And that would be to deprive the *praecognitum finis* of the ability effectively to form us, or to deprive it of the capacity to found a science (I.1.1).

The foregoing may be summed up *thesenhaft* in a number of short statements:

Cognitio Dei is *neutralized* without *credere Deo*. That is, when trust is subtracted, the integral form cannot any longer form the soul or lead the will toward friendship with God.

Cognitio Dei is *falsified* without *credere in Deum*. That is, when love is subtracted, a person's actions belie her well-formed statements.

Cognitio Dei is *diversified* in the presence of an Aristotelian demonstration. That is, when faith in a particular proposition is subtracted, the focus of faith narrows to what is more central to its friendship with God, without any change in faith's act.

III

*A Further Objection Answered
and the Significance of the Hypothesis
Assessed: Thomas and Barth*

7

Thomas and Barth

In the commentary on Thomas's Romans commentary, I have tried to show that the natural cognition of God functions properly—that is, is able to execute cognition's proper office of shaping the soul—only in the presence of *grace.* Natural cognition of God *without* grace is an anomaly, a residual, defective "cognition," so called only by courtesy that proves irrelevant to salvation except negatively, in increasing human fault, in showing our cognition of God to be a has-been. Natural cognition of God without grace is a self-consuming artifact, *un*natural, *de*natured, a paradox. Meanwhile, the praise of the natural knowledge of God without grace that some seem to detect in talk of preambles I identified as a misreading based on taking the *Contra gentiles* rather than Question 1 of the *Summa* as the governing text; preambles function differently, I argued, in the last stage of Thomas's development. They get transmuted into faith. The cosmological arguments fulfill the charge of sacred doctrine to leave no part of the world God-forsaken. The reading sought to take better account of the integrity of an Aristotelian science.

A Thomistic objection and Thomas's possible reply

An objection might, however, take another tack. A Protestant might still worry about passages that sound optimistic about the human intellect after the Fall. There *are* passages, a Protestant objector might concede, that imply that such knowledge is ineffective and therefore so called only by courtesy, cognition that is "mere cognition" because without faith. There are *other* passages, the objector might insist, that imply that such cognition is the product of a human faculty finite but effectively impervious to sin, or injured by it in a way that makes little real difference. Such a faculty would be able, Babel-like, to reach up to God. God would be subject to its deliverances. The cognition it gained would count as its own possession rather than as a gift of grace, the *plena possessio* of *scientia* as acquired habit, and it would impugn therefore the unexactedness and freedom of God's friendship. *Scientia*, not faith, would become the habit corresponding to sacred doctrine. Even if such cognition were ascribed to grace at some level, human control over it would belie the ascription. It would be tame grace. Indwelling grace would become grace domesticated. Grace freely given would become grace taken for granted. Grace and gratitude would come apart. The very concomitant attitudes that Thomas makes ingredient in the soul possessing effective knowledge would come undone. Grace bestowed upon the creature would become a creature of the creature's own. And finally human beings would be tempted "to worship and serve the creature rather than the Creator." The very conclusion that Thomas sought, with Paul, to exclude would then be upon him.

The seed of that undoing appears, the critic would say, in the one article on the necessity of grace that receives the answer that grace is *not* necessary. Of the articles of the form, whether a human being can do such-and-such without grace, only one returns an answer in the affirmative. That is the question whether a human being can recognize anything true without grace: *Utrum homo sine gratia aliquod verum cognoscere possit* (I-II.109.1). The answer is a qualified yes. It seems to clinch the objector's case to note that here we are not talking about whether a human being can know anything true "by nature," where "nature" causes semantic difficulties. Here the question is whether a human being can know anything true *without grace*. That matches the Protestant sense of "nature." It would seem therefore to present a clear case. And Thomas seems to say nothing that impugns the cognition of a human being without grace as less than perfect. The problem of sin gets limited to the will, and cognition seems to prove independent of the will after all.

Put another way, the conclusions I have reached in Parts I and II about the need of grace for effective knowledge and about Jesus Christ as the paradigm of demonstration sound more like the first objection of I-II.109.1 than like the reply. Here they are:

> On the first matter we proceed as follows. It seems that the human being without grace can recognize (*cognoscere*) nothing true.
>
> [Objection] 1. For the gloss of Ambrose [Ambrosiaster] on I Cor. 12:13— *No one can say "Jesus is Lord" except by the Holy Spirit*—says: *Everything true, by whomever it should be said, is by the Holy Spirit*. But the Holy Spirit dwells in us by grace. Therefore we are not able to recognize [*cognoscere*] truth without grace.

[*Sed contra*] But on the other hand there is what Augustine said in his *Retractions* 1:4: *I do not approve what I said in prayer: "God, you did not want them to know* [*scire*] *the truth unless they were clean." But it is to be responded that it is possible for many, even unclean, to know* [*scire*] *many true things.* But it is by grace that a human being is made clean. . . . Therefore a human being is able to recognize [*cognoscere*] truth by herself without grace.

[Corpus] I respond that to recognize truth is a certain use, or act [*actus*], of the intellectual light. . . . A use, however, brings about, if you like, a certain having been moved [*quilibet quendam motum*]. . . . The functioning [*actio*] of the intellect, and of whatsoever created being, depends upon God in two ways: in one way, insofar as it has from God the form by which it acts [i.e., as secondary cause]; in another way, insofar as it is moved by God to act [i.e., as primary cause].

. . . the human intellect has a certain form, namely the intelligible light itself, so that it is of itself sufficient for certain intelligible things that are to be known [*cognoscenda*]: for those things namely at the knowledge [*notitia*] of which we are able to arrive by sensible things. But the intellect is not able to perceive higher intelligible things unless it should be perfected by a stronger light, as by the light of faith or of prophecy, whence it is called the *light of grace*, insofar as it is superadded to nature.

Both lights, that of intellect and that of faith, are from God, and in that sense, both lights, one might say, are of grace. In that case, however, one would want to say that here there are really two sorts of grace—call them grace I and grace II—the first domesticated and, from a Protestant point of view, no grace. But why should the first light cease to be grace, just because God has graciously refused to withdraw it, just because God's punishment is not so severe as it might have been, just because God has graciously kept the human race in being long enough to save it? In those ways grace I resembles Luther's civil use of the law: both have nothing to do with salvation except that they keep the triumph of evil from becoming total, permanent, and final. The passage insists that the unsalvific cognition of God that the Gentiles have by the concrete powers of their created nature, insofar as it is true, is *also* to be ascribed in thankfulness to God, *also* not God-forsaken. Even Barth will speak of such knowledge (*Erkenntnis*) when he speaks of "secular parables of the truth."[1]

The passage leaves untouched, however, the assertion that such cognitions of the truth prove ineffective against the fallenness of the will, unless God should turn the will. The passage leaves untouched the assertion that what we recognize by the *super*natural light of grace we also truly recognize "by nature": the alternative, according to Thomas's usage, would be to say that we recognize something *un*naturally, which Thomas regards as a contradiction in terms (with the possible exception of rapture, which Thomas dislikes for a similar reason[2]). So: we may know some, unsalvific because not-will-converting truths about God by nature with the grace of creation, that is, by nature denatured but not ceasing to exist; and we may perceive other, salvific because will-converting truths about God by nature with the grace of salvation, that is, by nature restored to good working order so that God can point it beyond itself anew, towards the divine friendship that was God's purpose for it from the beginning.

In that context we may see the significance of this fact: Thomas's question is *not,* as the hyper-Protestant would expect, "whether the human being can know anything *preparatory for salvation* without grace." Similarly the objections do *not* defend the side the hyper-Protestant would expect, or something like "It would seem that the human being can perceive articles of faith without grace," leading to the *respondeo* that a human being could perceive only preambles without grace. That is not Thomas's question. Rather the objections open attack on a *different* front. The only objection worth making goes: "it would seem that the human being without grace can know *no* truth without grace." *That* is the objection obvious to Thomas. So the question is whether the human being can know anything true at *all* without grace, or, more pointedly, whether God can use people who are not Christians or Jews to teach people who are. The answer Thomas rejects would mean, generally, that there are some people God cannot move directly, and others whom God cannot teach through people unlike themselves. It would mean, specifically, that Thomas would have been prevented by grace from learning anything from Aristotle, and, furthermore, God would not have been able to move the mind of Aristotle in any case.

Thomas does not deny the objection altogether, but responds with a distinction. The distinction does come between two sorts of grace. It is *true* that a human being without grace can know *no* truth without grace, where the sort of grace required is the sort that keeps us alive and in being. But the rhetoric of the reply makes clear that that use of "grace" is an odd one; grace usually means the elevating sort that the purpose of which is to raise us above creation to friendship with God, and also, under the conditions after the Fall, to save us from sin. Elevating grace is still necessary for supplying the conditions that faith requires to the sentence *Credo Deum esse.* The sentence *Credo Deum esse* is called true because it is true when it subsists in the right sort of mind; but the wrong sort of mind can neutralize it. The mind of the unbelieving philosopher or of the demon can neutralize it. The neutralization is not, to put it as oddly as the situation deserves, somehow the fault of the *proposition.* In Thomas's system one must insist that the state of affairs participated in by the mind adhering, by means of that enunciable proposition, to the truth, does not change just because another mind, failing to adhere to the first truth, thinks the proposition with assent, in this case ineffectively. It is in virtue therefore not of the truth of the proposition, which enjoys truth only under the conditions of a right mind, but of the truth of the state of affairs, that Thomas says a human being may recognize some truth by the grace of creation that keeps one alive, even when that cognition is not yet of the sort that only the grace of salvation can deliver in faith, the sort that effectively reproduces its form in the soul so as to change the human being that holds it.

We can also see why Thomas had to answer the question as he did. That a human being can have *cognitio* of some truth without grace, which Thomas affirms at I–II.109.1, does not deny that the cognition in question is defective, and does not affirm that the cognition in question has anything to do with our elevation—except as it gets taken up into the nature that is shot through with *grace.* On the other hand, insofar as it is assimilable into the cognition that we have by *graced* nature, it is not false, but potentially participant in truth. It is this assimilability that Thomas affirms in the article. But the power of assimilation belongs to grace. To answer otherwise, therefore, would deny to grace the power to assimilate *anything at all* into its realm. Since human beings are created rational, that is, to deny the possibility would *impugn* grace by rendering us (as our rational selves) strictly irredeemable. Similarly, as we saw in Chapter 1, Thomas makes the intelligibility of things participant in their revealability. To deny them any intelligibility at all would be to deny to revelation the power to obtain any purchase in us.

Thus an additional nuance accrues to the conclusions of the previous chapter. Nature without grace—in the technical sense of God's will to save—does not concretely exist. It is by God's gracious will to elevate it that nature not so much *exists* as *persists.* It is *for the sake of God's original plan to elevate nature* that God mercifully allows nature to persist. Even here it is not as if the grace of creation provides a platform or substrate or all-too-human ground upon which for God to build. Even here it is rather that God's elevating purpose, God's intent to make *friends* of human beings keeps us alive and functioning. The grace that allows the Gentiles to have even the unsalvific and feckless cognition that they have *depends logically* upon the grace, in the sense of God's elevating will, that seeks to render that cognition effective. "Grace II" does not depend upon a "grace I" which is "really," as a hyper-Protestant objection would have it, no grace at all. Rather "grace I" is "no grace at all" only in the sense that it is no *independent*, no *separate*, no *different* grace at all, even if Thomas distinguishes it for the sake of analysis: it is nothing other than the grace of elevation working in advance, proleptically, under conditions of sin, to keep us alive and functioning until God's plan proceeds; it is not a human power so much as a divine mercy, no less so if we fail to recognize it as such. As a mercy under conditions of sin it is already not only God's elevating grace persisting because of God's remaining true to God's own purpose and promise; it is already God's *saving* grace. Otto Pesch puts it this way:

> It is easy to overlook: The justification of the sinner is no "new" dispensation of God's, but the carrying out of God's creatorly will over against the rebellious human creature. The dimensions of nature that remain *un*disturbed are therefore to be conceived of as the effectiveness by anticipation [*Vorauswirksamkeit*] of the grace that saves.[3]

So nature is a cross-section of God's plan. We misunderstand it if we consider it on its own. We must take the viewpoint of the whole, whether from creation forward, or from the eschaton back. From creation forward we see nature as the persistence (in the face of obstacles) of God's gracious plan to take us beyond ourselves to be God's friends. From the eschaton back we see nature as the anticipation (despite obstacles) of that same plan. It would be odd (if not violent) for God to befriend us without respect for our temporal condition; therefore we must not be surprised if God's purpose of befriending us has temporal, and to us in time therefore anticipatory effects. Glory follows grace just as what is first in intention is last in execution. After the Fall, nature can be understood only in terms of what lies before and after it. Nature, under conditions of original justice granted and lost, is God's not foreclosing on the plan of creation, and God's not preventing the anticipation of elevation, or a *place* for the plan to be carried out, and the execution to begin.

A Barthian objection and Thomas's reconstructed reply

Let us raise the stakes by pursuing the comparison with Karl Barth. Consider the following contrast between Barth and Thomas proposed by one of

the most convinced and convincing Barthians, George Hunsinger.[4] The recent date of his study—1991—reminds us that the reading he offers of
Thomas on nature is still current. He serves as a careful and interesting example of a whole class of possible critics. We will see whether Part II has
given us any leverage against it.

> By reviewing Aquinas's discussion of the justification of the unright-
> eous, the contrast between the two theologians can be sharpened. In
> what sense, Aquinas asks [I–II.113.10.], might this justification be consid-
> ered to be a miracle? Three possible senses of miracle are distinguished.
> First, insofar as a miracle is something which can be done only by divine
> power, justification can be considered a miracle. Second, insofar as a mir-
> acle is something which actualizes a possibility not inherent in nature,
> justification cannot be considered a miracle. Finally, insofar as a miracle
> is something which operates outside the usual order of cause and effect,
> justification may or may not be considered a miracle, depending on the
> circumstances. (In cases where an instantaneous conversion actualizes
> perfect righteousness in an individual all at once, as occurred with
> St. Paul, justification can be considered a miracle; otherwise, righteous-
> ness is perfected within the individual by grace as it operates inside the
> usual order of cause and effect.)
> It is the second of these points which provides the best contrast with
> Barth. Barth agrees with Aquinas that the justification of the unrighteous
> person is something which can occur only by divine power, but disagrees
> that in justification (and thus in salvation) grace actualizes a possibility
> inherent in human nature. Barth considers justification to be a miracle in
> the very sense that Aquinas rules out. Indeed, Barth must do so, precisely
> because he disallows a key premise articulated by Aquinas in this text,
> namely, that "the soul is by nature capable of or open to grace."

We have seen that such an assumption does not impugn but lauds grace,
does not render "nature" incoherent but preserves for it the possibility of
coherence, does not tie God's hands but bears witness to God's steadfast remaining true to God's own self, to God's creative purposes and elevating
promises, does not make grace a human creature but preserves nature as a
divine mercy. Still the standard charges recur: "If this premise is granted as
used by Aquinas, divine grace and human freedom must necessarily be conceived as interdependent in the work of salvation."

The charge is too strong. It is true to say that Thomas inter*defines* nature and grace. That is because we cannot understand properly functioning
nature apart from grace, and we cannot recognize nature, either as it con-

cretely subsists in the faithful or as it concretely subsists in the unfaithful, without knowing what its *end* is, a purpose that God graciously *bestows* upon it in elevating it. This much any Barthian should grant: we ought to define nature in terms of grace because it takes Jesus Christ to tell us what nature is. That is also the burden of the insistence of Question 1 of the *Summa*, as we have seen, upon the *praecognitum finis*, which is Jesus Christ, as necessary for understanding nature in terms of what God has in store for it. But to say that the conception of nature depends upon grace is different from saying "divine grace and human freedom must necessarily be conceived as interdependent in the work of salvation." That would be so only if human freedom contributed something *in*dependent in the work of salvation. But we have seen that contribution is different from cooperation, precisely because cooperation is entirely *de*pendent upon grace.

"Cooperation" language merely ensures that we do not do good *un*willingly. Barth too requires that we do the good *"gerne,"* eagerly; it does not change the point that Thomas deploys a technical term and Barth does not. If God moves the motive, that does not impugn but praises grace: "our mind both moves and is moved...whence the entire business [*operatio*] belongs to grace" and not, that is, to us as opposed to grace (I–II.111.2c and *ad* 2). The only alternative would be a sort of nature that could not undergo movement by God without becoming something else. Protestant thinking sometimes goes that way: anything moved by God must be by grace; grace and nature are mutually exclusive categories; therefore nothing moved by God can be natural. But such a nature would be almost incomprehensible to Thomas. The sort of thing that could not undergo movement by God without becoming something else could not be a creature, which was made to be God-moved. Or natures made for God could not be moved by God as their end, so that they not only fall away from God, but escape from God into nothingness. The objection eliminates creation by making it something immovable, and such absolutes are either divine or demonic in a non-Christian way. The objection, that is, resolves creation either into the sort of non-critter that a Manichean evil would be, or into the sort of non-critter[5] that God is.

For these purposes therefore it is misleading to abstract nature from the context of the divine plan and the concrete (supernatural) human end. Perhaps it is strictly possible to define nature apart from grace, in terms of human ordering, but given the *concrete* human ordering beyond itself, it is speculation of a pernicious kind, about how God might have treated us if God had not loved us as God does, and of a kind that Thomas disparages. In sacred doctrine at least, since it considers all things precisely as ordered to God, nature cannot appropriately be defined apart from grace. Grace does not however for that reason get defined in terms of nature. Rather for that very reason grace remains independent of nature, just because nature could not exercise any independent causality over against grace. The only causality that operates toward God is the causality by which God, working either within or without the will, calls all creatures according to their natures into the divine communion. Barth makes that move too, when he interprets creation as the "external ground of the covenant," and the covenant as the "internal ground of creation."[6]

Hunsinger would press his point, however. He would say that the very language of "capacity" and "openness" surreptitiously defines not only nature but grace too. Hunsinger would presumably appeal to the logic of question and answer in his reply.

The rejoinder to the point pressed makes both a concession and a demurrer. It is true that language works in a way that constrains answers, to some extent, in terms of the questions. We first understand the gospel stories *in time*, for example, because have learned language from our human parents. But that does not mean that the truth of the gospel stories or the significance of the concepts they convey depend *logically* upon the truths or concepts we have inherited. Rather the truths or concepts that come to us inherited *logically* owe their truth or helpfulness to their participation in the first truth. Thus the fact that our language makes the semantic range of words like "capability" and "openness" depend both upon what is open and what it is open to does not mean that the facts arrange themselves that way.

Second, Thomas would defend the sense of *"capax"* as entirely negative. Hunsinger's qualification "as used by Aquinas" undermines his case: the case fares better with the qualification "as read by others." Thomas denies that nature is capable of grace in the sense Hunsinger rightly fears, that of *finitum capax infiniti,* or the finite capable of the infinite. Rather Thomas regards nature as capable of grace in the sense of *God's* plan to save *that which* God created, or to carry through what God had begun. It is none other than God's own purpose that God saves. Thomas adduces a quotation from Augustine to clarify the remark in just that way. "Naturally the soul is open to grace" gets glossed as "is open to God *by grace.*" Nature is only open to grace *by grace.*

Hunsinger surreptitiously assumes that nature could be open to grace only by itself, since "graced nature" seems like a contradiction in terms to many Protestants. But it does not to Thomas. Grace clears its own room.

The word seeks to exclude the violence to nature that Barth also wants to exclude. But the misunderstanding, as we have seen, goes so deep as to need a reconceptualization. I shall propose two.

1. Hunsinger grants a concession earlier on the same page. It does not go far enough. Better, it goes back and forth—all the more reason for a reconceptualization. It says: "Although human freedom is certainly [in Thomas] in some sense conceptually subsequent to and dependent on divine grace, in another (if perhaps secondary) sense divine grace is nonetheless subsequent to and dependent on human freedom. By contrast, as previously suggested, Barth's position on such matters is always one which repudiates a scheme of conceptual interdependence in favor of a scheme in which divine grace cannot be understood except as conceptually prior to and entirely independent of human freedom." Had Hunsinger understood the force of the phrases "in some sense...in another (if perhaps secondary) sense" of his concession, he could not have written "by contrast," but would have to have written "in a similar way." The "other, secondary sense" in which for Thomas divine grace is conceptually subsequent to and dependent on human freedom is just another way in which Thomas reverses the usual polarities of conceptions so that the aspects of human freedom on which grace seems to depend (the usual suspects of the theology of controversy)— like cooperation, merit, preparation, perseverance, reason—become so many ways in which Thomas takes an apparent pretension to human autonomy, analyzes it, and finds grace. The language of subsequence and dependence tends finally to break down. For as long as the language of divine and human "agency" is in place it becomes difficult to *keep up* the task of conceiving of them as on two different levels. Yet everyone would insist, whether via an analogy of being or via an analogy of faith, on the distinction, because thinking of them as on two different levels keeps getting undermined by thinking of them as two levels of *the same sort of thing*. We do not want to give up the double language of agency—Hunsinger makes it, in a final chapter, his test case—but we misread Thomas if we do not notice how at every opportunity he puts up roadblocks against the conclusion that in comparing divine and human agency we have two levels of the same sort of thing. The verb "cooperate" exists just so that free will cannot be said to do the same thing as divine will and "operate" as a rival (I–II.111.2). "Merit" gets defined as if the dishes of a balance that would weigh us became buckets to uplift us (I–II.114). I take the images from George Herbert, whom I find almost perfectly to represent, willy-nilly, Thomas's integration of the biblical "merit"-talk into a *sola gratia* scheme:

Justice [II]

The dishes of thy balance seem to gape
　　　　Like two great pits;
　　　　The beam and scape
　　　Did like some torturing engine show;
　　　Thy hand above did burn and glow,
　　Daunting the stoutest hearts, the proudest wits.

But now that Christ's pure veil presents the sight,
　　　　I see no fears:
　　　　Thy hand is white,
　　　Thy scales like buckets, which attend
　　　And interchangeably descend,
　　Lifting to heaven from this well of tears.

It is more helpful to think of Thomas as treating the will as a *place* where God also works. Protestants tend to think of the will as a God-forsaken place. Thomas thinks of the will as another locus of divine activity. Better: "the will" is the name for the place where God primarily addresses, engages, and involves human beings. "The will" is also the name for the place where human beings primarily rebel against God. *For that very reason* God's activity in that place, God's taking that field, salvation's occurrence and working out just there can only be the work of grace alone. Thus the dense and elegant formulation of Bernard of Clairvaux: "The entire work is in the will *precisely because* the entire work is from grace."[7]

2. Imagine the nature-grace debate as a debate about what class of stories in the gospel to use to explicate the question of what it means to "hear" the word of God. Take Protestants as tending to imagine it this way. There are two candidates: the parables and the healings.[8] In the parables it is assumed (except perhaps in Mark) that human beings have an innate capacity to hear and understand: The one who has ears to hear, let that one hear. So it makes sense to talk about a human faculty, analogous to hearing, that takes in the word of God, a capacity for grace. That, Protestants take it, is the Catholic view.

But that view, imagine our Protestant continuing, is too optimistic. It does not take account of the stories in which the hearers notoriously *fail* to understand, and of the version in which Mark says (4:12) that Jesus speaks in parables in order that the hearers will *not* understand. Mention is made of human capacity only to emphasize human *in*capacity. Mention is made of public parable only to emphasize the private explanations to the disciples, so as to preserve divine freedom with regard to who understands and who does not. So the parable model of human response to God's word, or, if you like, of the human cognition of God, breaks down. Better to turn to another.

Take the Protestants, then, to see themselves as preferring a second model, that of the healing stories. Protestants want to emphasize the *reversal* by which it is none other than the *blind* who see, the *deaf* who hear, the *lame* who leap for joy. Similarly in Mark it is never the disciples, even with their parable explanations, who are said in the indicative mood to "follow Jesus": they are only commanded to do so, in the imperative, especially when like Peter they stray: "Follow after me, Satan": it is not until the episode *after* Jesus's sharp rebuke of Peter that Mark comes to say (10:52) of the healed Bartimaeus *alone* (the one whom Jesus had found blind and screaming by the side of the road), simply and without qualification, in the indicative rather than the imperative mode: "and he followed him."[9] It is *those* stories, the Protestant would say, to which we ought to turn to see what human capacities are like. There are none. The gospels describe them as *in*capacities: as blindnesses, deafnesses, lamenesses. They wait upon a miracle also in the *second* sense of the typology of miracles that Hunsinger quoted from Thomas above. To explicate blindness, deafness, and lameness as "openness and capability" flies in their face. The gospel knows eyes closed, ears stopped, walkers thwarted. Far better to take Barth's tack: that possibility follows from actuality. Better to talk about the sight of the sighted than of the "sight" of the blind. The latter is what we have seen Thomas up to in the Romans commentary: talking about the "cognition" of the ignorant.

That, I take it, explicates a certain sort of Protestant argument so far.

Thomas has a rejoinder. First he would observe that it cannot be wrong to *speak* of things that we cannot understand. The blind, the deaf, the lame are still defined, on the level of language, in terms of the capacities they lack, even if it does, as everyone admits, take grace to restore them. When we hear about the "ears of the deaf unstopped, the eyes of the blind opened," it is indeed ears and eyes that they possess, their own nature restored.[10] If we outlawed all talk of nature—of eyes and ears and legs—we might misread the biblical healing stories as *contrary* to nature, as "bestowing" upon us *un*human capacities that could only *violate* us. Thomas is afraid that in the absence of nature-talk the healing stories would look as if Jesus bestowed upon us not our own nature in return but faculties alien to us: not sight but radar, not ears but antennae, not two good legs but six.

Absent talk of nature, Thomas might fear, it becomes hard to distinguish metanoia from metamorphosis, the gospels from Kafka. It is the absurdity of grace's turning human beings into cockroaches, and not its independence, that Thomas wants to deny when he says that the human soul is open to grace *"naturaliter."*

We can even say something about the positive point of Thomas's talk about human faculties in terms of these stories. The characters in the gospel healing stories remain, by God's prevenient mercy, able to *use the words* that form a request for healing even as they remain also *unacquainted with the state* that they request. The presence of Jesus prompts the blind to ask for sight even without having experienced it. So there seems to be a place for *talk*, for linguistic place-holders, even where we do not have discursive intelligibility of the *quid est* to which we refer.

The full integrity of this talk depends, to be sure, upon its coming from a person who enjoys *effective use* of the faculty mentioned. Similarly the full integrity of the cognition of God depends upon the propositions' inhering in a mind united by faith with the first truth, and in that case the cognition is effective in the soul (is formed faith). But language retains a residual sense just when we know the *use* of the words. (Most human language proceeds in this mode, which is why Wittgenstein is helpful.) It retains that residual sense not because truth inheres in words and propositions, but because the usage in the community is not *entirely* divorced from the reality wherein the truth inheres. The requests of the gospel blind, deaf, and lame to be healed make sense because the sighted, hearing, and walking keep those words alive and in contact with the form of life in which they enjoy their full integrity. Similarly talk of the knowledge of God proceeds not because the cognition inheres in the propositions, or even, finally, because even one human being could, over a long period of time, reach some truth about God, and keep the community in touch with reality, but rather because *God* does not abandon us utterly. That God does not abandon us *utterly* means just that God mercifully preserves our nature from entire non-existence. God preserves some community with us, even that of God's wrath, and it is there, under God's *vindicta*, God's desire for self-justification as the promising God, that we encounter the cognition of God that human beings have "by nature." It is certainly not in virtue of something *in*dependently human—which if not meaningless would have to mean that which refuses, *against* nature, to depend upon grace, and that which therefore blinds, deafens, lames, and kills—that God, according to Thomas, preserves eyes, ears, legs, and lives. It *could not be*, as hyper-Protestants claim, that Thomas has

God preserve nature in virtue of anything other than its utter dependence upon grace. It is in virtue of nothing other than God's plan that in the meantime we retain only miraculously usable eyes, ears, legs, and lives. God preserves the blind for no other reason than that they may see, the deaf that they may hear, the lame that they may leap for joy: in the same way God preserves nature denatured to be restored and elevated, cognition dead that as faith it may live and have life abundantly. That is the pattern that Thomas seeks positively to preserve.

"Mainly, [Barth] believes, grace would not be grace—it would not be sovereign, free, gratuitous—if human freedom were not conceptually subsequent to and entirely dependent on it," Hunsinger concludes. Thomas believes that too, without qualification. Human openness to salvation, expressed either as unfallen reason or as willing cooperation, belongs on the side not of our contribution to a redemption from a sin wherein we cannot help ourselves, which is for Thomas too a contradiction in terms, but on the side of the persistent mercifulness toward us and faithfulness *ad intra* of God in the divine plan, a plan to elevate *this* creature, the very one whom God created open to friendship with God, and the very one that rebelled against it. It is the *blind* who see, the *deaf* who hear, the *lame* who leap.

So far the Barthians.

Assessment and significance of the hypothesis: Thomas and Barth in convergence on Romans 1?

Let us pursue the comparison with a return to the *Shorter Commentary*. I confine myself to Barth's comments on 1:18–32, some six pages. I regard them as parallel to longer discussions in the *Dogmatics*. Their brevity, their commentary-order and their commentary-context, parallel to Thomas's, give those comments great advantages for my purpose over the comments of the *Dogmatics*, without loss.[11]

Barth begins with a paragraph of rhetorical questions that he then devotes half the exposition, some three pages, to answering in the negative:

> Does Paul mean a second or even a first revelation apart from the one mentioned in 1.17 when now he suddenly introduces a *revelation* of God's *wrath* against all the ungodliness (irreverence) and iniquity (insubordination) of human beings, viz. of the Gentiles (1.18–32) and the Jews (2.1–3.20)? Has he abandoned his office as a messenger of the Gospel for a while in order to speak in the first place in an entirely different capacity as a religious interpreter of the human situation as such, as a Christian

student of the philosophy of religion and of history? This section has often been interpreted as if this were the case. Then that whole rather long section 1.18–3.20 would mean that Paul—as bad preachers are admittedly in the habit of doing—is leading off with a lengthy discussion of something quite different from his text, i.e. from the matter which he has already indicated clearly and unmistakably.

Can we regard him as capable of that?[12]

The practiced reader of Barth will gather from the tenor of those questions the tenor of the answer, just as the practiced reader of Thomas's articles will be able to predict a lot about the *respondeo* from the objections. That Barth will reassert Paul's office as an apostle and his standpoint as one who confronts the Gentiles with the gospel of Jesus Christ (p. 27) is almost obvious. What is not obvious is why Barth perpetrates just the same sort of misreading against Thomas as he ridicules in readers of Paul. Thomas's advocates and detractors, Barth chief among the latter, act as if Thomas had "abandoned his office as a messenger of the gospel for a while in order to speak in the first place as a religious interpreter of the human situation as such, as a Christian student of the philosophy of religion and of history." We have seen that the description applies no more to Thomas than it does to Paul. That is also true for many of the same reasons. In fact we may take Barth's defense of Paul to apply *tout court* to the proffered reading of Thomas. The overall shape of Barth's argument fits.

A number of particular features stand out.

1. Barth like Thomas makes God's wrath a form of God's grace. For Thomas we have seen that God's *ira* is God's *vindicta*, at once the self-justification by which God maintains the integrity of God's *promises* and the deliverance according to which God carries out the divine intention in creation (*In* Rom. 1:17–18, esp. §§102 and 109). For Barth we learn that Paul "sees the Gentiles as well as the Jews in the reflected light of that fire of God's wrath which is the fire of [God's] love," and that that love has endured "for a long time, yea always, since the creation of the world" (p. 28).

2. Barth like Thomas sees Paul as ascribing a knowledge of God to the Gentiles (whatever its status) in order to stake out as it were a certain field. Thomas, as we have seen, wants to render all true human cognition incorporable into sacred doctrine, wants to treat all things as *revelabilia* (*ST* I.1.3), and so to leave no realm God-forsaken. We could take Thomas therefore to be proposing the natural cognition of God to be an answer precisely to this question of Barth's: "How can the Gospel be God's almighty power (1.16), if the Gentiles could exculpate themselves by saying that God is a stranger to

them, that they are living in some forgotten corner of the world, where God is not God or cannot be known as God...?" (pp. 28–29). Both Thomas (*In Rom.* 1:19, §115) and Barth want to deny that question's presupposition. Yet it is in providing an articulation of that denial that Thomas's concept of concrete nature, nature always already shot through with grace, finds its point and purpose. It is a nature from which God has never entirely withdrawn the grace intended to elevate it, sustaining the creation, and here appearing as God's wrath: This nature is the "place" in which the Gentiles live, in which it would be false to say that "they are living in some forgotten corner of the world, where God is not God or cannot be known as God." That is the sense in which nature is graced, in which God refuses to leave us alone. Barth imagines that that nature or place is otherwise for Thomas; he continues to ask, expecting a negative answer, "if there were such a thing as a self-contained Gentile world, established, secure and justified in itself" (p. 29). But we have seen that Thomas's concrete nature is precisely *not* self-contained, precisely *not* "established, secure and justified in itself." To have security (*fiducia*) in ourselves and "ascribe good" or justify ourselves is for Thomas too precisely our Gentile sin (*In Rom.* 1:21, §129). Rather it is contained in grace, established in grace, and first secure and justified in grace, even if that grace first appears as God's delivering vindication. Barth's denial of *such* a Gentile world, a God-forsaken one, is the affirmation of a *natural* world, when we understand "nature" as Thomas does. It is the world in which, Barth and Thomas would agree, God's grace blows as wrath (*vindicta Dei*). And it is the same world in which, Barth and Thomas would agree, God's grace blows as gospel (*evangelica gratia, In* Rom. 1:16, §§97–99, which is of Christ, §102). One world, one grace. Barth defines that world negatively as one unforgotten by the grace of Christ; Thomas defines that world positively as one where the grace of Christ is necessary and sufficient; so that even the positive definition belongs in the inalienable context of grace, and has never, in fact, existed for its own sake.

3. Barth like Thomas is able, when it suits him, to distinguish between effective and ineffective cognitions of God—and even to preserve the word "knowledge" or "*Erkenntnis*" for the latter. "In spite of their *objective knowledge of God*[13] they have not rendered to [God] the honor and gratitude they owe..." (p. 29). Usually Barth reserves *Erkenntnis* for knowledge as a concrete formation of the soul, complete with obedience (*Gehorsamkeit*) and thankfulness (*Dankbarkeit*), much as Thomas reserves *cognitio vera* for the form that "leads human beings toward the good" (*In* Rom. 1:18, §112), which Thomas tends in the Romans commentary to follow

Paul in identifying with justice (§112) and gratitude (e.g., *In* 1:8, §45; 1:21, §127); that is how it works in the *Church Dogmatics*, too. But here, evidently, he is open to Thomas's way of dividing things up, and he finds it useful, perhaps even necessary, to resort to it, precisely in order to do justice to the usage of Paul. And that openness—so rare for Barth to assert, so difficult for Barth to give an account of—is just the place where Thomas anticipates the need of an articulate account and seeks, in the service of explicating precisely the necessity and efficacy and power of what he calls *gratia evangelica*, to supply one.

4. Thomas like Barth insists that as Barth puts it "Paul does not dream of paying the Gentiles anything resembling a compliment and of trying to find in their religions some point of contact for the understanding of the Gospel; on the contrary he is merely and simply calling them to faith in God's verdict." That is the reason why Thomas can turn around and characterize the cognition he has so carefully accounted for as one that effectively the Gentiles *lack*, because it paradoxically manages to leave them unformed. As Preller puts it, "Such 'cognition' of God that philosophy can produce is merely the clarification of what was there all the time—a felt ignorance."[14] That is why Thomas insists on accounting for human natural cognition of God in its full, salvific, graced rather than residual and defective form, why he describes it in Paul himself as involving "all virtues" (Prol., §1), and why he describes it even at Romans 1:20 as objectively trinitarian, whether the Gentiles recognize it as such or not: so that he has a contrast by which to render the Gentiles' relative cognition defective and their relative ignorance culpable (*In Rom.* 1:21, §127).

5. Thomas like Barth insists that this culpability leaves the Gentiles in a situation from which they cannot free themselves. "[Paul] starts by referring to the best the Gentiles have, or claim to have: their religion, which consists in one great confusion between the Creator and [the Creator's] creatures. If there is any position from which no bridge can possibly be built to the Gospel, to the knowledge of the living God, then this is it! Human religion, as radically distinguished from belief in God's revelation, always originates and consists in this confusion: in the mistaken confidence in which [human beings] want to decide for [themselves] who and what God is, which can only produce this confusion, i.e. idolatry. This mistaken self-confidence is the actual object of God's wrath." The contrast Thomas makes parallel to Barth's is not the intellectual one between sacred doctrine and *metaphysica*, but the one he describes when he says "IN THEIR THOUGHTS THEY BECAME EMPTY, in so far as they had trust [*fiducia!*] in

themselves, and not in God" (§129) and when he says "For the Apostle appears...to touch...natural theology, which the philosophers in the world observe, worshiping parts of the world, and with respect to this he says: *And they worshiped and served the creature rather than the Creator*" (§149 *in fin.*). For the natural cognition of God is neutral only when Thomas considers it in abstraction from the mind that holds it, and since Thomas, unlike the twentieth century, defines truth not in terms of propositions but in terms of the adequation of a thing to the *mind*, that is a fairly odd thing to do. In actual human minds Thomas evaluates the knowledge of God according to what use the human being puts it, which is to say the will, and there all the language of praise and blame is at home.[15] So Paul could "pay the Gentiles a compliment" only with regard to their use of their knowledge; but they use it ill, "subtracting from God's power and *scientia*...but rather they ascribed their good things to their own ingenuity and power...the light of wisdom having been taken away" (*In* Rom. 1:21, §§127, 129, 130).

6. Both Barth and Thomas want to talk about a *refusal* of God to abandon human beings, which Thomas explicates with the concept of nature and Barth explicates with his talk of a world unforgotten, as well as about a *delivering up* of human beings to their own sinful desires. Thomas can make the distinction as one between the will that sin affects directly (the delivering up) and the relatively upright powers of reason that sin affects indirectly (the leaving unabandoned) in every concrete human being. Barth replaces distinction with dialectic, so that talk of God's not abandoning the Gentiles to any place where God is not God gets juxtaposed with talk of God's abandoning the Gentiles to their own desires. That dialectic is saved from contradiction just if we read it in Thomas's terms: the place where God does not abandon us is the place God's grace sustains for us in our concrete nature, and by the grace of God it is in just that God-sustained place that our falling down occurs.

7. Barth like Thomas insists that "human beings are without excuse, because, having the knowledge of God, they still do not render [God] honour and thanks as God. It is unquestionable that knowledge of God is here ascribed to the human being in the cosmos, and knowability is ascribed to God" (*CD* II/1, p. 119, translation slightly modified). Of course this knowledge, in Barth as in Thomas, is no independent knowledge, but depends, for Barth, upon the "revelation of the grace of God in Jesus Christ," as for Thomas upon the *evangelica gratia Christi*. And for Thomas as for Barth it proves effective only as that knowledge is "fundamentally surpassed, but

at the same time also included, in a higher knowledge, and, despite its limitation, raised into this higher knowledge" (*CD* II/1, p. 116)—much as for Thomas too the natural cognition of God is taken up into sacred doctrine by the technical means of parsing it as *revelabile* or subordinating it to the primary demonstration in the humanity of Jesus Christ.

8. Both Barth and Thomas want to affirm that what God primarily reveals is God's own self in Jesus Christ. For Barth Jesus Christ is the primary form of the threefold Word of God, incarnate, written, and preached. For Thomas Jesus Christ must also be the real, light-giving aspect of the Revelation in order to ground the new *scientia* of sacred doctrine as other revelations grant to other Aristotelian disciplines the first principles that give them rise. For both Barth and Thomas scripture is the place from which one mounts arguments, for Barth as the second form of the Word of God, for Thomas as the propositional form of the first principles to which sacred doctrine must attend and return in order to exercise its scientific character. And for both Barth and Thomas the scripture witnesses, whether as the Word's secondary form, or as *scientia's* propositional aspect, to Jesus Christ as the argument that trumps or absorbs all others. True human words from the secular sphere "are true in their supposed and implied, if not always immediately apparent, connection with the totality of Jesus Christ and his prophecy, and therefore as they indirectly point to this, or as this indirectly declares itself in them" (*CD* IV/3, p. 123).[16] That statement could well serve as a summary of the move that *Thomas* makes in articulating sacred doctrine's overarching unity and integrity in Question 1, or in construing *cognitio naturalis* in the context of God's delivering wrath and the gospel grace of Christ in Romans 1.

This is all by no means to deny that large and important differences remain between Thomas and Barth. But it is to say that they are differences that distinguish different human beings on the side of the angels, rather than one on the side of the angels and one on the side of the Antichrist. To find Thomas and Barth in convergence in their commentaries on Romans—not just on any book, but on *Romans*—is to find them in convergence in the place where for both the *Summa* and the *Dogmatics* the account of the natural knowledge of God is at home. Convergence between Thomas and Barth on the natural knowledge of God also goes a long way toward increasing the significance of Part I's account of sacred doctrine's *scientia* as scripturalist and christoform. It should dispense, too, with many objections that Protestants may still harbor toward that account. "*Spitzenleistung*," indeed!

The account raises new objections, to be sure. To explain how both students of Barth and students of Thomas came to agree on their divergence would require an account of how both Barth and Vatican I represented opposing responses to Kant. That is a topic for another day. But in an epilogue, as a "concluding unscientific postscript," I will tender some speculations.[17]

EPILOGUE

The Common Thomas of Barth and Vatican I

I

Let us return to the passage quoted in the introduction in which Barth sums up his attitude toward Thomas Aquinas.

> Natural theology was able, ... after the rediscovery of Aristotle, to get the upper hand over medieval theology, which at last and finally became apparent in the formulas of the First Vatican Council (in the canonization of Thomas Aquinas as its supreme achievement [*Spitzenleistung*]).[1]

No one will miss the way in which Barth sees Thomas through Vatican I—more precisely, through Vatican I and *Aeterni Patris* both interpreted despite his explicit protestation to the contrary *in malam* if not *pessimam partem*.[2] His first mention of Vatican I quotes the famous line "God, the principle and end of all things, is certainly able to be recognized [*certe cognosci posse*] from created things by the natural light of human reason"[3] and assumes, without asking whether fallen or unfallen nature informs the question, where the "light of reason" comes from or whether it in this case or ever acts alone, whether the "certainly" indicates self-evidence or inference, how "principle and end of all things" and "from created things" might bear or demand crypto-theological interpretations, or what degree of knowledge or ignorance "recognized" (*"cognoscere"*) suggests; without asking, in short, whether Vatican I intends and manages to say any more than Paul does, Barth assumes that something nefarious is in play, that the assertion functions in the hands of the Vatican fathers as it would in post-Kantian Protestant theology, where the dialectic of subject and object, creature and God have in their continual seesawing largely elided the theater of the glory of God, the world God created apart both from human perceptions and uses of it and in a different way also from God, the scene of Christ's passion, the world which continued in Vatican I and up through von Balthasar's *Theodramatik*[4] to give God and rational creatures in Catholic theology a differ-

ent place and context. When Barth stood Schleiermacher on his head he reversed subject and object as if the known and the knower put an end to the
matter, as if rational creatures exhausted creation, so that he can make
nothing of "all things" except "our thing" and nothing of "from created
things" except "from us alone," so that Vatican I's natural knowers of God,
if there be any, become *ipso facto* human beings lost, as so many human beings curved in upon ourselves. On Barth's reading they cannot even by the
power of God elevating precisely their natures be or become human beings
lost, rather, in wonder, love, and praise.

Because Barth takes the doctrine of God as basically a reflection on
God's trinitarian name he takes the question of the use of the term *"Deus"*
in the document as a question about *which God* Vatican I intends—the
God, in Pascal's phrase, of the philosophers or the God of the Bible. After
the question gets stated in that way, of course, the answer becomes inevitable. Barth asks for example whether the characterization *"Deus noster"* refers the name to the God of Jesus Christ: he answers no. He does not
consider whether the Council might like Thomas have in mind the Father
of Jesus Christ and be reflecting on the ways in which the all-too-human
term "god" might appropriately and analogically—even, in the analogy of
faith—be applied to that divine person. He therefore takes the analysis of an
analogical description of the Father of Jesus Christ for an analysis *manqué*
of that one's being: "The intolerable and unpardonable thing in Roman
Catholic theology is that the question is put in this way, that there is this
splitting up of the concept of God, and hand in hand with it the abstraction
from the real work and activity of God in favour of a general being of God
which [God supposedly] has in common with us and with all being."[5] That
proposition is of course one that Thomas, at least, denies in a remarkably
explicit, thoroughgoing, and consistent way (e.g., I.3.5). We shall have occasion below to return to this business of how differently Thomas and Barth
deploy the term "God."

Barth's misunderstanding reaches the point of rendering natural theology not just mistaken but unintelligible to him: "The battle was already
fought and the positive presentation of the knowability of God already lay
behind us when we realised, and tried to explain, that with this presentation we had affirmed the very thing which Vatican [I] denies, and we denied
the very thing which it affirms. And it was only as we asked the astonished
question: How was such a thing possible, anyway? that step by step we became involved at all in a supplementary treatment of the claims and
promises of natural theology in general and as classically embodied in Vati-

can [I]."[6] The unintelligibility however comes not, Thomas might say, from any unintelligibility of natural theology *in se*, but from an unintelligibility that Barth unnecessarily builds into it, an unintelligibility *ad hominem*. It says less about Vatican I's concept of God or, *a fortiori*, Thomas's, than about Barth's own or, better, the difference and distance that plausibly intervene. Mutual unintelligibility need not however end in utter untranslatability. For as I said in the Preface, "[t]he more you and I seem to differ on some topic, the less reason we have for thinking we are discussing the same topic after all.... Too much divergence ceases to be divergence altogether: it merely changes the subject."[7]

That said, it becomes all too easy to tell a story about how Barth might have arrived at just such a position as he held. The entire progress of the Enlightenment from Locke forward and of both its Protestant admirers from Schleiermacher and its Catholic opponents culminating in Vatican I, *Aeterni Patris*, and schools of twentieth-century Thomists all conspire to prepare him for and confirm him in it.

II

Consider these features of *Aeterni Patris*. Like the *Contra gentiles* but unlike the *Summa Theologiae* it divides human knowledge into two domains, one accessible, one inaccessible to reason.[8] Not only that, but those truths accessible to human reason, so far from the *Summa's* "frequent admixture of error," *Aeterni patris* apparently foresees as "immediately perceptible by all human beings, without *any* admixture of error."[9] It is in that context that Leo XIII goes on to speak of their being "acknowledged by the mere [= purely?] natural light of reason, demonstrated with appropriate proofs and vindicated even by pagan philosophers" and quotes in support of Romans 1:20—reading in the English, amusingly enough, "the invincible" for "the invisible things of God." The context of *Aeterni patris* puts an apparently quite different light on such concepts as "natural," "demonstrate," "appropriate," "vindicate," and Romans 1:20 altogether, so that it becomes easier to see how Barth, seeing Thomas through them, might misread him.

But Leo goes on. The way of philosophy opens to all human beings "a smooth and easy way" to the faith, and in another metaphor it supplies "foundations...well and truly laid."[10] The two-story system of the handbooks follows naturally if not necessarily from such remarks, as well as the *amplius via* that Thomas denies in I.1.8. "We are therefore indebted to human reason for this great, preeminent benefit"—so Leo draws a conclusion—"that it enables us to demonstrate the existence of God." No matter what "enables" might mean, it is apparently from that ability that we learn to trust revelation, rather than the other way around. For "[t]he clear consequence"—a second conclusion—"is that human reason is disposed to place the most ample confidence and authority in the Word of God."[11] It looks as if the sciences of human reason judge and authorize sacred doctrine, just the reverse of what Barth in *Church Dogmatics* I/1 and Thomas in *ST* I.1.8 assert and insist, and as if it is demonstrations that provide the suppressed subject for the disposing. Hence the apparent plausibility of Barth's reading of Thomas.

One might, to be sure, interpret not only Thomas but even *Aeterni Patris* more congenially than that. The project would require putting the context (of accessible and inaccessible truths and of such phrases as "without any admixture of error") *itself* into context, a context still larger where the doctrine of the creation of the *world* and *not*, in Enlightenment fashion, the human intellect, grounds the assertions, so that they serve no general anthropology of the sort of which Barth ought rightly to be afraid, but the objective reality of a creation that exhibits its own evidence in what von Balthasar does and Barth might regard as an aesthetic rather than Enlightenment-conceptualized scientific way. *Aeterni Patris* just *might* bear an interpretation that moved it in the direction of the proof from nature instead of "natural science" (whatever that is) that Barth upheld in the letter to Carl Zuckmeyer: "On the contrary, I would gladly concede that *nature* does objectively offer a proof of God, though the human being overlooks or misunderstands it. Yet I would not venture to say the same of natural *science*, whether ancient or modern."[12] So that we should not think that senility had already set in when Barth wrote that (May 1968), I submit that he might have been describing a similar insight here, toward the beginning of the dogmatics, at greater length and with more care:[13]

> The concept which lies ready to our hand here, and which may serve legitimately to describe the element in the idea of glory that we still lack, is that of beauty. If we can and must say that God is beautiful, to say this is to say how [God] enlightens and convinces and persuades us....It is to say that God has this superior force, this power of attraction, which speaks for itself, which wins and conquers, in the fact that [God] is beautiful.... [God] does not have it, therefore, merely as a fact or a power. Or rather, [God] has it as a fact and a power in such a way that [God] acts as the One who gives pleasure, creates desire, and awards with enjoyment. And [God] does it because [God] is the One who is pleasant, desirable, full

of enjoyment, because first and last [God] is alone that which is pleasant, desirable, and full of enjoyment. God loves as the One who is worthy of love as God. That is what we mean when we say that God is beautiful.

A reinterpretation of *Aeterni Patris* might continue as follows: It is in fact a scriptural citation, "for by the greatness of the beauty, and of the creature, the Creator of them may be seen so as to be known thereby" (2 Peter 1:16), that warrants the assertion about God's demonstrability which is in any case asserted merely as "enabled." The statements about the consequence of human reason's placing confidence in revelation for that reason may possibly apply to unfallen or concrete nature (rather than to the nature that Barth imagines for them), or they may refer to a practical consequence about the *temporal* order in which human beings learn things as opposed to the logical order according to which as Leo would hardly deny sacred doctrine remains subalternate not to human philosophizing but to the *scientia Dei et beatorum*.

III

But surely Barth and Vatican I had irreconcilable intentions even if their texts prove more malleable than we would have thought. To compare their intentions in reacting to Kant I appeal to three sorts of *pre*knowledge as a historico-theological conceit.

By "*pre*knowledge" I mean no foreknowledge in the sense of *scientia media* but a term to hold together three sorts of knowledge whose names Thomas deploys the prefix "pre-" intentionally or unintentionally to mark: the *praeambula fidei* ("preambles to the faith," or metaphysics), the *praecognitum finis* ("something foreknown of the end," or revelation as included God's gift to human beings of an integral supernatural end), the *prae-incipia* or *principia scientiae* ("the first principles of the science" of sacred doctrine, or the articles of faith).

The very first question of the *Summa* tells us by what necessity a human being needs revelation besides philosophical disciplines. *Aeterni Patris* answers a different question, for what purpose a human being needs philosophy. In doing so however it implicitly commends Thomas's answer, and a commendation puts its own question into a different context. Given that, as I.1.1 puts it, revelation is necessary in respect of a particular end, namely the salvation of human beings, a determination that it reveals as graciously single, unitary, and final, it is necessary that they have something foreknown, or a *praecognitum* of it. The matters that Leo discusses count neither as *praecognitum* nor as principles but as preambles. It is important that we observe the distinctions among these three types of pre-knowledge. They prepare the human being for salvation in distinct ways, so that it is correct in each case to pay them, *praecognitum finis, principia* (= *articuli*) *istae scientiae, praeambula fidei,* the compliment of a certain necessity, but to conflate them is to undermine the distinctions that Thomas creates them to maintain, and to perpetuate the misreading that Barth shares with almost everyone in the century after Vatican I. Leo may defend the preambles in the strongest terms, it will appear, without at all impugning the distinct necessity of the *praecognitum* in view of something else, as long as his readers keep the differences straight.

Praecognitum, principia, and *praeambula* possess their various necessities in view of different ends. I will take them in reverse order. It is clear— Thomas makes it explicit—that the *praeambula* possess no necessity in view of human salvation as such. By "as such" I mean that nothing prevents someone from taking preambles on faith without following their demonstrations. How large that category is Thomas leaves open. Necessity in view of salvation as such—it is the burden and accomplishment of I.1.1 to establish—pertains to the *praecognitum finis.* The preambles possess however for that very reason a necessity of their own, a necessity in order that the reason of the human being be not divorced from but involved in its elevation by grace. It is a necessity of integrity. If Thomas did not by some such process assume reason (as Barth also does) into the process of salvation it is hard to see how he might explicate its redemption. Here too what is not assumed is not redeemed. So far, that is, from revelation's building upon reason's foundation as the two-story system of the handbooks would have it, revelation suspends reason in its net. The point of the preambles is that reason should rest in that net and not slip through it. Thus Thomas says that reason is able to demonstrate the proposition "God exists," but that it need not (I.2.2 *ad* 1). He expects that some people will prove unable to follow the Five Ways, that to do so will take great time and effort, and that they will suffer admixture of error (I.1.1). That describes no foundation as the Enlightenment came to think of it. Rather it describes an option that to its joy faith may exercise by use of reason as helpmeet on the way to understanding. To deny some such role for reason would exempt it from the orientation of the entire human being toward our unitary supernatural end and leave it in principle out of the *via in Deum* which is Jesus Christ, so that they would cease to be human beings whom God saved, agents of their own acts, and become creatures bereft of their proper mark. The process of elevation itself would then destroy the divine image, shatter the integrity proper to the human creature, and create a division in God's plan and self. The matter of the creature's integrity deserves more drawing out, for it is that that the Enlightenment threatened and that that Vatican I's Enlightenment critique and Karl Barth's upending of Schleiermacher sought each in their divergent ways to preserve. Hence a pair of diagnostic questions: what sort of creature results, in Thomas-like terms, from that integrity's failure, and how may we deploy Thomas's analysis to characterize the theological attempts at its repair?

Descartes had notoriously driven a wedge between mind and body, dividing sense-impressions therefore from their role in thought, as Thomas's Aristotelian realism could not allow. Thomas did however know of rational creatures in whom mind and body suffered something like that dissociation. With the caveat that in that case unlike Descartes's the rational creatures lacked bodies altogether we may summarize the difficulty like this: If Descartes created the mind-body problem often ascribed to him, then (Thomas might say) he had begun to confuse human beings with angels. He had lost the psychosomatic unity that marks the human creature and come up with a sort of angel in a body.

The confusion got worse. Kant went on despite his intentions and disclaimers to move the entire sensory world inside the mind. The phenomena left the body insufficiently intelligible, and the body that the mind had long animated and lately inhabited was finally lost. The embodied angel with which Descartes had begun proceeded in Kant to shed a body it had long ceased to make sense of its need for. Two further results followed: in a corresponding loss, described with polemical flourish by Hans Urs von Balthasar in his little book *Cordula*,[14] the mind lost with the body also the world, an angel set free from the matter now not only of a human body but even of an earthly home; and in a further split implied though unstated in Nicholas Wolterstorff's article "The Migration of the Theistic Arguments," Locke divided the mind between the intellect and the will in a way that brought the embodied or disembodied human angel to resemble the third of Thomas's rational creatures, the demons.

To such problems Protestants and Catholics offered differing solutions. Protestants following Schleiermacher accepted the split between subject and object that Kant had wrought and worried lest God too be absorbed without intelligible remainder into the human mind. It was therefore the independence of God and the gratuity of grace that they saw threatened and that they sought in turn to protect. Thus even as Barth insists upon God as subject, never object, and upon revelation as in no way deducible, as he thought Schleiermacher to have found it, from the structures of the human mind, he remained ontologically upon the subject-object seesaw while noetically revelation if not ordinary sense perception recapitulated the way in which Thomistic angels received the data upon which their minds might work: by God's gracious infusion. It was a way of insisting on the *praecognitum*, Thomas's name for revelation's gratuitous necessity, and in its purpose of blocking the Schleiermacherian move it succeeded. Indeed the *praecognitum* on which Barth might be said from Thomas's point of view to have fastened furnished in its objective aspect as revelation arguably *the* weapon appropriate to the protection of God's independence and grace's gratuity.

The priority of the noetic moment in Barth—according to which, in spite or better just because of the objectivity of the reconciliation that God works for us in Christ, everything that makes for its this-worldly effectiveness rests on our recognition or *Erkenntnis* of it—also reflects his picking up, sometimes in communitarian or ecclesiological, often in Enlightenment individual fashion, that element of Christian logic that Thomas calls the *praecognitum finis*—to which Thomas too, in his own way, accords in I.1.1 a certain necessity for the working out of God's salvific purpose—so that Thomas's precognition becomes *mutatis mutandis* Barth's recognition, or *Erkenntnis*.

Meanwhile Catholics had seen the problem's other aspect and sought another solution, although later they would be in danger of recapitulating the Schleiermacherian progress. They saw the human being disembodied by its enlightenment as a rational creature dispossessed of its psychosomatic integrity, its elevation to angelic heights attended by the danger and actuality of a greater fall. The human being had acquired the marks with which Thomas had characterized those who "believe and tremble," namely the demons. It was such a dissociation of intellect from will that gave rise to the Enlightenment's idolization of objectivity as an intellectual attitude. Objectivity, or evidence, belongs in Thomas, excuse the tautology, to— objects. No extramental objects, however, could any longer legitimate their claims to existence. So the Catholic Church first approached the disintegration of the human creature's mind from body and intellect from will by restoring its home. The tack, somewhat indirect, angled thus to take objectivity from the realm of intellectual attitudes and return it to the world. To do that one would insist upon the evidence, as Thomas would say, of signs. (The interpreted evidence of objects apprehended by a mind moved

by the will toward the good, not the diamondized evidence of mental objectivity apprehended by a mind alienated from its Creator, would supply "objective evidence" properly so called.) It was a world moreover available to
the senses, the senses not of an angel but of a body with will and passions. It
was important, that is, that God not infuse sense impressions into our
minds as into those of the angels, and that sense impressions have something other than noumena to be of. And it was important that the world of
which we had or might have impressions maintain enough independence
over against us to remain God's creation rather than ours. Such independence or difference from our minds furnished the creation with a necessary
susceptibility to various interpretations, however evident the truth of one
in itself. The gap, that is, between the world and us reopened a gap between
evidence in itself and evidence to us. The gap left room for concupiscence
and history and for real interaction therefore between us and God. World restored, body regained, subjectivity repulsed. Or so we may ascribe the hopes
to the attempt.

Of the three sorts of *pre*knowledge that Thomas mentions, the one that
holds together the body, the senses, and the world is that of the preambles.
In its differing circumstances the first Vatican Council and its thinkers
made something of them that Thomas in his did not. Nominalists and real-
ists had other concerns. Whatever Thomas does with them, the Five Ways
possessed in his time something of the quality of a set piece. The late nine-
teenth-century West could not however any longer take theology's cosmological claim for granted. It is therefore thus that Leo XIII found himself
praising the natural powers of human reason, those that connect us by body
and sense to the natural world, and thus that he found himself mentioning
the Five Ways as natural knowledge's summit. So far from seeking to promote an Enlightenment anthropocentrism, Leo sought instead to break it—
just by praising those aspects of the human being that depended "by nature" on something independent of and over against it. In positing natural
knowledge he sought to dispossess it; in praising it he sought to put it in
its place. The strategy avoided the Protestant seesaw and made sense of
the doctrine of creation, Christianity's means of staking a claim upon the
world. Grace's object includes creation as a whole and the creature as a
whole, the whole world and the whole human being, no societies excepted
and no faculties uninvolved: we may call it (on analogy to "total depravity")
total gratuity, an exceptionless claim. The preambles insist that "even" the
deliverances of the world, the senses, and human reason remain subject to
God's deployment for a salvific purpose: even they, preambles insist, re-

main within the grace's possible or actual reach. Vatican I and *Aeterni Patris* might be said, from Thomas's point of view, to have fastened upon *the* weapon appropriate to guarantee the human creature's integrity and grace's universality.

It remains to say a word about the third and most constitutive sort of preknowledge that Thomas deploys, the first principles of sacred doctrine as *scientia*, to which this book has been devoted. A little about how *principia* exercise in turn a necessity peculiar to them may add to the plausibility of this Thomas-eye interpretation of Enlightenment and post-Enlightenment theology. The *principia* are the articles of faith. I called them "most constitutive" because it falls to the articles (among other things) to determine (among other things) faith's content. Both Catholics and Protestants have called upon them when the nature of salvation, rather than its gratuity or integrity, is at stake. Of course all three aspects hang together. Thus it is that when Barth sees that it is the doctrine of the Trinity that Schleiermacher's reduction has materially lost he masses the whole witness of the revelation to restore it. Thus it is too that Catholic theology since Kant, whether pre-, Neo-, or post-Thomist, bears a plausible reading as a reflection, now less, now more successful, upon the doctrine of creation. Appeal to faith's articles also occasionally appears as a response, for example, to the tendency of historical criticism to separate the Jesus of history from the Christ of faith, since as it assigns the crucifixion to the first and the resurrection to the second it tends to leave unintelligible the proposition that it was the one crucified, dead, buried who on the third day rose.

Only time will tell whether the strategy of *Aeterni Patris*, with von Balthasar in the late twentieth century, may, after Kuhn's demythologization of natural science, prove a better one for getting beyond Kant. For the next century however it failed in one way after another. Natural science tended in its turn to establish a God-free realm, and Vatican I, in promoting the natural knowledge of God, generated numerous attempts to promote a knowledge of God founded upon natural science. Almost no one, indeed, made any distinction. Even those who did found it imprudent, until perhaps von Balthasar's theological aesthetics, to try making anything better of it. It was under those circumstances of failure that Barth wrote to Carl Zuckmeyer that he did in fact believe in a natural knowledge of God, just not any knowledge of God based upon natural science, "ancient or modern." Yet we may characterize Thomas's casting of sacred doctrine as *scientia*, and his taking up into it all things whatsoever, as an attempt that manages to make use of natural science—namely Aristotle's account of *scientia* as arising from and attending to a real *revelation*—in a way that Barth, when he excluded it "both ancient and modern," had left out of account. And we may characterize Thomas's natural knowledge of God, just where it makes use of cosmological arguments, as one that depends for its effectiveness on attitudes of justice and gratitude that only grace working through nature could supply.

Notes

Notes to the Preface

1. Otto Hermann Pesch, *Die Theologie der Rechtfertigung bei Martin Luther und Thomas von Aquin: Versuch eines systematisch-theologischen Dialogs* (Mainz: Matthias Grünewald, 1967). See also his *Thomas von Aquin: Grenze und Größe mittelalterlicher Theologie* (Mainz: Matthias Grünewald, 1988), and articles cited in the text.

2. Jeffrey Stout, "What Is the Meaning of a Text?" *New Literary History* 13 (1982):3–4.

3. Nicholas Wolterstorff furnishes a good example of that approach, contrasting the projects of Thomas and Locke. See his article, "The Migration of the Theistic Arguments: From Natural Theology to Evidentialist Apologetics," in *Rationality, Religious Belief, and Moral Commitment*, ed. R. Audi and W. J. Wainwright (Ithaca, N.Y.: Cornell University Press, 1986), 38–81.

4. Stout, "What Is the Meaning of a Text?" 8.

5. Ibid., 8.

6. Ibid., 5–6.

7. Meanwhile, there are three authors to whom I constantly refer. They are Otto Hermann Pesch, whom I have already mentioned; Michel Corbin, *Le chemin de la théologie chez Thomas d'Aquin*, Bibliothèque des archives de philosophie, nouvelle série 16 (Paris: Beauchesne, 1974); and Victor Preller, *Divine Science and the Science of God: A Reformulation of Thomas Aquinas* (Princeton, N.J.: Princeton University Press, 1967).

8. See for example Alasdair MacIntyre, "Too Many Thomisms?" Chapter III of *Three Rival Versions of Moral Enquiry: Encyclopaedia, Genealogy, and Tradition* (Notre Dame, Ind.: University of Notre Dame Press, 1990), 58–81.

Notes to Chapter One

1. In so doing it bears a great affinity to the work of Pesch, who argues that, properly understood, Thomas leaves room for Luther's innovations.

2. In those ways, too, it tacitly carries forward the Barth-interpretations of

Catholics like Hans Küng, Karl Rahner, and Hans Urs von Balthasar. See Hans Küng, *Justification: The Doctrine of Karl Barth and a Catholic Reflection,* 2d ed., trans. Thomas Collins et al. (Philadelphia: Westminster, 1981); Karl Rahner, e.g., "Questions of Controversial Theology on Justification," in his *Theological Investigations,* vol. 4, trans. Kevyn Smith (Baltimore: Helicon, 1966), 189–218; and Hans Urs von Balthasar, *The Theology of Karl Barth,* trans. Edward T. Oakes (San Francisco: Ignatius, 1992).

3. That work has been begun by Michel Corbin, who makes a few scattered if suggestive comments, and by Nicholas Wolterstorff, "Migration of the Theistic Arguments," esp. 38–39 and 81, n. 2.

4. Ibid., 81, n. 2.

5. *In* Rom. 1:25, §145; and *ST* II–II.94.1, both times quoting Augustine, *De civitate Dei* 7.5.

6. That is just a sampling. Influential have been, both when I agreed and when I did not: Jeffrey Stout, *The Flight from Authority: Religion, Morality, and the Quest for Authority* (Notre Dame, Ind.: University of Notre Dame Press, 1981), and *Ethics After Babel: The Languages of Morals and Their Discontents* (Boston: Beacon, 1988); Alasdair MacIntyre, *After Virtue: A Study in Moral Theory* (Notre Dame, Ind.: University of Notre Dame Press, 1981), *Whose Justice, Which Rationality* (Notre Dame, Ind.: University of Notre Dame Press, 1988), *Three Rival Versions of Moral Enquiry* (Notre Dame, Ind.: University of Notre Dame Press, 1990), and *First Principles, Final Ends, and Contemporary Philosophical Issues* (Milwaukee: Marquette University Press, 1990); and George Lindbeck, *The Nature of Doctrine: Religion and Theology in a Postliberal Age* (London: SPCK, and Philadelphia: Fortress, 1984). But none of these books will be cited much, either in support or in dissent.

7. Stout, *Ethics After Babel,* chap. 8, "The Voice of Theology," 163–188.

8. The thoughts on Locke in "Migration of the Theistic Arguments," although not on Thomas, appear at book length in Nicholas Wolterstorff, *When Tradition Fractures* (New York: Cambridge University Press, 1995). Future citations of Wolterstorff refer to "Migration."

9. Where doubt (I think) indicates primarily a lack of adherence of the will to the good. Debating out of a desire to manifest the truth is laudable. Thinkers of the Enlightenment (like thinkers of any period) might fall into either category, but it has been more characteristic of *post*-Enlightenment hermeneutics of suspicion to follow the medievals in devoting much methodological consideration to the adherence or lack of adherence of a thinker's will to the good.

10. For a history of the Enlightenment career of that notion, see Hans W. Frei, *The Eclipse of Biblical Narrative: A Study in Eighteenth and Nineteenth Century Hermeneutics* (New Haven, Conn.: Yale University Press, 1974).

11. Karl Barth, *Fides quaerens intellectum. Anselms Beweis der Existenz Gottes* (Munich: Christian Kaiser, 1931); and in English, *Anselm: Fides Quaerens*

Intellectum: Anselm's Proof of the Existence of God in the Context of his Theological Scheme, trans. Ian W. Robertson (Richmond, Va.: John Knox, 1960).

12. Karl Barth, *Die Kirchliche Dogmatik*, 4 vols. in 12 (Zürich: Zollikon, 1932ff.). ET: *Church Dogmatics*, ed. and trans. G. W. Bromiley and T. F. Torrance (Edinburgh: T. & T. Clark, 1936ff; 2d ed. of vol. I/1, 1975). Here, vol. II, part 1, p. 127, translation modified. Hereinafter cited like this: *CD* II/1, p. 127.

13. *CD* II/1, p. 82, emphasis added.

14. *A Late Friendship: The Letters of Karl Barth and Carl Zuckmayer*, trans. Geoffrey Bromiley (Grand Rapids, Mich.: Eerdmans, 1982), 42. Barth dates the letter 7 May 1968. German: *Gesammtausgabe: Briefe*, V, p. 286, §286.

15. "Scientia naturalis...res a Deo procedentes considerat" (*In* John, prol., §9). I adopt the translation of James Weisheipl, trans. and ed., *Commentary on the Gospel of St. John* (Albany: Magi, 1980), 26, which I discuss below.

16. Karl Barth, *A Shorter Commentary on Romans* (Richmond, Va.: John Knox, 1959), 28, emphasis added.

17. I mimic the phrase, modified from a technical term of different range coined by Wilfred Sellers, that appears at the end of Preller, *Divine Science*, "the material moves of faith," 266–273.

18. The "Paul" in question may or may not differ from the "Paul" delivered by historical criticism; I mean a figure with enough in common with the traditional reading that both Thomas and Barth would recognize an appeal to him as authoritative and potentially challenging.

19. For a Wittgensteinian account of how texts and interpreters influence traditions, see Kathryn Tanner, "Theology and the Plain Sense," in *Scriptural Authority and Narrative Interpretation*, ed. Garrett Green (Philadelphia: Fortress, 1987), 59–78.

20. Discussion at the end of Part II of this essay.

21. That is not to say that Thomas "proves the existence of God," or even thinks he does. The Five Ways "involve the claim that certain propositions, e.g., 'God exists,' are true; but they do not involve the claim that we know in what way these propositions predicate intelligible characteristics of an intelligible subject" (Preller, *Divine Science*, 31).

Note too that by "cosmological" (not Thomas's term) I merely mean not ontological and not transcendental, i.e., his arguments, not Anselm's or Schleiermacher's.

22. Karl Barth, *Kurze Erzählung des Römerbriefes* (Munich: Christian Kaiser, 1956); *A Shorter Commentary on Romans*.

23. Etienne Gilson, *The Christian Philosophy of St. Thomas Aquinas*, trans. L. K. Shook (New York: Random House, 1956), 9. The passage is quoted and discussed in Marshall, "Aquinas as a Postliberal Theologian," *The Thomist* 53 (1989): 389–390.

24. I owe the observation to Bruce Marshall.

25. *"Narrativus."* In *Sent.*, prol., art. 5. I owe the reference to Marie-Dominique Chenu, *La théologie comme science au XIIIᵉ siècle*, 3d rev. ed. (Paris: J. Vrin: 1957), 66.

26. See the Marietti edition: *Super epistolas S. Pauli lectura*, 2 vols., 8th rev. ed., ed. Raphael Cai, O.P. (Turin and Rome: Marietti, 1953), I, vi–vii.

27. James A. Weisheipl, O.P., *Friar Thomas D'Aquino: His Life, Thought, and Work* (Garden City, N.Y.: Doubleday, 1974), 250 and preceding discussion. See also the annotated bibliography, 355–406. Otto Pesch, in "Paul as Professor of Theology: The Image of the Apostle in St. Thomas's Theology," *The Thomist* 38 (1974): 589, n. 8 also prefers the Paris dating. He calls the arguments of Henri Bouillard on the point "incontestable," citing Bouillard's *Conversion et grace chez saint Thomas d'Aquin* (Paris, 1944), 225–241.

28. See Corbin, *Le Chemin*, ch. III, section IV: "Le passage de la *Somme contre les gentils* à la *Somme théologique* (livres II et IV)," 643–692.

29. Weisheipl reports a view that the *Contra gentiles* is *contemporary* with the *Secunda pars* of the last *Summa*—making the beginning of the *Contra gentiles* later than that of the *Summa theologiae!*—only to describe it as unconvincing and "contrary to all known facts" (p. 360). That aside, it would be very interesting to have a report about the probable influence of the *first* commentary on Romans upon the composition of the *Contra gentiles*. Since we have neither the text nor much of a date for Thomas's first *lectura in Romanos*, however, a comparison seems impossible.

Notes to Chapter Two

1. For additional texts and other arguments see Otto Hermann Pesch, *Theologie der Rechtfertigung*, sections "Christozentrik—nein und ja," 581–585 and "Gotteslehre und Christozentrik," 864–866.

2. Thomas's tendency to announce single propositions that go on to govern large bodies of text comes in for explicit consideration when we look at the structure of his Romans commentary.

3. Corbin, *Le chemin*, 717–718.

4. Dogmatic Constitution on Divine Revelation (*Dei Verbum*), I.2. Corbin notes the same correspondence in *Le chemin*, 698, n. 8.

5. Corbin, *Le chemin*, *passim*: that is one of the main theses of his book.

6. Ibid., e.g., 716, 804. n. 64.

7. Ibid., 491–680, esp. from 652.

8. See ibid., e.g., 705, 713, 741, 745, 759–760, 798–799, et al.

9. For a history of attempts, internal and external to theology, to relate Aristotle and the Bible, see Chenu, *La théologie comme science*. On Thomas, Chenu needs supplementation and correction by Corbin.

10. "[I]n captivitatem redigi[re] omnem intellectum in obsequium Christi," quoted, e.g., in I.1.8 *ad* 2 *in med.*

11. Gloss, contemporary with the *Summa*, from *In* 2 Cor. 10:5, §352: "quod quidem fit quando id quod homo scit, totum supponit ministerio Christi et fidei." That is also a description of what Thomas is up to in the apparently non-christological sections of the *Summa:* he is placing all his knowledge in the service of Christ and of the faith. Cf. the discussion in Marshall, "Aquinas as Postliberal Theologian," 400–401.

12. Corbin, *Le chemin*, 717.

13. Terence Irwin, *Aristotle's First Principles* (New York: Oxford, 1988), 7. Thomas did not miss this in works contemporary with the *Summa;* see, for example, *In metaphys.*, bk. 5, *lect.* 1, *in fin.*, where he writes that Aristotle "reduces all the aforesaid uses [of the word "first principle"] to what they have in common; and he says that what is common in all the uses spoken of is, that something be called a first principle, that is first, whether in the being of a thing,...or in the becoming of a thing, or in the cognition of a thing."

14. Alasdair MacIntrye, *First Principles*, 4. See also 1–7.

15. Irwin, *Aristotle's First Principles*, 7.

16. Examples also from ibid.

17. "Postquam philosophus in primo libro determinat de *principiis rerum naturalium*, hic determinat de *principiis scientiae naturalis*" (*In phys.*, bk. 2, *lect.* 1, *in init.*).

18. Thus we need not worry whether particular candidates for first principles—elements or atoms or quarks—go far enough down to count as truly "first." We do not call them "first" to make an *arche* into a Cartesian foundation; we call them "first" principles to distinguish them from inner and final principles. Cartesian scrupulosity would only exasperate Aristotle or Thomas. Precisely because of their inseparability from explanation, first principles need not, indeed cannot go all the way down. Explanation always furnishes a context. In fact, any beginning of a thing in the world that furnishes a good enough beginning (*positio*) for a particular explanation can count as a first principle for that purpose. See Chenu, *La théologie comme science*, 72–73, note 1, paragraph 1, and Thomas, *In Post. Anal.*, bk. 1, *lect.* 5, no. 7.

19. See Jonathan Lear, *Aristotle: The Desire to Understand* (New York: Cambridge University Press, 1988), chap. 2, section 1: "Nature as an inner principle of change," 15–26.

20. I.1.5 *ad* 1, citing Aristotle, *Metaphys.* II.1, 993b9; I take the rendering of the internal quotation from the Blackfriars edition. The same distinction in unity appears when Thomas distinguishes two senses of formal object: he identifies the form as it directs the development of things as "on the part of the thing itself" (*ex parte ipsius rei*), and the same form as it directs the develop-

ment of a rational soul coming into conformity with the world as "on our part" (*ex parte nostra*) (II–II.1.6 *ad* 2).

21. Liddell, Scott, Jones et. al., *A Greek-English Lexicon*, rev. ed. with supplement (New York: Oxford, 1968), svv. *"epistêma"* and *"epistêmê."*

22. Corbin, *Le chemin*, 717.

23. Irwin's words again, *Aristotle's First Principles*, 7.

24. Corbin, *Le chemin*, 717.

25. Ibid.

26. Ibid. The whole paragraph follows Corbin.

27. Ibid.

28. Ibid.

29. Ibid., 718; emphasis added.

30. Ibid., 717. This paragraph abbreviates an argument that Corbin presents over pp. 709–727.

31. Better, he interpolates it. In one of the oddest deliverances of Thomas text-criticism, it appears that the text about quasi-subalternation was written after the highpoint of the subalternation doctrine, although it appears in an otherwise earlier work. So the highpoint of subalternation theory appears at *In Boethium de Trinitate* q. 2, art. 2, *ad* 5, while the qualification of quasi-subalternation appears at *In Sent.*, prol., art. 3, solution to questiuncula 2. The dates are: *Sentences*, 1254–56; *De Trinitate*, 1256; interpolation into the *Sentences*, between 1256 and probably 1258; *Summa theologiae*, 1266–73. See Corbin, "Annexe: Le problème textuel de l'article 3 (qa 2)," *Le chemin*, 202–205, for bibliographical and manuscript references.

32. *In Phys.* bk. 1, *lect.* 1 *in init.* There is nothing to prevent the revelatory power of a form to strike us first in a new interpretation rather than a new discovery; it belongs to form to reveal itself at once in minds and things.

33. Corbin (*Le chemin*, 733) quotes and rejects, as considering only the propositional aspect of first principles, the following interpretation from John of St. Thomas: "Theology takes its first principles from faith for this life, for inferring its conclusions and reasoning [*ratiocinando*] about God: so that faith reflects upon things immediately revealed, whereas theology reflects upon things deduced [*illata*] from them, which are called revealed mediately or virtually" (*In Iam partem*, q. 1, disp. 2, art. 5). Note the multiple changes that reading requires John of St. Thomas to make. John speaks of "theology" rather than sacred doctrine; he takes first principles from faith, not revelation; he interprets the word "virtual" by creating a distinction between two sets of *propositions*, rather than between propositions and reality; and he introduces words like *"ratiocinando"* and *"illata"* that heighten the sense of intellectual mechanism. Each of those changes works to conceal first principles' real aspect. For further discussion of *Konklusionstheologie*, see Corbin, *Le chemin*, 813–816. Cf. also *In Heb.* 1:1

§557, where *virtute* covers at once a conclusion in a premise and an effect in a cause.

34. Ibid., 717–718.

35. For more on the *scientia* enjoyed by angels, and its usefulness as a test case for human knowing, cf. Preller, *Divine Science*, 71, 78–80.

36. I owe the warning to Joseph DiNoia.

37. *In metaphys.*, prol.

38. Lear, *Desire to Understand*, 230.

39. That is the burden of *Metaphys.* 7.7–9, especially 1034b9.

40. See *Phys.* 8.

41. David Burrell, *Knowing the Unknowable God: Ibn-Sina, Maimonides, Aquinas* (Notre Dame, Ind.: University of Notre Dame Press, 1986); Chenu, *La théologie comme science*; Preller, *Divine Science*, 4.

42. *In Rom.* 1:19, §114; similar language recurs, e.g. at I.12.13 obj. 1 and *ad* 1.

43. MacIntyre's *First Principles* also holds the four aspects inalienably together, although he neither distinguishes them as I do nor does he, in that volume at least, treat Thomas as a practitioner of more than "the theology that pertains to metaphysics" from which Thomas takes care to distinguish sacred doctrine (I.1.1 *ad* 2 *in fin.*).

44. Lear, *Desire to Understand*, 310. In its own context the remark sounds all too Hegelian: "[S]ince [Aristotle's] God is a first principle of all things, and is (at least partially) constituted by self-understanding, it would seem that this understanding is itself a cause or principle of all things. Understanding [the understanding that human beings (also) have] is itself a force in the world" (p. 9). "Thus the understanding of first principles—philosophy—is not an understanding of something that exists independently of that understanding. . . . Philosophic activity, then, is one of the basic forces in the universe. This, of course, is a misleading way of putting a deep truth about Aristotle's world. 'Philosophical activity' is a name we give to substantial form only belatedly..." (p. 310). Perhaps that is what happens when "transcendence" remains within the world. In any case reformulation can only help. For more of what Thomas does, see for example I.14 (God's *scientia*) to I.16 (truth).

45. For an Aristotelian (and Wittgensteinian) reformulation of Freud, see Jonathan Lear, *Love and Its Place in Nature: A Philosophical Interpretation of Freudian Psychoanalysis* (New York: Farrar, Strauss & Giroux, 1990).

46. *Metaphys.* 1.2, 982b28–983a11.

47. *Sic: Metaphys.* 8.5.3, 1048a11. Thomas's irregular citations of the *Metaphysics* give historians clues about whose translations he was using and therefore when he was writing.

48. I come to say more about that in a chapter that draws conclusions from Thomas's Romans commentary.

49. Preller, *Divine Science*, 32.

50. "[D]iscernendo scilicet credenda a non credendis" (II–II.9.1 *in fin.*).

51. Cf. Preller, *Divine Science*, 241.

52. On the compatibility of divine providence with contingency and freedom, see I.22.4. For the use of the adverb *"infallibiliter"* to describe how things happen according to God's providence without imposing necessity on them (i.e., founding contingency and freedom), see I.23.6. For an account of the whole, see Kathryn Tanner, *God and Creation in Christian Theology: Tyranny or Empowerment?* (Oxford: Basil Blackwell, 1988), 36–119, esp. 46–48.

53. "Lest anyone want to confine [*cogere*] scripture so to one sense, that other senses be entirely excluded, that in themselves contain truth and are able to adapted to scripture, preserving the literal sense" (*De potentia* q. 4, a. 1, c., *post init.*). See discussion in Bruce Marshall, "Absorbing the World: Christianity and the Universe of Truths," in *Theology and Dialogue: Essays in Conversation with George Lindbeck*, ed. Bruce Marshall (Notre Dame, Ind.: University of Notre Dame Press, 1990), 69–102, esp. 90–97. Were I fighting a battle on another front, I would want to make more of that strain in Thomas. See Eugene F. Rogers, Jr., "How the Virtues of an Interpreter Presuppose and Perfect Hermeneutics," *Journal of Religion* 76 (1996).

54. For explication and critique, see Preller, *Divine Science*, especially 55–62.

55. Ibid., 65. Here and below I retain his italics and his use of single quotation marks for concepts.

56. I do not mean to invoke Karl Rahner's explication of the *"Vorgriff auf esse,"* but only to give the notion a name.

57. Preller, *Divine Science*, 70–71.

58. Ibid., 239, citing *In* Heb. 11:1, notes that Thomas calls faith "a kind of beginning, as it were [*quasi quoddam inchoativum*]" of the vision the blessed have of God.

59. Cf. ibid., 241: "God does not exist in...formal clarity in the intellect of the believer. The mode of faith's participation in the science of God [the science that God enjoys] is causal and analogical. The first truth is both the first and final cause of the existence in the soul of the believer of the intentions of faith. The form in which we possess the science of God is not the form in which God...possesses that science, but an *analogue* of that form. The manner in which that 'state of mind' called "faith" exemplifies or is isomorphic with the intentional being of God is known only to God and the *beati.*"

60. I.43.5; cf. I–II.90 and 109 proemia; I–II.106.1, esp. in biblical quotations.

61. A phrase I owe to Victor Preller.

62. Preller (*Divine Science*, 232–233) puts it like this: "Scripture is itself a created analogue of God's act of self-knowledge as expressed in his Word or inner speech. Conformation of the mind to the intention of sacred scripture effects the conformation of the soul to the Second Person of the Trinity."

63. For a similar analysis of Barth, see Bruce McCormack, *Karl Barth's Criti-*

cally Realistic Dialectical Theology: Its Genesis and Development, 1909–1936 (Oxford: Clarendon, 1995), chap. 8, 327–374.

64. "Scientia naturalis...res a Deo procedentes considerat...Evangelium Ioannis, quod divisim scientiae praedictae [moralis, naturalis, metaphysica] habent, totum simul continet, et ideo est perfectissimum" (*In* John, prol., §9).

It is tempting to take the matter further. When Thomas comes to consider ethics, metaphysics, and natural science there, he calls the Gospel of John most perfect in containing them all at once. The perfection of John consists in the simultaneity or entirety of his vision. Natural science, Thomas says, considers things *"a Deo procedentes."* The formulation calls attention to itself because it is not one that natural science would bestow upon itself. Neither Aristotle nor the moderns would describe natural science as considering "things that proceed from God." Thomas is referring to the real orientation of natural science toward God—indeed, if Pesch is right, toward "the Lord Jesus"—that John sees (*Rechtfertigung*, p. 581, n. 10, citing *In Io.*, prol., §1, quoted below). As so oriented, natural science studies—not *realia* anymore—but *revelabilia*. In John, that is, natural science is re-oriented, trans-formed. In John, Thomas says nothing to indicate that the imperfection of those sciences consists in their not actually pursuing *revelabilia*. Otherwise, we learn in *In Io.* 1:9, §125 (a section that I will comment upon at the end of this chapter), they can even be described as having "false light." Rather, in this passage their imperfection lies merely in not being *"simul."* The way lies open to suppose that Thomas is not only re-*orienting* natural science but re-*defining* it. Here, that is, natural science properly so called is subsumed into sacred doctrine to the extent of becoming a branch of it. We could construct such a discipline. It would be an explication of creation which would generally and for the most part work in relative independence from the biblical *litterae*. It could not be modern creation science, for that would be to consider things as *revelata*, not *revelabilia*. Thomas's Aristotle commentaries could not take this approach, of course, and remain commentaries upon Aristotle instead of Genesis. In the *Summa* the long anthropology of the *Secunda*, however, may constitute such an attempt. The John commentary gives us grounds for calling that treatise not just "the anthropology that pertains to sacred doctrine" but anthropology properly so called. To say that the anthropology of the *Secunda* constitutes anthropology proper is not to say that it is more correct than (say) Freud. It is simply to say that it proceeds by believing God, although there are many ways of so proceeding in detail, and that when it does so it may still claim to speak to anthropology that proceeds otherwise according to the permission of I.1.6 *ad* 2. Karl Barth gives a history of "biblical cosmologies" in *CD* III/2, pp. 4–6, of which he prefers that of Polanus. He rejects them because the Bible does not contain any detailed account of the cosmos. But that is again to pursue the matter as one of *revelata* rather than *revelabilia*. Weisheipl, *Commentary on the Gospel of St.*

John, 26, brings out the oddity by translating with "as": "natural science... considers things as proceeding from God."

65. MacIntyre, *First Principles*, 23, 25. For a short, to-the-point discussion of the controverted relation of the two figures of science in Aristotle, see 23–29. For their relation in Thomas, our accounts diverge.

66. "[S]ecundum Philosophum in I *Poster.* [I.1.4, 993b21], *una scientia est quae est unius generis subiecti*" (I.1.3 obj. 1). Although the quotation appears in an objection, the reply does not deny, and the response presupposes it. According to the chronology in Weisheipl, *Friar Thomas D'Aquino*, 375, the *Posterior Analytics* belongs between 1268 and 1272. The *Summa* dates from 1266–1273.

67. MacIntyre, *Three Rival Versions*, 84–85.

68. Preller, *Divine Science*, 232, citing *In Post. Anal.*, bk. 1, *lect.* 1.

69. Corbin, *Le chemin*, 694–695.

70. Thomas does know of an inspiration in which God is revealed to human beings in abstraction from the free use of their capacities; it goes by the name of rapture (II–II.175). Unlike scripture, it is for that very reason incommunicable in principle to any other human being in this life. See Preller, *Divine Science*, 193. I find a theory of inspiration requiring human freedom as a special case of the vocation by which God works in all human beings implied in Thomas's prologue to his commentary on the Pauline epistles; see Chapter 3.

71. Preller, *Divine Science*, 233, 242.

72. Ibid., 233–234.

73. Ibid., 239.

74. Ibid., 242.

75. Ibid., 234.

76. Ibid., 263.

77. Ibid., 242.

78. "Secundum doctrinam Ecclesiae intellectis sane," II–II.5.3 *ad* 2. For discussion see Marshall, "Aquinas as a Postliberal Theologian," 377–378 and Pesch, *Rechtfertigung*, 725–728. For the way in which scriptural interpretation is to be adapted to the best deliverances of extrascriptural inquiry so far, see the preceding note to *De pot.* 4.1c.

79. Why does Christ need to argue from scripture? As Preller puts it (*Divine Science*, 248–249), "Christ appeared to the apostles to establish the fact of the resuscitation, which is what is taken by faith to be a cause of salvation. As an article of faith, however, the resurrection cannot be seen, but must be believed; for the object of faith is not the fact, but the causal efficacy of the fact in the order of salvation—in Heilsgeschichte. That must be proved out of scripture, even with the resuscitated body standing before the believer. To prove by scripture is to presuppose the intentionality of faith. Ultimately, that which is believed is God himself, since he is the principle of that causal order known-by-faith as the 'order of salvation.'"

80. Cf. Corbin, *Le chemin*, 855–857, for an argument in favor of the coherence of the scientific and scriptural elements of Question 1.

81. For a complementary statement of the matter, which also takes into account texts from the *Contra gentiles*, see Corbin, *Le chemin*, 697–700.

82. Cf. I.82.1, which identifies the "necessity of an end," discussed in Corbin, *Le chemin*, 695.

83. For discussion and bibliography, cf. Pesch, *Rechtfertigung*, 652–655.

84. "Grace perfects nature," taken for granted in I.1.8 *ad* 2, I.2.2 *ad* 1, and elsewhere. For evaluation of the texts in Thomas and the secondary literature on the phrase, see Pesch, *Rechtfertigung*, 519–526.

85. *Metaphys.* 7.9, 1034b9.

86. Cf. Corbin, *Le chemin*, 723, citing *Post. Anal.* I.2 (72a14–20) and I.13 (78b35–39). See also Chenu, *Théologie comme science*, 73, nn. 1–2, and 81, n. 1.

87. "An end must be something foreknown [*praecognitum*] to human beings, who ought to order their intentions and actions into an end" (I.1.1).

88. Thomas relies on this conceptualization throughout his Romans commentary, and I will be developing it there. On Thomas's resistance to speculations that depart from the concrete decisions of God recorded in the scriptures, see III.1.3c and *In* 1 Tim. 1:15, §40, discussed in Marshall, "Thomas, Thomisms, and Truth," *The Thomist* 56 (1992): 514–515, n. 32. In those passages the question dismissed is whether God would have been incarnate, if human beings had not sinned. In the present case the question is even farther removed from the concrete course of salvation history: Suppose God had made human beings without grace (I.95.1, esp. *ad* 4).

89. For an account, remarkable for the closeness of its explication of the text, of how the move to *revelabilia* defines and unifies sacred doctrine in the *Summa*, see Corbin, *Le chemin*, 727–743.

90. Ibid., 733–735, persuasively argues the insufficiency of those explications.

91. Ibid., 741. See also 743, esp. n. 32.

92. *De pot.* q. 4, a. 1, c., *post init.*

93. That is a reading of the Fourth Way of I.2.3, a consequence of God's perfection (I.4.1) and goodness (I.6.1), and conforms to the rules for speech about God (I.13.3 and I.13.6).

94. In that article *"scientia divina"* seems to function as a synonym for *"scientia Dei et beatorum,"* at just the place where Preller's book, *Divine Science and the Science of God*, makes its title distinction.

95. Pesch, *Rechtfertigung*, 583, n. 10, his emphasis. The christocentricity follows from Thomas's claim to be explicating "secundum quod Dominus Iesus tripliciter est contemplatus" in *In* John prol., §1.

96. "Now there is in those things which we confess of God a twofold mode of truth. For certain things are true of God which exceed the entire faculty of human reason, as that God is one and three together. Yet other things belong to

those which reason can also (or even reason can) attain, such as that God exists, God is one, and other things of this sort, which the philosophers also (or even the philosophers) demonstratively prove of God, led by the light of natural reason" (*Contra gentiles*, I.3.2). Here too I could translate *"etiam"* as "even" rather than "also." But "also" brings out better the doubleness of the twofold mode of truth, as opposed to the singular integrity of sacred doctrine as *scientia* in the later *Summa* (I.1.3). See the discussion in Corbin, *Le chemin*, 535–544.

For the difference of the scheme of the *Contra gentiles* from that of the *In Boethium de Trinitate*, see p. 559. For the difference between the scheme of the *Contra gentiles* and that of the *Summa Theologiae*, see 700–709, esp. 705; and 727–743, esp. 741.

97. Corbin, *Le chemin*, 705. I owe my attention to the word *"etiam"* to the discussion in Corbin, 700–709.

98. By *Contra Gentiles* II.4.1 Thomas is writing: "Now it is palpable from the foregoing that the doctrine of the Christian faith considers creatures insofar as a certain likeness to God rebounds from them, and insofar as an error about them leads to an error in things divine. And so the foregoing teachings, philosophy too, are placed under another rationale. For human philosophy considers creatures according as they are of such a kind: whence too different parts of [natural] philosophy are found according to the diverse kinds of things. The Christian faith, however, considers them not insofar as they are of such a kind, for example, fire as it is fire, but *insofar as it recalls the divine heights and in some way is ordered to very God.*" With that, despite the language of similitude and representation, Thomas is well on the way to subalternation of formal rationales. See the discussion in Corbin, *Le chemin*, 652–666.

By *CG* IV.1.9, furthermore, Thomas is willing to add a third mode to the first two: "The third [human cognition of things divine] is according as the human mind will be elevated to those things which are to be intuited as perfectly revealed"—a cognition which promises to overcome the division. It is the intuition the blessed will share with God, a future cognition against which, according to the *Summa*, God in sacred doctrine grants an advance. See Corbin, 671–680.

For an overview of the progress of the theory of theological science from the *De trinitate* through the *Contra gentiles* to the *Summa*, see Corbin, 709–727.

99. Corbin, *Le chemin*, 682. According to the likeliest datings, Thomas completed the *Contra gentiles* in 1264. Already within it, by textual evidence, he was changing his course. But thereafter (1264–1273), just before or contemporary with the *Summa*, he seems to have composed an enormous volume of work: *De potentia, De malo, De spiritualibus creaturis, De anima, De virtutibus in communi, De caritate, De correctione fraterna, De spe, De virtutibus cardinales, De unione verbi incarnati, In Psalmos, In Ioannem, In Romanos, In I Corinth. 1–10, Commendatio sacrae scripturae, In Peri hermeneias, In Post.*

anal., In phys., In de caelo et mundo, In de generatione, In Meteora, In de anima, In metaphys., In Eth., In Pol., In de causis, De perfectione spiritualis vitae, Contra retrahentes, De unitate intellectus, De aeternitate mundi, Compendium theologiae, De substantiis separatis, De regimine principium. See the catalogue in Weisheipl, *Friar Thomas D'Aquino*, 355–405.

100. "This science surpasses other speculative sciences with regard to certainty at least, since other sciences have certainty from the natural light of human reason, which is able to err; this one, on the other hand, has certainty by the light of divine knowledge, which is not able to deceive.... For it does not accept its first principles from other sciences, but immediately from God by revelation" (I.1.5c and *ad* 2).

101. Quoting II *Metaphys.* [I.1.2, 993b9] at I.1.5 *ad* 1. I owe the translation to the Blackfriars edition.

102. It orders the ends of all other practical sciences to its own: "The end of this doctrine, insofar as it is practical, is eternal beatitude, to which, as the ultimate end, all other ends of practical sciences are ordered" (I.1.5 *in fin.*). The ends of speculative sciences get taken up into that movement, too. For the article begins: "Since this science is speculative with respect to one thing, and with respect to another it is practical, it transcends all others, speculative as well as practical." It would detract from the science's dignity (and unity) to think it a virtue just that it did both things, speculative and practical, precisely as *different*, as a jack-of-all-trades. Rather it pursues them together from their God's-eye *union*, and it is *so* that it is higher, beside which the separation makes mere points in an analysis: "Sacred doctrine, consisting in one thing together, extends itself to those things that pertain to diverse philosophical sciences, on account of a formal rationale that stretches into diverse things: namely, according to how they are cognizable by the divine light. Whence although among philosophical sciences some are speculative and some are practical, *sacred* doctrine comprehends both under itself, as God, in every science, enjoys self-recognition, too, as well as recognition of those things that God has made" (I.1.4).

103. I owe my attention to the repetition and placement of the thesis in article one to the excellent discussion in Corbin, *Le chemin*, 700–702.

104. *In I Sent.*, prol., art. 5, quoted in Chenu, *Théologie comme science*, 66.

105. A qualification he elaborates upon in the immediately following paragraph of the reply *ad* 1: "And so also no confusion follows in sacred Scripture: since all senses are founded upon one, namely the literal, from which alone an argument can be drawn, but not from those things which are related according to allegory." For more on this passage, see Henri de Lubac, *Exégèse médiévale*, vol. II, part 2 (Paris: Aubier, 1964), 272–285; and Rogers, "Virtues of the Interpreter."

106. *Quaestiones quodlibetales* n. 7, q. 6, a. 2, obj. 1. Although the definition comes from an objection, the reply does not deny but uses it.

107. *Quaestiones quodlibetales* n. 7, q. 6., a. 2, *ad* 1.

108. "The allegorical sense pertains to Christ not only as regards the head, but also as regards the members...But the moral sense pertains to the members of Christ as agents [*proprios*] of their own acts, and not according as they are considered members....So the allegorical sense pertains to Christ as he is head of the church militant, justifying it and infusing grace....Christ's true body itself, and those things which were done in it, are figures of Christ's mystical body, and those things which are done in it, as in it, namely in Christ, we ought to take an example for living. In Christ also the future glory is demonstrated to us in advance [*praemonstrata est*]; whence those things that are said literally of Christ's head itself, are able to be expounded both allegorically, referring to his mystical head; and morally, referring to our acts, which ought to be reformed according to it; and anagogically, in that in Christ the way to glory has been demonstrated to us [*in quantum in Christo est nobis iter gloriae demonstratum*]." *Quod.* n. 7, q. 6, a. 2, *ad* 2-5.

109. "Principale autem in doctrina fidei Christianae est salus per crucem Christi facta" (*In* 1 Cor. 1:18, §45 *in med.*). Cf. discussion in Marshall, "Thomas, Thomisms, and Truth," 522-523.

110. The translation simplifies matters. In the original Thomas compares not only *scientia* and *Verbum*, but also the way in which they relate differently to God *in se* and to God as God of creatures, so that we get a double analogy. It goes like this: "[S]icut Dei scientia Dei quidem est cognoscitiva tantum, creaturarum autem cognoscitiva et factiva; ita Verbum Dei eius quod in Deo Patre est, est expressivum tantum, creaturarum vero est expressivum et operativum" (I.34.3 *post med.*). Both *facio* and *exprimo* can mean "to form," but the second conveys the more precise connotation of "press out according to a mold."

111. *In* John 14, *lect.* 6, §1958. I owe the citation to Marshall, "Thomas, Thomisms, and Truth," 523.

112. *In* Rom. 1:20a: §115 *"Secundo"*; §117 *"Aliud"*; §122 *in init.*

113. Believers do receive a "gift of understanding" (*donum intellectus*, II–II.8), but in a different sense. The gift is not such as to render the understandings strictly "knowable" or *scibile*. The next question, on the gift of *scientia*, denies that possibility (II–II.9). Compare Thomas's definition of faith as the substance of things not seen at II–II.4.1.

114. I owe my first attention to this appearance of the word *"demonstrare"* to a remark by Alasdair MacIntyre. See also Michel Corbin, "La Parole devenue chair (lecture de la 1re question de la *Tertia Pars* de la Somme Théologique de Thomas d'Aquin)," chapter 3 in *L'inouï de Dieu: Six études christologiques* (Paris: Desclée de Brouwer, 1980), 109-158.

115. Thomas uses *"demonstrare"* and *"demonstratio"* in a variety of ways, to be sure, just as any Latin author would, which we will survey in a moment. But he has unusual resources for holding that variety intelligibly together,

among them his christology, his doctrine of analogy, and the way he constructs sacred doctrine as a science.

116. "Now the end (*finis*) of a demonstrative syllogism is the acquisition of *scientia*" (*In Post. Anal.* bk. 1, *lect.* 1, §8).

117. The questions of the explicitness of faith and of the approach to truth of nonChristians in Thomas are too complex to be treated here. But see, among other places, II–II.2.7 and II–II.5. The explicitness of the faith required varies according to time, person, and circumstance, and even those who have no explicit faith may have implicit faith. Thomas seeks to preserve two principles: Salvation is always in Jesus Christ, and God alone knows the true natures of things with complete adequacy. Salvation may not bypass Jesus Christ; even implicit faith is, perhaps reflexively unknown to the believer, nevertheless in him. "What is really going on 'in the mind' or 'in the soul' is adequately represented only in the intentional being or Word of God" (Preller, *Divine Science*, 265). My access to the state of my own faith is no better than my access to anything else earthly: it is a *revelabilium*. (I–II.112.5 *in init.* and *ad* 4). Therefore Aquinas calls our knowledge of our state of grace strictly "conjectural" (I–II.112.5 *in fin.*).—Aquinas does leave room for Luther's insistence on *Heilsgewißheit*, but it arises under different rubrics; see Pesch, *Rechtfertigung*, 748–757.

118. The whole paragraph that opens the *Tertia Pars* reads as follows (my emphasis): "Quia Salvator noster Dominus Iesus Christus, teste Angelo, "populum suum salvum faciens a peccatis eorum" (Mt. 1,21), *viam veritatis nobis in seipso demonstravit,* per quem ad beatitudinem immortalis vitae resurgendo pervenire possimus, *necesse est ut ad consummationem totius theologici negotii,* post considerationem ultimi finis humanae vitae et virtutum ac vitiorum, de ipso omnium Salvatore ac beneficiis eius humano generi praestitis nostra consideratio subsequatur."

119. Preller, *Divine Science*, 243, emphasis modified.

120. For an excellent explication of how this sentence functions in Thomas— although it attends to other features of the account than the ones that have to do with the "demonstration" complex—see Bruce Marshall, "Thomas Aquinas's Logico-Semantic Explication of 'This Man Is God'" in his *Christology in Conflict: The Identity of a Saviour in Rahner and Barth* (Oxford: Basil Blackwell, 1987), 176–189.

121. *In* John 1, *lect.* 8, §188. I owe the quotation to Bruce Marshall, "Thomas, Thomisms, and Truth," 524.

122. A claim many would dispute. Preller argues at length that the Five Ways not only fail, they also contradict each other (*Divine Science*, 108–178), but that those things do not undermine Thomas's purpose, which is to show that we are ordered to that which we cannot know or understand (179–182).

123. *Quod.* 10.4.1 obj. 2. (The reply distinguishes between what is manifest

in se and to us, but denies neither the role of first principles nor the comparison with light.)

124. *In* John 1:9, §125.

125. I owe this way of putting the matter to Gretchen Breese.

126. Specifically, in this case, Thomas sets things up so that the more sacred doctrine pursues the description of *De anima* 3, the more it fulfills the charge of 2 Cor. 10:5, which we have already seen. See *De veritate* 14.1, which ends as follows: "But since the intellect is not in this way terminated in one thing, so that it is carried through to its own proper [end]...hence it is that its restlessness [*motus*] is not yet quieted [*quietatus*]....For in so far as [a true termination] comes from itself, [the intellect] has not satisfied [that condition], and it is not terminated in one thing, but it is terminated only extrinsically. And thus it is that the intellect of the believer is said to be captivated, because it is held by alien termini, and not proper ones. II Cor. 10:5: *bringing back in captivity all understanding*, etc." Note that the quotation ends "into obedience to Christ." I owe my attention to this passage to Gretchen Breese.

127. *In* John 14, *lect. 2 ca. med.*, quoting Ps. 85(86):11.

128. III.9.2. I owe my attention to the passage to Preller, *Divine Science*, 253.

129. Cf. the interpretation, borrowed from Gregory, of the story of doubting Thomas, at II–II.1.4 *ad* 1, which comes in for discussion in my Part II.

130. Preller, *Divine Science*, 251. The third sentence comes before the first two in the original.

131. *In* John, prol., §3.

132. Pesch, *Rechtfertigung*, 865.

133. Gilson, *Christian Philosophy of St. Thomas*, 9.

Notes to Chapter 3

1. Karl Barth, *A Shorter Commentary on Romans*, 26. An explicit comparison of Thomas and Barth on Romans will close chapter 7.

2. Compare the complementary and confirmatory article of Otto Pesch, "Paul as Professor of Theology: The Image of the Apostle in St. Thomas's Theology" (cited in Chapter 1, n. 27), 584–605. It is more wide-ranging and correspondingly less text-specific. It also makes less of the thick doctrinal connections between the portrait of Paul and such loci as election, vocation, and inspiration.

3. The Romans commentary follows Preller's rule to call the knowledge of God possessed by human beings in this life only *"cognitio."* Thomas brings the matter up explicitly, as we shall see.

4. According to the best historical information available to him at the time. It seems likely, although I will not be arguing this, that the way in which Thomas relates divine and human authorship of biblical texts has the (largely unexploited) resources to entertain a great deal more tension among the human

authors (as between Pauline and Lukan accounts of Paul's activity) than anyone considered in the thirteenth century. Pesch makes a similar claim in his "Exegese des Alten Testamentes bei Thomas," *Die Deutsche Thomas-Ausgabe* (Graz, Vienna, Cologne: Styria, 1933ff.), vol. 13, p. 701.

5. Text and paragraph numbering follow the Marietti edition cited in Chapter 1. The *prologus* and Romans commentary appear in vol. 1, 1–230. I will cite them in the text by Prologue or *"In"* (for *"In Romanos"*) chapter and verse, plus the Marietti paragraph number. The translation is mine, and may vary according to the uses to which I put it; I know of no standard English (or other modern-language) translation. The typography also follows the Marietti edition and requires a little explanation. Thomas's text appears in plain Roman type. Section numbers added by Marietti and the text of the verse currently being commented upon appear in SMALL CAPITALS. Thomas's quotations from the Bible and others appear without quotation marks in *italic* type. (In general, that has the advantage of causing the structure of Thomas's citation of authority, especially scriptural authority, to stand out.) Biblical verse numbers added by the Marietti editors appear here as there in the text without square brackets to segregate them. Other sources identified in the Marietti notes I have moved into square brackets within the text.

6. My appreciation for the Aristotelian ramifications of form has been stimulated by Lear, *The Desire to Understand*, chap. 2, "Nature," 15–54. I owe to Lear for example the language of "fashioning": he suggests "four fashions" as a replacement for the usual "four causes" (28–42).

7. The phrase titles a section in Lear, *Desire to Understand*, 15–25.

8. Christ comes from without, but works from within. Or in theological terms, he is both *extra nos* and *intimum*.

9. See discussion in Pesch, *Rechtfertigung*, 518–521, esp. paragraph 4, and additional texts cited at n. 16. I follow Preller's suggestion that "Aquinas gives us not so much proofs of the existence or unity of God, as arguments for asserting the proposition 'God exists' or 'God is one'" (*Divine Science*, 31). He refers there to Victor White, O.P., "The Unknown God," in *The Unknown God* (London: Harvill, 1948).

10. In both the *Institutes* (III.14.7) and a Romans commentary of his own (at Rom. 3:24), John Calvin used a four-cause analysis for incorporating Christ into his account of *justification*. Even promising attempts—such as Wilhelm Niesel's—to read his doctrine of election as similarly Christ-informed have however no texts so congenial to rely on. See Wilhelm Niesel, *Theology of Calvin*, trans. Harold Knight (Grand Rapids, Mich.: Baker, 1980), chap. 12, section 1: "Election in Christ" (pp. 159–169); and H. Paul Santmire, "Justification in Calvin's Romans Commentary," *Church History* 33 (1964): 294–313, esp. n. 47, which quotes four-cause analyses of justification from both Luther and Trent.

11. Karl Barth devotes *Church Dogmatics* II/2, §33, "The Election of Jesus

Christ," to rendering election christocentric. He faults those, including Thomas (*CD* II/2, 106–107), who restrict the predestination of Jesus Christ to his human nature (III.24.1). For Barth wants the predestination of Jesus Christ to be the eternal self-determination of God's own character in order to exclude the possibility of a *decretum absolutum* in perilous abstraction from the revelation in Jesus. But the place he cites (III.24.1) is the wrong place to look for Thomas's contribution to the question of God's eternal self-determination for human beings. God's eternal self-determination for human beings comes under the relation of mission and procession. The one eternal procession of the Son has a temporal *terminus*, which is his mission (I.43.2 *ad* 3), and that is for grace making graced alone (I.43.3), quite apart from the Fall. That Thomas seeks to follow the scriptures in talking about the incarnation as a remedy for sin (III.1.3) does not affect God's self-determination for us in the missions of the persons.

12. "Know" here, in the Vulgate of Thomas's quotation, is *"scire."* In the Romans commentary he makes nothing of the word. Does he here at least tacitly allow Paul a *scientia* of divine things that he elsewhere denies? In the commentary on 1 Cor. 2:2, §75, where the quotation is at home, he takes *scire* in his usual agnostic way. That is, he takes seriously the negation, that Paul knows, in the sense of *scire,* nothing; and the affirmation, that Paul knows, in the sense of *scire,* Jesus Christ, he takes not of Paul as knower but, glossing the passage by reference to Colossians 2:3, of Christ, where all the wisdom and science of God are *hidden.* In short, the verse does not mean to Thomas that Paul has *scientia* of his own, even in Christ; it does mean that Paul knows, in the sense of *scire,* where *scientia* is located: it is hidden in Christ for the blessed in heaven. That explication confirms the distinction of the *Summa* about the Spirit's gift of *scientia*—it allows one to know, in the sense of *scire,* what propositions to *believe* (i.e., by trusting in the *scientia* of Another), but not to possess them as *scientia* of one's own.

13. Pesch makes these remarks about Thomas and the *sola* with regard to justification ("The Image of the Apostle in St. Thomas's Theology," 594–595): "[In] explaining Romans 4:5, Thomas exposes himself to a second challenge of his thought by the Apostle. He does exactly that which offended Catholic exegetes so much in the case of Luther: without hesitating he joins the 'sola' to the 'fides,' the 'alone' to the 'faith,' and interprets the verse to mean: the sinner receives...justification 'by faith alone without works.'" The text (correctly quoted but mis-cited by Pesch) has:

330. Then when [Paul] says BUT TO ONE [WHO DOES NOT WORK], etc., he shows how eternal reward [*merces*] is related to faith, saying, BUT TO ONE WHO DOES NOT WORK, namely do external works [*exteriora opera*]... THAT ONE'S FAITH WILL BE REPUTED, namely alone, without external works [*scil-*

icet sola, sine operibus exterioribus], AS JUSTICE .... For from the fact that one believes in the justifying God [*in Deum justificantem*], one places oneself under God's justification, and so receives its effect....

331.... And this exposition is literal, and according to the intention of the Apostle [!], who takes power from what is said in Gen. 15:6, *it was reputed to him as justice*, which has tended to be quoted [*consuevit dici*] when that which is the least on anyone's part is reputed to one gratis, as if one had done the whole.

And therefore the Apostle says that this reputing would have been out of place, had the justice been from works, but is only appropriate [*solum habet locum*] when it is [based] on trust [*ex fide*].

14. See *In* Rom. 8:35, §722.

15. I owe my attention to this possibility to Victor Preller.

16. Note that Thomas also devotes *lectio* III of Chapter 1 (*In* 1:4) to the verse, "Qui praedestinatus est filius Dei."

17. *ST* I.23.3 notwithstanding. For discussion see Pesch, *Rechtfertigung*, 849–855. He summarizes: "1) Reprobation is not, like predestination, a positive act of God's will. 2) The question of salvation is not open any more, but decided. 3) The responsibility for the loss of those not predestined does not rest with God" (p. 855, n. 32, crediting H. Vorster, *Das Freiheitsverstandnis bei Thomas von Aquin und Luther* [Göttingen, 1965], 195).

18. *In* Isaiah 30:27.

19. Cf. also Henk J. M. Schoot, *Christ the 'Name' of God: Thomas Aquinas on Naming Christ*, publication of the Thomas Instituut te Utrecht, n.s., vol. 1 (Leuven: Peeters, 1993).

The phrase "Who is," which Thomas calls the name most appropriate to God (*ST* I.13.11), evidently enjoys its supreme appropriateness in respect of another purpose.

20. Way 1, "and by this everyone understands (*omnes intelligunt*) God"; Way 2, "which everyone names (*omnes nominant*) God"; Way 3, "which everyone calls (*omnes dicunt*) God; Way 4, "and this we call (*dicimus*) God"; Way 5, "and this we call God" (I.2.3). Whether the differing conclusions indicate different audiences or standards for the arguments is a question for another day; see Preller, *Divine Science*, chap. 3.

21. For Thomas goes on to say:

And thus as the angels carry [*deferre*] divine illuminations to us, as distant from God, so the apostles carried the teaching of the gospel from Christ to us. And as in the Old Testament, after the law of Moses, the prophets are read, who were handing down [*tradere*] the teaching of the law to the people—according to Mal. 4:4: *Remember my servant Moses*—so also in the New Testament, after the gospel, the teaching of the Apostles is read, who handed down to the faithful what they had heard from the Lord, according to I Cor. 11:23: *I received from the Lord what I also delivered to you.*

22. See also Barth's discussion of the rejected as place holders for the elected (*CD* II/2, 477ff.).

23. Karl Barth, *CD* II/2, 506.

24. Pesch gives three different categories of ways in which Thomas allows Paul to form him in "The Image of the Apostle," 593–605.

Notes to Chapter 4

1. Pesch, "The Image of the Apostle in St. Thomas's Theology," 602.

2. Thus Luther too distinguishes between *Gesetz* (accusing law) and *Gebot* (liberating commandment): "Das ist die Summe des ersten Gebotes: nicht verzweifeln, sondern vertrauen, Gott fürchten und ihn lieben über alles, er will nämlich, daß man ihm aus ganzem Herzen glaubt" *WA* 39 I/581, 9, quoted in Pesch, *Rechtfertigung*, 43.

3. Thomas Domanyi, *Der Römerbriefkommentar des Thomas von Aquin: Ein Beitrag zur Untersuchung seiner Auslegungsmethoden*, Basler und Berner Studien zur historischen und systematischen Theologie, vol. 39 (Bern: Peter Lang, 1979), 194–195. See "Plan und Gliederung des Römerbriefes," 193–201. The book contains only one analysis of actual content in the Commentary, Romans 5:12; the subtitle's reference to "*Auslegungs*methoden" is seriously meant.

4. "[V]irtu[s] evangelica gratiae [est] omnibus hominibus in salutem…est necessarium ad salutem…est efficax sive sufficiens" (*In* 1:18, §109).

5. The *coniunctio* is threefold, Thomas continues, and includes the grace of union, or the incarnation of Jesus Christ; the grace of adoption, or the salvation of the faithful; and the glory of fruition, or the final enjoyment of God by the blessed in heaven. For more passages concerning friendship with God, which is a theme more discussed than cited in Aquinas scholarship, see *ST* I–II.100.2 ("*communitas…hominum ad Deum*"), I–II.100.5 ("*quandam communitas seu res publica hominum sub Deo*"), I–II.99.2 ("*amicitia hominis ad Deum*"); for discussion and additional texts, see Pesch, *Rechtfertigung*, 415, esp. n. 16.

6. Translation modifies Blackfriars.

7. "Credere Deum non convenit infidelibus sub ea ratione qua ponitur actus fidei. Non enim credunt Deum esse sub his conditionibus quas fides determinat. Et ideo nec vere Deum credunt: quia, ut Philosophus dicit, IX *Metaphys.* [1051b25], in simplicibus defectus cognitionis est solum in non attingendo totaliter" (II–II.2.2 *ad* 2). The passage will receive a full discussion in Chapter 6.

8. Latin appears below, p. 124.

9. In Latin, "Postquam Apostolus ostendit quod x, hic incipit/ostendit quod y." See "Plan und Gliederung des Römerbriefes," 193–201 in Domanyi, *Römerbriefkommentar,* esp. 197.

10. Domanyi, *Römerbriefkommentar,* 194.

11. Pesch, *Rechtfertigung,* 489. For the first clause he cites *CG* IV.52, *In Rom.* 5:12 (§416), *De malo* 4.2 *ad* 1, and *ST* I.–II.85.1, and for the second *ST* I.95.1c, I.100.1c, *De malo* 4, 1c *ca. med.,* 4.4 *ad* 1, 4.8c, 5.1c, and *CG* IV.52.

12. I.100.1c and *ad* 2. The rational soul is not passed on "naturally," but is "conferred" by God.

13. Pesch, *Rechtfertigung,* 491, material in brackets from 490.

14. For a discussion of I–II.109.1, which might seem to furnish an objection to this, see Chapter 7.

15. See Pesch, "Allwirksamkeit," in *Rechtfertigung,* 840–849 and 866–867. With some elegance he implies a distinction without a difference between Luther's concept of Allein*wirksamkeit* (368–377) and the concept of All*wirksamkeit* (840–849) he ascribes to Thomas. (Unlike the text itself, the table of contents mistakenly prints *"Alleinwirksamkeit"* for both sections.)

16. Cf. the *Summa's* deployment of Romans 1:20 to ground an appeal to a natural law (I–II.93.2 *ad* 1), which I study in a future article. Note that the Jews' knowledge of the Law will not be in vain, since "all Israel will be saved, non particulariter sicut modo, sed universaliter omnes" *In Rom.* 11:26, §916. For more, see my contribution to Stephen Fowl, ed., *A Critical Reader in the Theological Interpretation of Scripture* (Oxford: Basil Blackwell, forthcoming) and Steven C. Boguslawski, *Aquinas' Commentary on Romans 9–11,* doctoral dissertation, Yale University, forthcoming.

17. Cf. Romans 6:1–2, 15; 7:7, 13.

18. I owe this way of putting the matter to an unpublished paper by David Yeago. Part III will suggest that the observation holds true also for Barth.

19. But the knowledge of sacred doctrine gained by study alone in abstraction from faith formed by love (as in "someone instructed in moral science," or religious studies generally) is nevertheless sufficient for teaching (I.1.6 *ad* 3).

20. The alternative is one that Thomas also presents in his commentary on 1 Corinthians:

> The human being has deviated from the rectitude of the divine cognition [*a rectitudine divinae cognitionis*] on account of vanity of heart. Whence it says in Jn. 1:10: *He was in the world, and the world was made by him, and the world did not recognize [cognovit] him.* And therefore God led the faithful to the salvation-bearing cognition of God [*ad sui cognitionem salutiferam*] by certain other things, which are not found in the reasonings of creatures either, in order that by worldly human beings, who consider only the rationales of things human, [those other things]

might be regarded as foolish. And of that sort are the patterns [*documenta*] of faith" (*In* I Cor. 1:21, §55 *post med.*).

I owe the citation to Bruce Marshall.

21. I owe to Joseph DiNoia the observation that characterizations of grace as free and unexacted leave it conceptually empty, whereas a notion of fellowship, such as appears in Thomas, specifies its content. The observation leaves open the question of how to evaluate theologically the ascription of that particular content to grace.

22. Barth, *Shorter Commentary*, 27.

Notes to Chapter 5

1. Chapter 7 will take up an objection that such optimism is in question after all.

2. 102...In one way [the verse is interpreted] of the justice by which God is just, according to Ps. 10[11]:8: *The Lord is just and loves just deeds*. And according to that reading, the sense is that *the justice of God*, by which namely God is just in promise-keeping, *is revealed in him* ["*in eo*," for which one expects "in it," namely the gospel, but Thomas glosses this way] namely in the human being believing the gospel, since that one believes that God has fulfilled what God promised about Christ having to be sent; and this OUT OF FAITHFUL-NESS, namely of the promising God [*ex fide, scilicet Dei promittentis*]—Ps. 144[145]:13: *The Lord is faithful in every word.*—TO FAITH namely of the believing human being.

James Samuel Preus's book *From Shadow to Promise: Old Testament Interpretation from Augustine to the Young Luther* (Cambridge, Mass.: Harvard, 1969) credits Luther's use of the concept of promise but misses similar remarks in Thomas.

3. Or another way, it may be understood as of the justice of God by which God justifies human beings. For the justice of human beings is called that by which human beings, by their own powers, presume to justify themselves, below in chapter 10[:3]: *Ignoring the justice of God and seeking to establish their own, they have not been put under the justice of God*. Which justice indeed is revealed in the Gospel, in so far as human beings are justified by the promise of the Gospel [*per fidem Evangelii*] in accord with what time it may be, whence he adds FROM PROMISE TO PROMISE [*ex fide in fidem*], that is from the promise [*ex fide*] of the Old Testament proceeding to the promise [*in fide*] of the New Testament, since according to each human beings are justified and saved by the faithfulness [or promise] of Christ [*per fidem Christi*],

since by the same promise [or faithfulness] they believe [him] to be coming by which we believe [him] to have come; and therefore it says in II Cor. 4:13: *Having the same species of faith we believe on account of what we are speaking of. (In* Rom. 1:17, §102)

4. Marshall, "Aquinas as a Postliberal Theologian," 374.

5. Wolterstorff, "The Migration of the Theistic Arguments," 71.

6. In the *Summa* Thomas analyzes the definition into faith's *act* and faith's *habit.* The *act* of faith belongs in the intellect: it is "to think [*cogitare*] with assent" (II–II.2.1); it is the *habit* of faith that belongs in the will: it directs the intellect "to assent to things not seen" (II–II.4.1).

7. Thus it matches Luther's demand that faith have assurance (*Heilsgewißheit*) without complacency (*securitas*). See Pesch, *Rechtfertigung,* 262–282.

8. *In* Rom. 4:3, §327. I apply Thomas's analysis of an act in the excursus of Chapter 7.

9. Preller, *Divine Science,* 32. I retain his distinction between single and double quotation marks. At *De Trin.* I.2.1 *ad* 1, Thomas says that it is known (*"scitur"*) of God that God is: but that usage is qualified there in three ways. First, we know that God is precisely as unknown (*"ignotus"*), which is the culmination (*"maxime perficisse dicimur"*) of our cognition of God in this life. And second, the context, confirmed by words like *"perficisse"* and "in this life" (*"in statu viae"*) indicates that the cognition of faith is included. Third, Thomas's *De Trinitate* sets up sacred doctrine as a science in a way distinct from that of the *Summa,* if Corbin (*Le chemin,* 709–727) is right.

10. Preller, *Divine Science,* 180.

11. *In Post. Anal.,* bk. I, lect. 15, no. 1. Thomas also devotes *lectio* 15, nos. 1–4 to the subject.

12. George Lindbeck, *The Nature of Doctrine* (cited in Chapter 1), 64. See also Bruce Marshall's discussion of the remark and its critics in "Aquinas as a Postliberal Theologian" and "Thomas, Thomisms, and Truth" (*passim*).

13. Marshall, "Aquinas as a Postliberal Theologian," 364–365.

14. The modern discussion began with Gilbert Ryle, but see more recently Clifford Geertz, *The Interpretation of Cultures* (New York: Basic Books, 1973), 6–7.

15. I owe my attention to the distinction, and its association with the wink-twitch example, to Victor Preller. Some English translations do not distinguish Thomas's *"actus"* and *"actio"*—or worse, sometimes represent and sometimes *reverse* the distinction.

16. Pesch, *Rechtfertigung,* 735–737. I have removed paragraphing and some emphasis, and transposed the material appearing here in parentheses from a footnote (n. 95) at that place.

17. RSV. Thomas's Vulgate reads: "Invisibilia enim ipsius a creatura mundi,

per ea quae facta sunt, intellecta conspiciuntur, sempiterna quoque eius virtus et divinitas."

18. *Shorter Commentary*, 27–28.

19. Preller, *Divine Science*, 29, n. 41.

20. Cf. discussion in Marshall, "Aquinas as a Postliberal Theologian," 54.

21. *ST* I.1.1 and, even more explicitly, *De Trin.* III.1 *ad* 1: "a human being frequently fails in that she supposes to be a demonstration what is not." I owe the reference to Bruce Marshall, "Aquinas as a Postliberal Theologian," 394, n. 95.

22. *Shorter Commentary*, 28, emphasis added.

23. I owe the language of "claim upon" to Joseph DiNoia, *The Diversity of Religions: A Christian Perspective* (Washington, D.C.: Catholic University Press, 1992), 130.

24. *"Proportionata"* is an adjective from *"proportio,"* which according to Varro and Cicero translates Greek *"analogon"* (see Lewis and Short's *Latin Dictionary, s.v. "proportio"*). Thomas is putting the matter as strongly as possible here. Despite all claims made by Protestants and Catholics for and against the analogy of being, Thomas here excludes the essence of God from the class of things susceptible to it.

25. See Wolterstorff, "The Migration of the Theistic Arguments," where John Locke serves as the principle representative of modernism (esp. 38–56).

26. See Karl Barth, *Anselm: Fides Quaerens Intellectum* (cited in Chapter 1).

27. Pesch, *Rechtfertigung*, 865.

28. The last sentence has in Latin the sequence *"manifestavit...legeretur,"* which must be translated "manifested...might be read"—a possibility that was open in the past, not "has manifested...might be read"—a possibility open in the present: that would require *"manifestavit...legatur."* (Nor is it a closed possibility in the past, "manifested...might have been read": that would require *"lectus sit"* or *"esset."*) Perhaps Eden was the only actual time of that preterite *"manifestavit."* See I.94.2–3.

29. Or so I read III.43.1 *ad* 3 in conjunction with II–II.5.2 *ad* 1–3.

30. "The demons hate it [*displacet*] that the signs of faith are so evident that by them they are compelled [*compellantur*] to believe" (II–II.5.2 *ad* 3).

31. See for example the *felix culpa* passage in III.1.3 *ad* 3, and a stronger version at *In* 1 Tim. 1:4, §40 (the latter discussed in Marshall, "Thomas, Thomisms, and Truth," 514–515, n. 32); the question of whether suffering is to be ascribed to the divine nature in III.46.12; and the death of God ("*mortem Dei," "Deus moriatur"*) passage at *In* 1 Cor. 1:23, §47. For discussion of the last see Bruce Marshall, "Aquinas and Luther on Deciding What Is True," unpub. ms., pp. 4, 13.

32. I owe the distinction between the logic of belief and the logic of coming to believe to remarks by Hans Frei.

33. As Preller insists: "No action, no thought, no intention or decision of

[the human being] possesses the slightest soteriological value apart from the grace of God [I–II.109.5–6]. The conformity of the mind to God is an aspect of salvation. Thus, there can be no *movement* of the mind to God apart from the initiative of God.... There can be no natural power of *coming to know* God" (*Divine Science*, 28–29, original emphasis).

34. See I–II.85.3 on *"ignorantia"* as a consequence of *"originialis iustitia subtracta."* For recovering the possibilities of the Romans commentary, however, we would probably have to follow Thomas through the intervening passages to the Adam and Christ passage of Romans 5:12ff. The commentary on that verse makes no mention of Adam's *scientia*. And although it is the only passage that Domanyi undertakes to analyze, he confines himself almost entirely to methodological remarks about *quaestio* format and historical remarks about accounts of hereditary transmission of original sin (259–266).

35. I am grateful to Robert Jenson for the gloss, offered in response to a query.

Notes to Chapter 6

1. Who counts as a Gentile is a fluid issue, because once the definition of "non-Jew" is left behind, the concept behaves with the uncertainty of "the apparently unsaved," the identities of whom are not susceptible to human discovery. Cf. II–II.2.7, II–II.10.6. As Preller restates those passages, "We cannot, then, *know* that we have truly informed faith—that there is in our 'souls' that intentional image of God which conforms us to [God]. There is no more in the conscious mind of the true believer than *may* be present in the conscious mind of the nonbeliever.... [I]t is quite possible that God...has 'seized' the will and affections of [human beings] who—for one reason or another—do not assert the truth of the propositions of faith" (p. 265). I hope to investigate the question of Gentiles in a future article. Steven Boguslawski, O.P., is writing a dissertation at Yale on Thomas's commentary on Romans 9–11, including a translation of those chapters, where crucial texts will be.

2. For textual and exegetical support for this interpretation, see Corbin, *Le chemin*, esp. 643–691.

3. More on that passage appears in the next chapter.

4. For textual and exegetical support of this interpretation, see Corbin, *Le chemin*, 741–743.

5. According to Preller. See *Divine Science*, 22–25 (in general) and 108–178 (in detail).

6. Among them is also a *scientia* "under the conditions that faith requires" (II–II.2.2 *ad* 3) that "adds to the merit of believing" (II–II.2.10). How that works will form a chief subject of the excursus.

7. Marshall, "Aquinas as a Postliberal Theologian," 353–402, esp. 370–387, and more recently his defense against critics in "Thomas, Thomisms, and

Truth," 499–524. I am grateful to Marshall for discussion and citations of texts. Marshall also identifies the analysis by Aquinas with a modern analysis dependent upon it by George Lindbeck, where the three aspects appear as ontological, categorical, and intrasystemic truth, (357–363), citing Lindbeck, *The Nature of Doctrine*, 47–52 and 63–69.

8. II–II.51.2 *ad* 3.

9. E.g., "Credere Deum esse unum, credere Deum esse factorum coeli et terrae, credere Deum esse propter nos homines et propter nostram salutem descensum de coelis, incarnatum, et hominum factum."

10. On account of its correlation with faith's material object, Marshall argues for "to hold beliefs about God" as a sufficiently broad translation of *"credere Deum"* ("Aquinas as a Postliberal Theologian," 379).

11. "But the human being, on account of the vanity of his or her heart, strayed from the rectitude of the divine cognition [*a rectitudine divinae cognitionis deviavit*]. Hence it says in John 1:10: *He was in the world, and the world was made by him, and the world did not recognize* [*cognovit*] *him*. And therefore God has led the faithful to a salvation-bearing cognition of God [*ad sui cognitionem salutiferam*] by certain other things, which are not found in the reasonings of creatures, in order that by worldly human beings, who consider only the rationales of human things, might be reputed foolish" (*In* 1 Cor. 1:21, §55 *in fin.*). The passage follows immediately upon Thomas's quotation of Romans 1:20. See discussion in Marshall, "Thomas, Thomisms, and Truth," 512–515.

12. Cf. *In* John. 6:44 (*lect.*4): "But if one is not elevated, it is not a defect on the part of the one drawing, to whom, *in se*, nothing is lacking; but it is on account of an impediment in the one who is not drawn. For we are able to speak in one way, as pertains to this, of the human being in the state of integral nature [*in statu naturae integrae*], and in another way [of the human being] in the state of nature corrupted; for in integral nature there was not any impediment prohibiting this being drawn [*tractio*], so that then all human beings were able [*poterant*] to be sharers [i.e., generally] in this being drawn. But in corrupt nature all are equally prohibited by the impediment of sin from this being drawn; and therefore all [i.e., individually] need to be drawn."

13. Pesch, *Rechtfertigung*, 735–737, quoted above, p. 120.

14. I owe to Victor Preller both the insight that for Thomas human freedom is always habitual and the current notion of intelligibility.

15. I owe my attention to this article to Cathy Kaveny.

16. I–II.1.1c, quoting II *Sent.* d. 24 c. 3.

17. I owe the horizon metaphor to Cathy Kaveny.

18. Preller, *Divine Science*, 181.

19. Wolterstorff, "Migration of the Theistic Arguments," 72. Although speculative science constitutes "a certain kind of sharing" in the beatific vision (in

that both are characterized by metaphors of vision), nevertheless "perfect beatitude cannot consist essentially in speculative *scientia*" (I–II.3.6).

20. Ibid., 71.

21. The only cognition we have of God is cognition of God's effects. But some of those effects, namely the effects of grace, carry us much further toward an identifying description of God, which would be like being able to identify the one coming as Peter without knowing whether Peter was (say) a human being or an angel. So it is that one of the effects of grace by which we know God is the incarnation (III.1.1 *s.c.*), and the incarnation is as a particular human being (III.16.11)—as identifiable as Peter. On the latter passage, see Marshall, *Christology in Conflict*, 176–89 (cited in Chapter 3, n. 120).

Notes to Chapter 7

1. *Church Dogmatics* IV/3. The phrase forms the title of the excellent Epilogue (pp. 234–280) to George Hunsinger's *How to Read Karl Barth: The Shape of His Theology* (Oxford: Oxford Univerity Press, 1991). Hunsinger's comments on Thomas will come in for extensive comment below. Hunsinger sums up Barth's doctrine in the words of John Calvin: "Whenever...we meet with heathen writers, let us learn from the light of truth which is admirably displayed in their works, that the human mind, fallen as it is, and corrupted from its integrity, is yet adorned by God with excellent talents. If we believe that the Spirit of God is the only fountain of truth, we shall neither reject nor despise the truth itself, wherever it shall appear, unless we wish to insult the Spirit of God." Hunsinger (p. 234) quotes John Calvin, *Institutes* II, ii, xv in the translation of John Allen (Philadelphia: Presbyterian Board of Publication, 1902).

2. II–II.175. See the commentary by Hans von Balthasar in *Die Deutsche Thomas-Ausgabe* (cited in Chap. 3), perhaps the most extended treatment of Thomas by him: Hans Urs von Balthasar, "Die Entrückung," in *Die Deutsche Thomas-Ausgabe* 23:372–409. Von Balthasar is editor of the entire volume, *Besondere Gnadengaben und die zwei Wege Menschlichen Lebens*, which covers II–II.171–82.

3. Pesch, *Rechtfertigung*, 526. The paragraph concludes a section called "Natur und Gnade," under the chapter "Macht und Ohnmacht der Sünde."

4. Hunsinger, *How to Read Karl Barth*, cited above with approval. The quotations that follow all come from p. 146.

5. I owe the word "non-critter," used of God, to Robert Gregg.

6. *CD* III.

7. Bernard of Clairvaux, *De gratia et libero arbitrio* (PL 1027) quoted in Hans Küng, *Justification: The Doctrine of Karl Barth and a Catholic Reflection* (cited in Chap. 1), 266.

8. My usage of the parable metaphor here is entirely different from the terminology of "secular parables" by Barth.

9. I owe my attention to the narrative significance of that sequence to Richard Hays.

10. I intend this account as a *reformulation* of Thomas, but he does use the same metaphor literally: "As neither were the eyes which Christ gave to the one born blind of another sort than the eyes that nature produced" (I.94.3 *ad* 1).

11. The closest parallel comes at *Church Dogmatics* II/1, 118-23, where even the wording is similar. Cf. also I/2, 304-307.

12. Barth, *Shorter Commentary*, 24, translation slightly modified.

13. Emphasis added. Cf. the fuller context (p. 28, emphasis added):

> The world which has always been around them, has always been God's work and as such God's witness…Objectively the Gentiles have always had the opportunity of knowing God…*And again, objectively speaking, they have always known* [*God*]. In all that they have known otherwise, God as the Creator of all things has always been, objectively speaking, the proper and real object of their knowledge, exactly in the same sense as undoubtedly the Jews in their Law were objectively dealing with God's revelation.

14. Preller, *Divine Science*, 29, n. 41.

15. Hunsinger (*How to Read Karl Barth*, 255-256) sums up Barth's objections to natural theology like this: It advances three "unfortunate things: falsifying abstractions, neutral generalizations, and nonexistent capacities." But in Thomas, I have been arguing, grace makes abstract nature concrete, the analysis of an act particularizes and evaluates generalizations so as to leave neutrality behind, and nonexistent capacities are spoken of only to follow Paul in something like the way that Barth himself attempts to do. Thomas affirms their nonexistence not in terms of simple absence, but in more complex terms of ineffectiveness and culpability—which is the point of their nonexistence.

16. As quoted in Ibid., 264. The entire chapter (234-280) is an elegant account of that feature of Barth.

17. An abridgment of this chapter, with material from Chapters 1 and 6, will appear under the title "Thomas and Barth in Convergence on Romans 1?" in *Modern Theology* 12 (January 1996).

Notes to the Epilogue

1. *CD* II/1, p. 127, translation modified.

2. I include *Aeterni Patris* because it provides apparent grist for Barth's mill although it goes unmentioned there. (The reference at II/1, 656f. applies to the Molinist controversy.)

3. "Deum, rerum omnium principium et finem, naturali humanae rationis lumine e rebus creatis certe cognosci posse," *CD* II/1, p. 79, quoting the *De fide catholica* of Vatican I, chap. 2, *De revelatione* (Denzinger, no. 1785).

4. See Hans Urs von Balthasar, *Theodramatik* (Einsiedeln: Johannes, 1973–1983), vol. 1, section I.A.: "Dramatik zwischen Ästethik und Logik," 15–22.

5. *CD* II/1, p. 84.

6. *CD* II/1, p. 164–165, translation slightly modified.

7. Jeffrey Stout, "What Is the Meaning of a Text?" (cited in the Preface), 5–6. See also chap. 3 of Alasdair MacIntyre's *Three Rival Versions of Moral Enquiry*, 58–81, "Too Many Thomisms."

8. Consult the English translation in Jacques Maritain, *St. Thomas Aquinas: Angel of the Schools*, trans. J. F. Scanlon (Sheed & Ward, 1948), appendix I (134–154). The present assertion occurs on p. 136.

9. Reading "human beings" for "men" and adding my emphasis from Maritain (ibid., 136).

10. Ibid., 138. I serve notice here that I am marshaling evidence for the plausibility of what charity must call a *mis*reading; it turns out that the smooth and easy way and the foundations well and truly laid come separated by a paragraph in praise of creation's *beauty*, which Barth himself might, we shall see, admit as ("unscientific") evidence of God's existence and in praise of precisely revelation, so that the order of reason and revelation in the handbooks' two-story system might arguably admit of reversal on the basis of a reading even of *Aeterni patris* itself.

11. Ibid.

12. *A Late Friendship: The Letters of Karl Barth and Carl Zuckmayer* (cited in Chap. 1), 42.

13. *CD* II/1, pp. 650–651. Hans von Balthasar quotes the passage as an anticipation of his approach in *The Glory of the Lord: A Theological Aesthetics* (New York: Crossroads and San Francisco: Ignatius, 1982), 55–56.

14. Hans Urs von Balthasar, *Cordula, oder der Ernstfall* 3rd. ed. (Einsiedeln: Johannes, 1966), 48–64. ET: *The Moment of Christian Witness*, trans. Richard Beckley (San Francisco: Ignatius, 1994).

Index